International Standards Desk Reference

Your Passport to World Markets
ISO 9000
CE Mark
QS-9000
SSM
ISO 14000
Q 9000
American, European, and
Global Standards Systems

Amy Zuckerman

amacom

American Management Association

New York • Atlanta • Boston • Chicago • Kansas City • San Francisco • Washington, D.C.
Brussels • Mexico City • Tokyo • Toronto

In loving memory of
Anita Diamant,
Paul "Tiny" Stacy,
and
Nancy Ann Kramer,
who dedicated their lives to the
pursuit of truth and justice.

Library of Congress Cataloging-in-Publication Data

Zuckerman, Amy.
    International standards desk reference : your passport to world
  markets, ISO 9000, CE Mark, QS-9000, SSM, ISO 14000, Q 9000
  American, European, and global standards systems / Amy Zuckerman.
       p.   cm.
  Includes bibliographical references and index.
  ISBN 0–8144–0316–6 (hc)
    1. Export marketing.   2. Quality control—Standards.   3. Quality
  assurance—Standards.   I. Title.
  HF1416.Z78   1996
  658.8'48—DC20   *96–35564*
                                                                        CIP

Printing number

10 9 8 7 6 5 4 3 2 1

Contents

Foreword

The CEOs of nearly 100 leading North American and European national and international corporations expressed their concern, at the November 1995 Transatlantic Business Dialogue (TABD) in Spain, that product standards, testing, and certification are the most important impediments to international trade. The prominence of these nontariff trade barriers today is brought about because of the elimination over the past few years of tariff trade barriers through such global and regional trade agreements as the World Trade Organization (WTO) and its predecessor, the General Agreement on Tariffs and Trade (GATT), and the North American Free Trade Agreement (NAFTA) between the United States, Canada, and Mexico.

Internationally accepted standards and conformity assessment practices related to product testing, certification, and quality assurance are desired by industry and consumers everywhere. The ideal goal is to have a single standard and corresponding conformance measure, if required, to be accepted globally, irrespective of where that conformance measure is conducted.

Cooperative development of standards among nations is required to achieve this goal. This will lead toward building the confidence necessary to accept test data, inspection reports, and conformity assessments conducted by other entities worldwide. Some government and private-sector efforts such as the Joint Business Development Committee's Standards Working Groups with Latin America and nations in the former Soviet Union as well as the Mutual Recognition Agreement negotiations between the United States and the European Union are achieving this important goal.

Amy Zuckerman exposes these issues in a succinct and clear manner. She provides information on practical approaches to achieving global market acceptance. Actual cases serve to illustrate the issue.

The challenges facing the United States in the global market are depicted by Zuckerman as being attributable in large part to the uniqueness of the U.S. standards and conformity assessment system. She highlights the value for reviewing our basic needs in standards and conformity testing as we address a growing global market. Her approach yields recommendations beyond those that have resulted from recent studies commissioned by the United States Congress.

Anyone engaged in international trade will find that not only is this book provocative with regard to the standards policy issues facing our nation, but more importantly, it contains practical and necessary information for doing business in today's global marketplace.

Dr. Stanley I. Warshaw, P.E.
Senior Policy Advisor for
Standards and Technology
U.S. Department of Commerce
Washington, D.C.

Preface

- A major thread manufacturer working with the automobile industry can't decide whether to pursue ISO 9000 or QS-9000 certification, the Big Three's new quality program. Does he need a QS-9000 certificate to sell directly to a Big Three distributor in Brazil and Europe?
- An exporter of customized machinery learns that he must earn a CE Mark to enter the European Union. He doesn't know what the CE Mark is or how to qualify for the EU product standard.
- Manufacturers face implementing ISO 14000, a new international environmental management system standard. What can they do to prepare for this process?
- An American electronics company is contemplating suing the German government to gain product entry into that country. The company has passed European Union product conformance standards but is not in compliance with German standards. Under EU law, the EU standards should supersede national standards, but the German government is not backing down. A showdown is expected in the Ministry of Justice in Luxembourg, the official court of the EU.
- American toy manufacturers complain to government officials that European directives regarding the health and safety of toys are geared to favor Danish manufacturers. It so happens that the chairman of the committee developing the requirements in this sector is Danish.

It is evident from these examples that international standards are proliferating, as are international standards programs. Businesses in the United States and abroad are confronted with an ever-growing, confusing array of programs and requirements.

Conversations with multitudes of business leaders and executives in both the U.S. and Europe reveal rampant confusion about standards in general and international standards programs in particular. Differentiating between product standards and quality assurance standards is proving confusing enough, let alone tracking these developments internationally.

Standards come in many different forms. Product standards, health and safety standards, and quality assurance, or process, standards provide a few examples illustrating how standards function in the world. Some standards are strictly voluntary; others are strictly mandatory. As in the case of ISO 9000, for example, a strictly voluntary standard may become mandatory at the insistence of a customer, a nation, or a national bloc.

Standards are the glue that will bind the new world order; they will unite Canada with Vietnam and Malaysia with the new Russia. But when misused, they can also become potent protectionist weapons. Meeting a variety of different foreign standards—not to mention redundant conformity assessment practices—can be costly, at best. At worst, foreign standards can delay entry into a foreign market, acting as a trade barrier.

Efforts are taking place worldwide to harmonize standards to allow for free-flowing international trade. These efforts, which usually take the form of mutual recognition talks, involve time and effort. Businesses must be able to cope with existing, not to mention emerging, standards programs while their governments and standards institutions negotiate.

International Standards Desk Reference: Your Passport to World Markets is designed to meet the growing needs of companies worldwide to understand and be aware of developments on the international standards front, developments that will surely affect their operations in the months and years to come. The book provides:

- Concrete information on standards institutions worldwide, the players, and the power blocs that are forming around standards.
- Information on various new and ongoing standards programs and how best to implement those programs, whether they are in the areas of quality assurance, the product itself, or health and safety. Some programs targeted for more in-depth treatment include ISO and ISO 9000 derivatives like QS- and Q 9000, as well as the European Union's product standard, the CE Mark, and the upcoming environmental management standard ISO 14000.

After reading this highly informative how-to guide, businesspeople will have the knowledge they need to:

- Pick and choose among programs that will affect their future
- Implement the programs they decide on in the most cost-effective way possible
- Keep up with international trends that may mean time and financial expenditures in the months and years to come
- Function in an international standards arena
- Investigate in each country/region (1) program qualifications, restrictions, compliance issues and (2) foreign government regulations that will affect their operating in that region

Information Sources

The information presented in this guide was culled from a myriad of sources—both governmental and private-sector—worldwide. It's important to note that international standards developments are ever-changing.

Moreover, this is a highly politicized topic. Many national standards bodies are government-operated, and their policies may reflect national political interests. Other standards bodies derive a good portion of their revenue from standards sales. That means there is not always consensus internationally on what is "correct" regarding standards and their use.

For these reasons, many experts were asked to lend their time to reading this material for accuracy and to offer their viewpoints on what is taking place in the international standards arena. The following experts served as reviewers and "editors" for this guide in what became a true team effort:

Dale Misczynski of Motorola Corp. edited the entire manuscript at two stages of its creation; Roger Frost of the International Organization for Standardization (ISO) Press Service provided major revisions of the ISO sections; Dan Reid of General Motors edited the QS-9000 chapter; Q 9000 expert Marsha Ludwig-Becker provided a great deal of the information that makes up the Q 9000 chapter on military standards; Frank Doherty of the Pentagon edited the Q 9000 chapter; Alan Barber, a European Union standards official, edited the European section, and other EU officials read through the CE Marking chapter; Marty Chizek of Weinstein Associates both provided information on CE Marking and edited this chapter; Stanley Warshaw, senior policy advisor for standards and technology at the Department of Commerce, edited the U.S. government material; Rick Clements provided background and lent his expertise to the material on ISO 14000; Diego Betancourt of Polaroid Corp. and Bob Walsh of the American National Standards Institute (ANSI) provided much of the material on Strategic Standardization Management, and members of the ANSI public relations staff had internal experts review the ANSI material.

Acknowledgments

This book would not exist without the support and guidance of many individuals worldwide. However, there are six individuals whom I want to thank particularly for encouraging my work in the international standards arena—work that has led to the publication of this book.

They are my editor, Anthony Vlamis, whose continued faith in me and this topic has helped me through many a difficult period; Dale Misczynski and Richard Buetow of Motorola, who have provided tutoring on the subject; Stanley Warshaw of the International Trade Administration (ITA), who opened my eyes to international standards developments; Ned Hamson, who first published my material in the *Journal for Quality Participation*; and J. W. Kisling of Multiplex and the National Association of Manufacturers, who long ago enlisted me to fight the good fight for small businesses.

In corporate and institutional America, thanks also go to Pat Earnest and Rita Jones of the Motorola Quality staff for their tremendous back-up support; to David Ling of Hewlett-Packard for providing research information; to Dan Reid of General Motors, Dan Whelan of Ford Motor Co., and Rad Smith of Peat Marwick and Bob Kozak of Entela for help on the QS-9000 chapter; to private consultant Marsha Ludwig-Becker for the huge amount of work she performed on the Q 9000 chapter; to Diego Betancourt of Polaroid for the information on strategic standardization management; to Bob Walsh, Marilyn Hernandez, and Elaine Ferst of the American National Standards Institute (ANSI) for providing reams of information and fact checking; to Rick Clements of the National ISO 9000 Support Group for the time and effort that went into the ISO 14000 chapter; and to Marty Chizek of Weinstein Associates for his help on the CE Marking chapter.

Members of the United States government have also provided a great deal of time and support. They are Charles Ludolph, Roger Rensberger, Maureen Breitenberg, Gary Carver, and Laurie Cooper of the Commerce Department. Thanks also to Helen Delaney and Rene van de Zande of the U.S. Mission to the European Union, and also to Frank Doherty of the Pentagon for pinch-hitting at the last minute.

On the international front, thanks to Larry Eicher, secretary general of the International Organization for Standardization (ISO) for his personal time, as well as to ISO public relations staffers Roger Frost and Anke

Varcin, and Kevin McKinley, Peter Ford, and Reg Shaughnessy, who are prominent members of ISO technical committees. Also to Hans Peter Werner of the World Trade Organization (WTO); Will Deken and Harry Gundlach of the Dutch Council for Accreditation (RvA). Thanks for on-going transatlantic help to Jacques McMillan, Antonio Silva Mendes, Michel Audoux, Jurgen Wettig, and Giles Allen of the European Union's Directorate-General III, Industry; and to David Stanger of the European Organization for Testing and Certification (EOTC) and Alan Barber, formerly with EOTC.

Quite a few magazine editors nationwide have offered encouragement. Thanks to Brad Stratton of *Quality Progress*; Jean Murphy of *Traffic World*; Bryan Berry of *New Steel*; Felecia Stratton of *Inbound Logistics*; and Tony Juncaj of Automotive Industry Action Groups' Actionline.

This project would not exist without the quality work performed by my researchers: Eddy Goldberg, Suzanne Vlamis, Laura Sylvester, Harvey Fenigsohn, and Abayah Sthrestha. Thanks to David Biederman for his early research support, to Alex Saenz for his humor and ability to track down errant editors, and to Jacquie Flynn for her assistance at the developmental stage of the editorial process. In the world of academia, special thanks to Phil Green of the Smith College political science department for his help with outreach on this subject, and John Blydenburg of Clark University for ongoing advice.

Then there are the many support personnel and friends who kept me going during the long writing and editing period. They are the cafeteria staff at Amherst College, including Kevin Stokes, Rose Rogalski, Carolyn Gonzales, Michele Triggs, and Ed Trudeau; David Lovelace and Maria White of the Montague Bookmill; Scott Plotkin and Peter Laitmon, who offered technical support; Bob Armstrong of the Worcester Committee on Foreign Relations for providing a trial run; Ronald and Dea Massaut, who provided hospitality overseas; Alan Hurwitz, Dennis Ravenelle, Andrea Goodman, Bob Solari, Sally Okulski and Jewel Greco, Jayne Pearl, Randy Bernard, Bruce Carson, Stanley Wiater, Nina Belmonte, B. Michael Zuckerman, Richard Rice, Julie Redstone, and Marianne Zurn for giving their time and advice; and my mother, Florence Zuckerman, and Lilli and Michael Egan, for financial and emotional back-up, and my daughter, Julia Beth "Bubbles" Biederman, for keeping me laughing.

Two additional people deserve special recognition for both their personal and technical support. They are my copy editor, Barbara Horowitz, who has gone way beyond the call of duty, and my partner, Nathaniel "Nat" Herold, whose ongoing love and support not only saw me through the completion of this project, but has made all the difference.

1

An Introduction to International Standards and Standards Development

Questions the Reader Will Find Addressed in This Chapter

1. What are standards and how are they applied internationally?
2. Why are some standards mandatory and others voluntary?
3. What is the origin of international standards?
4. How are international standards used and misused?
5. What are the major international standards systems?
6. What is the interplay between standards systems?
7. How are government-related standards programs financed?
8. What are international standards bodies?
9. What is the ISO/IEC system?
10. How does ISO interact worldwide?
11. How are standards set internationally?
12. What is the standards development process?
13. What is the standards communication infrastructure?
14. What are national differences?
15. What is growing standards conformity?
16. How are European standards coming to the fore?
17. Why do standards developments need to be tracked internationally?
18. What are some basic terms pertaining to standards?

Introduction

Standards have always affected business in the pocketbook. Manufacturers cannot compete for military contracts without meeting special standards. Earning a testing lab stamp of approval for an appliance may be

1

required for market entry, as well as a means of winning consumer confidence and sales.

In a burgeoning global economy, standards have taken on even more economic significance. Businesses are finding that they must meet new international standards criteria—sometimes earning certificates and marks at high cost—to compete in the international marketplace. For this reason, it is becoming increasingly crucial for businesses to be aware of how standards are developed and to constantly track those standards that will directly affect them.

Companies with the resources to do so should also become directly involved in international standards forums through the technical committees and advisory groups that develop standards. Even attending conferences relating to standards provides an opportunity to offer input to the process.

To become involved in standards activities means understanding how standards are developed, the various systems operating worldwide to develop standards and testing practices, and the nations, individual companies, organizations, and individuals—the players—that make this loosely knit system work.

In terms of regionally based standards systems, the American and European are the most highly developed worldwide. Operating concurrently is a private-sector international standards system where nonprofit organizations create global standards for business and government use. All the systems operate quite differently, each with its own unique set of governing bodies and players.

These systems—as well as emerging standards bodies worldwide—will be examined in full to provide companies the understanding they need to adequately keep tabs on international standards trends. In addition, there are chapters that explore new and evolving standards that businesses will encounter in the global marketplace.

What Are Standards and How Are They Applied Internationally?

Standards come in many forms and are used in many ways. They may affect the quality of our medicine, ensure that mechanical parts are interchangeable, or dictate that products be produced in a standardized fashion. Standards may be used to evaluate job performance or even to make sure that clothing and bedding are sized properly.

This book is about international standards, so the focus here is largely on industry standards, because most of the buying and selling that makes up international trade involves manufactured goods or raw materials.

Service companies also operate overseas and also face requirements to meet quality standards. Their concerns are addressed primarily in sections dealing with quality-related standards like ISO 9000, the international quality assurance standards series. ISO refers to the International Organization for Standardization.

In the industrial or manufacturing sector, standards deal mainly with

- The physical makeup of a product (e.g., steel)
- Creating standardized dimensions, such as in finished paper or containers
- Allowing for uniformity of parts such as screws, or conformity of equipment such as computers
- Product performance (i.e., the final product meets the design specifications, as in a car engine)
- Health and safety requirements for products and equipment (to prevent fires, explosions, electric shocks, chemical and radiation hazards, and so forth)
- Controlling the environmental impact of products and processes
- Creating a common international communication base
- Process (i.e., how a company operates)

Within the manufacturing sector, standards can be further categorized to reflect units of measurement, statistical methods, or quality management techniques. Then there are standards that guide the drafting of standards, known as the format of standards, the principles of variety reduction (so-called preferred numbers), and modular coordination.

What makes up a standard—its technical content—varies considerably depending on the problem it is designed to address. In general, standards are designed to address specific problems, so the vast majority deal with specific products or services, whether they be detergents on the manufacturing side or the transfer of banking funds on the service side.

Engineering design and calculation standards account for a large number of existing standards, whether they govern the design of concrete structures or calculate the thermal insulation of buildings. Many such standards form the basis of national building codes.

Another important area of standardization is that of communication and information exchange. Standards devoted solely to this purpose are called terminology standards. Besides containing terms and definitions related to the product or service in question, they include definitions, explanatory notes, illustrations, and examples. For instance, standardized graphical symbols used in the building trade help promote international trade through a common code. Quite a few international standards are devoted to harmonizing these sorts of codes on a worldwide basis.

Example: Electronics Industry

That standards can be potent tools—and weapons—is evident in how Microsoft has managed to make its industry standards relating to operating systems the norm. In the process, the software giant has dominated the world market.

As noted in the *New York Times,* "In understanding the two-decade history of Microsoft's increasing control over the computer software industry, nothing matters more than its strategic management of these points of interconnection: the creation, marketing and then manipulation of standards. . . . Microsoft has a mail standard, called simply MAPI (mail application program interface). It has a new telephone standard, for letting software interact with telephone equipment: TAPI. It is belatedly but feverishly working on a proprietory online multimedia document-publishing standard code-named Blackbird. Microsoft abhors industry-wide standards-setting: its pattern, with increasing consistency, has been to refuse to cooperate with any standards procedures but its own. . . .

"Microsoft is by no means the only company that seeks to exploit private standards. Netscape itself is playing a dangerous game with the standards that gave rise to the World Wide Web: creating proprietory 'extensions' that work only with its own software and hoping that its market dominance will be enough to make them stick. The history of I.B.M.'s downfall in the P.C. industry is a history of failed attempts to impose standards by fiat" (*New York Times Magazine,* November 5, 1995).

Standards and Foreign Trade

The U.S. economy is dependent on foreign trade for survival. Most recent government records show total U.S. exports more than doubled from 1985 to 1993, from $218 billion to $464 billion. Largely fueling this export burst are advanced technology products, which since the early 1980s have produced trade surpluses in the billions of dollars, offsetting trade deficits in non-advanced technology products every year since 1982.

Standards and conformity assessment practices—testing and certification—are crucial links to maintaining market presence overseas. When trading partners agree on standards and conformity assessment—called harmonizing—then trade can flow freely. When there is disagreement, or governments and trading partners impose their own standards and conformity assessment, goods and services can actually be shut out of foreign markets.

Advanced technology products, many of which face overseas government regulation, are particularly vulnerable in this regard. More and more, industry and government officials recognize the need to harmonize standards and conformity assessment practices to maintain open markets, not simply for the benefit of multinational corporations but also to help small and midsize companies that are becoming more dependent on international trade for their survival.

Voluntary vs. Mandatory Standards

Throughout the developed world, the vast majority of industrial standards are considered voluntary. There are exceptions where governments mandate certain standards, especially in the fields of health and safety, food and drugs, and environment. (When governments mandate standards, they become laws or regulations.) Also, customers may require conformity to standards or even proof of certification, obviating the voluntary nature of a standard. This is common practice with the International Organization for Standardization's 9000 series, for example.

Companies worldwide often seek standards certification because they know that they could well be shut out of markets if they do not conform to the accepted standards of that market. The standards in place may be voluntary, but companies know that in some countries (Japan, for example) "voluntary" usually means mandatory in practice.

Origin of International Standards

The electrotechnical field initiated international standards efforts at the turn of the century through the formation of the International Electrotechnical Commission. Some attempts were made in the 1930s to develop international standards in other technical fields, but World War II thwarted those efforts.

After the war, there was a need to create a wider array of international standards to meet the needs of an evolving worldwide economy. Even at that stage, there was awareness that disparity of standards from country to country and region to region meant higher costs for exporters and possible barriers to market entry. Meeting in London in 1946, delegates from twenty-five countries decided to create a new international organization to facilitate the international coordination and unification of industrial standards. This new organization, the International Organization for Standardization (ISO), began to function officially in February 1947. (Because the name International Organization for Standardization would have had different acronyms in different languages, it was decided to use an acronym derived from the Greek *isos,* meaning equal. The short form of the organization's name is always ISO.) It was not until ISO was created that an international organization devoted solely to international standardization came into existence.

Use and Misuse of International Standards

International standards play a major role in the functioning of a global economy. Nations utilize standards for trade, transport, and communications as well as for science and technology. Industry and service sectors worldwide use standards to unite world markets. In the international marketplace, standards developed through voluntary processes become valuable tools for binding markets, nations, and regional economic blocs. They represent a broad-based consensus of all interested parties, from producers (exporters) to users (importers) to governments, consumers, and even academia.

When misused, however, standards can become trade barriers. Those informed in the standards scene—especially nations and industries that actively participate in developing international standards—understand that standards can greatly influence the market. One game is to write into standards provisions that favor products of an individual company or nation. Another is to impose national or regional testing or certification practices—called conformity assessment—on foreign competitors.

Example

In the mid-1990s, a Mobil Oil quality manager complained that a competitor was attempting to develop standards that would benefit its market position by serving on an ISO technical committee overseeing oil and gas matters. Such complaints are not uncommon, which is why multinationals vie to place their representatives on international standards technical committees.

Because of such abuses, the General Agreement on Tariffs and Trade (GATT) contains quite a few provisions calling for the removal of standards as technical barriers to trade and harmonization of standards worldwide. There is recognition that standards can function both as market unifiers and as means of barring or slowing market entry. The Agreement on Technical Barriers to Trade binds signatory governments to adopt international standards as a basis for national standards and technical regulations.

When applied internationally without malice or market manipulation, standards can offer the following benefits on a global basis:

- Provide optimum economic solutions to repetitive technical problems in the design, manufacture, packaging, transportation, and delivery of goods.
- Protect health, safety, property, and the environment against hazards owing to the production, use, and disposal of products.
- Provide rules for preventing and fighting fires and explosions and for controlling chemical, radiation, and other hazards.
- Ensure interchangeability, interoperability, and compatibility of products and services within one industry and between industries.
- Yield overall savings in design, production, handling, storing, ordering, and use of goods and services.
- Provide a solid basis for assessing quality of products and services. Their application facilitates contracting and ordering of goods and services and the assessment of their quality, and reduces disputes over specifications and quality.
- Create a universal guide for the best means of establishing and assessing quality management systems. Suppliers are provided a guide for improving the quality of products and services while buyers, ideally, are provided confidence that the goods and services offered are up to high-quality levels.
- Facilitate communication in most fields of human activity.

Major International Standards Systems

The procedure for creating and disseminating international standards is examined in-depth in Chapter 8. Some information pertinent to this chapter is introduced here.

There are really two international standards systems operating simultaneously, and sometimes in tandem. Nations and regional economic blocs, as well as international standards bodies, all contribute to standards development internationally.

Example

Sometimes national or regional standards are mandated for entry into a market, affecting manufacturers worldwide. This is the case with the European Union's CE Mark, a product certification standard. As discussed in Chapter 7, EU directives mandate that companies earn a CE Mark in a variety of industries or face having their products barred from European sale.

Major international standards bodies develop international standards to help industry, consumers, and governments worldwide. This is the case with ISO 14000, a new environmental management standard now in draft form. ISO is developing ISO 14000 in response to industry and government requests to help them focus and better manage their environmental efforts.

Industries worldwide, in the meantime, are also major contributors to national, regional, and international standards systems. Although some industries and industrial associations—or even individual companies—may dominate worldwide industry standards development, there is no worldwide industry system per se. Instead, industry representatives serve as the backbone of national, regional, and international standards systems and programs.

U.S. standards organizations serve as the secretariats, or committee administrators, for approximately one hundred ISO technical committees. Secretariats include a mixture of government and private-sector organizations, with the emphasis on the private sector. The Society of Automotive Engineers, the American Society for Testing and Materials, and the National Fire Protection Association are among the U.S. private-sector organizations heavily represented at ISO.

Note: The issue of private-sector (industry) standards is discussed more fully in Chapters 2, 3, and 6, which deal with the American and European standards systems. Private-sector standards are also discussed in Chapters 4, 5, 7, 9, and 10, which describe new or ongoing standards programs.

Example

The Big Three automakers have created a joint quality program—QS-9000—that they plan to mandate for worldwide use among their supply base. QS-9000 employs the ISO 9000 international quality assurance standard coupled with industry-specific criteria. This is an example of an industry utilizing a preexisting standard as the basis for a worldwide quality program.

System A: National and Regional Standards and Accreditation Bodies

Throughout the developed world there is a tendency among governments to allow national standards-setting and standards-certification bodies a great deal of operational latitude. Each country or region has in place (or is creating) different types of accreditation mechanisms to promote market confidence that standards are being developed and assessed impartially and, in turn, meet standards of excellence and quality. The following are three recommendations from ISO officials for principles that should govern any standards body no matter how it is constructed:

1. It should have legal status as the body responsible for preparing national standards. In cases where there are numerous national standards bodies, one body (usually a federation) takes responsibility for representing the country's standardization interests at the international level.

2. The supporting membership of national standards bodies should represent all relevant interests—government, industry, professional institutions, consumer bodies, and research organizations.

3. The preparation of standards should be carried out in a spirit of openness through special committees in which all the main interests concerned are represented. Standards-writing committees should consult with all interests concerned and attempt to achieve consensus before making a decision.

Most governments support their national standards development bodies and provide for official national representation in international standards development organizations. The English government, for example, charters the British Standards Institution (BSI), and the Deutsches Institut fur Normung (DIN) has a memorandum of understanding with the government of Germany. In Japan, which provides a special case, 205 private-sector trade associations and professional societies work with the responsible government ministries to develop standards. These standards operate in addition to the national standards the Japanese private sector develops under the aegis of the Ministry of International Trade and Industry (MITI) and the Japanese Industrial Standards Committee.

Like standards bodies in the western European countries and Canada, U.S. standards organizations are private entities. As discussed in Chapter 2, the U.S. government plays a less direct role in standards development and regulation than do most governments worldwide. The U.S. government is an active participant in the overall standards scene but does not regulate or administer voluntary standards programs. Some government agencies, such as the Department of Defense, the Environmental Protection Agency, and the National Institute of Standards and Technology, are dues-paying members of the American National Standards Institute (ANSI), the major standards-coordinating body in the United States. ANSI occasionally receives federal funding for specific programs. In these indirect and piecemeal ways the U.S. government does provide ANSI some funding, but not enough to run the organization.

Note: In eastern Europe and Russia standards operations are strictly government run. In other countries the lines between government and private-sector standards efforts are less clear-cut. A government may provide 100 percent funding for standards activities but farm out work to private entities. The Japanese government is in charge of standards activities, for example, but it assigns the creation, publication, and dissemination of standards to private organizations.

How Government-Related Standards Programs Are Financed. Although most governments subsidize their standards efforts, ISO records show wide variation in the sort of support its national member bodies receive. Annual budgets of ISO member bodies range from less than one million to more than sixty million Swiss francs. Governments in Japan, Mexico, Korea, and most of eastern Europe fully finance standards efforts. In Canada and in most countries in western Europe and South America, the national members receive a portion of financial support—ranging from 15 percent to 90 percent—from their governments.

When governments do not directly finance standards efforts—as is the case in the United States—or offer only partial support, then standards bodies are forced to raise money. Most do so through membership fees, sales of publications, certification fees, and so forth.

System B: International Standards Bodies

The international standards system is explored more fully in Chapter 8. The two major international standards bodies are ISO and the International Electrotechnical Commission (IEC).

1. *ISO.* ISO is a worldwide federation of 118 national standards bodies, each representing a country. The ISO Central Secretariat in Geneva coordinates the development of standardization and related activities worldwide. In this regard, the ISO works to

- Facilitate the international exchange of goods and services
- Develop cooperation in the spheres of intellectual, scientific, technological, and economic activity

In its preparation of international standards, ISO brings together the interests of producers, users (including consumers), governments, and the scientific community. This work is carried out through more than twenty-eight hundred technical bodies. Approximately forty thousand experts from all parts of the world participate each year in ISO technical work, which to date has resulted in the publication of 10,060 ISO standards.

The Central Secretariat ensures the flow of documentation throughout the member bodies, clarifies procedure with committee secretariats, administers the voting processes, and publishes the draft and final versions of the international standards that are developed. The result of this activity is ISO international standards whose scope includes all fields except electrical and electronic engineering standards.

2. *IEC.* IEC members are from forty-two national committees, each from a participating country, representing the electrotechnical interests of the country concerned. The individual national committees include manufacturers, users, governmental authorities, and teaching and professional bodies. Most national committees are industry- and government-backed.

Over the years, numerous liaisons have been established between ISO and IEC committees. For example, a joint ISO/IEC technical committee has been established in the field of information technology.

The ISO/IEC System

IEC was formed in 1906. When ISO came into being forty-one years later, the two entities agreed that the IEC would continue to handle all matters regarding worldwide electrical and electronic engineering standards. ISO handles all other international standardization issues. ISO also agreed to consult IEC in all cases that involve any electrotechnical interests. To ensure the necessary technical coordination, ISO and IEC have established a joint ISO/IEC Technical Programming Committee.

Taken jointly, ISO/IEC standards cover all industrial sectors. They provide a large body of reference documents dealing with technical specifications for goods and services; test methods; quality assurance; protection of health, safety, and the environment; units of measurement; symbols; terms; and definitions in many fields.

The primary function of the ISO/IEC system is to garner consensus in the creation of international standards. The process of negotiation and developing consensus between countries is carried out through the national members of ISO and IEC.

Every member body has the right to participate in any of the international technical committees and subcommittees established to draft standards in the different fields. The work of the technical committees and subcommittees is highly decentralized, with technical committees meeting worldwide. On average, there are fifteen meetings taking place on any given workday throughout the world. Approximately forty thousand volunteer delegates participate in the actual creation of international standards.

Central offices for both ISO and IEC are maintained in Geneva, Switzerland, where a small staff carries out the planning and coordination of technical committee work and international meetings.

International Telecommunications Union

The International Telecommunications Union (ITU) prepares recommendations that cover the technological concerns of the telecommunication industries, from telephones to radio to cable TV and beyond. ITU is not involved in standards affecting the information flow on the information highway. As one ITU member explained it, ITU is involved in "the pipe, not the pipeline." The organization is also located in Geneva and works quite regularly with ISO/IEC on development of standards.

ISO, IEC, and ITU Interaction

ISO, IEC, and ITU are the three principal international standardization bodies. They maintain a joint mission statement that commits them to formally coordinate their efforts in overlapping fields of activity, such as information technology. These efforts reflect the growing interactivity worldwide taking place in the telecommunications and broadcasting technologies.

On the technical level, the playing field for joint collaboration between the three organizations is the Joint Technical Committee (JTC) 1, Information Technology. JTC 1 is actually a joint ISO/IEC committee that includes input from ITU-T when appropriate. (ITU-T is the acronym used to denote the ITU's standardization sector.)

Example

ISO, IEC, and ITU on occasion stage joint seminars. The three organizations also maintain a joint President's Coordination Group. The presidents of all three organizations annually issue a joint World Standards Day message on October 14. Moreover, the ISO/IEC Guide 59 Code of Good Practice for Standardization names the ITU as one of the three apex organizations (along with ISO and IEC) that coordinate voluntary standardization processes on the international level.

Also, through the IT (International Telecommunications) Strategies Cooperation Group, the three organizations focus on proposals for the harmonization of IT planning efforts by standards bodies at national, regional, and international levels.

ISO Worldwide Interaction

Approximately five hundred international organizations participate in ISO work, maintaining a special liaison status with ISO. These include all U.N. specialized agencies working in similar fields. ISO works on a consulting basis with the U.N. Economic and Social Council (ECOSOC) and on an equivalent status with nearly all other bodies and specialized agencies in the U.N. system.

Some of these international bodies make a direct technical contribution to the preparation of ISO standards. Others, particularly the intergovernmental organizations, contribute to the implementation of ISO standards, utilizing them in the framework of intergovernmental agreements.

Here are some ways that international organizations connect with ISO:

- International organizations may make proposals for the preparation of ISO standards in a new field in the same way as ISO member bodies.
- International organizations may be granted "liaison" status with technical committees and subcommittees. Liaison status consists of two categories: (1) "A" (makes effective contribution to the work, including the right to submit papers, attend meetings, and participate in discussions) and (2) "B" (wishes to be kept informed only).
- International organizations that can make an effective contribution to the implementation (or prevention of implementation) of ISO standards are expressly invited to comment on all relevant drafts of standards.
- Technical committees are instructed to seek the full and, if possible, formal backing of the main international organizations in liaison for each ISO standard in which these organizations are interested.

International Guides

ISO and IEC, through ISO's Committee on Conformity Assessment (CASCO), publish a series of international guides to help with documentation for certification and other conformity assessment matters. These publications also provide guidelines for implementation of ISO/IEC standards on the national, regional, and international level.

The first edition of the ISO/IEC *Compendium on Conformity Assessment* came in 1985 in response to requests from users about the results of ISO/IEC work on conformity assessment, the catchall term for testing and certification practices (see "Basic Terms" later in this chapter). In the spring of 1995, ISO/IEC issued the third edition of the *Compendium* to reflect advances in conformity assessment techniques.

Interplay Between Standards Systems

A great deal of interplay—and politicking—occurs between industry, national/regional standards development organizations, and international standards bodies:

- National standards bodies make up the membership of organizations such as ISO.
- Industry or standards development organization representatives from a multitude of countries sit on and chair the technical committees of the ISO and other organizations—committees directly

responsible for the development and promulgation of international standards.

- Sometimes national standards—whether developed through government auspices, the private sector, or a joint effort—are adopted as international standards. When this occurs, it is through the auspices of international standards bodies such as ISO.
- Conversely, there is a growing trend for countries to adopt international standards for national use.

The "Underground" Standards System

Both nationally and internationally standards activities have become politicized to such an extent that high-ranking members of ISO technical committees have complained publicly about the jockeying for control of committees and secretariats on the part of both private companies and governments. As in any system, there are rules that govern the majority and an underground system that reflects how things are really accomplished. Knowing the right route into a standards organization or the key players may mean the ability to break or stretch the rules and allow valuable access and input that will benefit an individual company, industry, or even national or regional economy.

Example

Access to key European Union standards organizations and committees is officially off-limits to foreigners. However, high-ranking U.S. standards officials report it is common knowledge that knowing the "right" person may mean entry into this officially closed system.

How Standards Are Set Internationally

In general, standards can be set in a number of ways:

- Through the market, on a de facto basis
- By government, through the regulatory process
- Through a voluntary consensus process

Note: The consensual approach is the stated approach of most international standards bodies. In practice, however, chairmen of ISO, IEC, and other working groups and committees may wield formidable power.

As explored in later chapters, standards are set differently throughout the world. In some nations the government and standards body are one and the same, while in others, such as the United States, standards organizations are strictly private entities. Some countries set up quasi-independent standards organizations that the government funds.

In the United States, the private sector sets almost half of all standards as part of a voluntary consensus process. All or most of the key players, including government, participate (see Figure 1-1). This system reflects the American preference for laissez-faire, keeping government hands off business and letting the market rather than government create the "rules."

The Standards Development Process

Again, international standards development is discussed more fully in Chapter 8. However, as a guide to more informative reading, one should be aware that implied consensus is key to international standards creation. The *ISO/IEC Guide 2* considers a standard "a document established by consensus and approved by a recognized body that provides . . . rules, guidelines or characteristics for activities." By "consensus," ISO/IEC means "general agreement characterized by the absence of sustained opposition . . . by any important part of the concerned interests and by a process that takes into account the view of all parties concerned."

In general, the usual procedure for developing standards involves the following stages:

1. Establishing the need for a standard to address a problem or situation in industry or trade.
2. Creating a technical committee or utilizing an ongoing committee to draft the standard in question. Committee members must represent the right amount of expertise coupled with proper representation of major producers, users, and professional groups concerned with the outcome.
3. Distilling the ideas put forward and actually drafting the standard. The process often involves sorting out a variety of conflicting solutions that cater to different interests and then accepting the most reasonable compromise.
4. Conducting testing and research to verify and validate the technical content of the standard. Sometimes testing is used to resolve differences that arise during the drafting stage.
5. Repeating the consultation and modification procedures employed during the initial drafting stage, if necessary, until consensus is reached.
6. Presenting the standard for formal approval to the standards organization's worldwide membership.
7. Periodically reviewing the standard, once it is accepted, published, and publicly disseminated, using the same consultation and technical committee procedures to update and revise it, if necessary.

Figure 1-1. Participants in U.S. standards development.

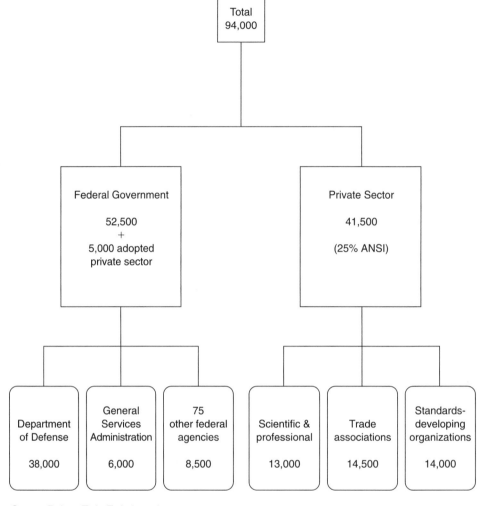

Source: Robert Toth, Toth Associates.

The Standards Communication Infrastructure

Communicating information on standards development and implementation worldwide is a vital function of the international standards infrastructure. Standards organizations in most countries maintain libraries
where interested parties can obtain information on international and regional standards on demand. In developed countries, most standards
information services offer what is called Technical Help to Exporters
(THE). Through this service, information is made available about foreign

standards and technical regulations relating to certain markets and includes such tailored services as comparative studies of regulations in several countries, procedures and formalities for submitting products for type testing, and requirements for obtaining approval for import into foreign countries. THE services may also cover diagnosis of a product to determine the degree of conformity to the standards and technical regulations it may have to face in foreign markets.

Because of increasing global reliance on electronic communications, ISO now maintains ISONET, an international information network. Although not entirely computerized, some titles, abstracts, and full texts of basic documents are kept on electronic media (such as CD-ROMs), which facilitates obtaining information in a given field via on-line access to standards-related databases.

National Differences

Despite many years of effort to harmonize standards, national standards still exist and often predominate in specific countries. Anyone who travels widely knows about the need to take along electrical current converters because electric current and supply voltages differ, especially between the United States and various European countries. Because of such differences, it is impossible for the United States to directly adopt IEC standards. The United States, in this case, is out of sync with the rest of the world, as it is in its failure to adopt the metric system. These differences exist because the push to globalize world markets cannot always transcend individual cultures and philosophical traditions. Even in Europe, where the European Union directives are law, many countries still tacitly require national product standards for entry into their individual markets (see Chapter 7).

Some international standards are endorsed as national standards as originally written, whereas others are translated for publication as national standards. As a result, equivalent texts are often available in two or more languages. ISO standards are always published in both English and French, and usually in Russian. They may be endorsed without change to become an AFNOR (France), DIN (Germany), or SFS (Finland) standard.

The Push for Standards Conformity

There is an escalating trend to adopt ISO and IEC standards as national standards. *ISO/IEC Guide 3* explains how to identify international standards functioning as national standards. In general, the country's standard designation code is coupled with ISO or IEC prefixes (e.g., an IEC standard adopted in Germany may read DIN / IEC 383).

A small number of the standards adopted by the American National Standards Institute bear the designation ANSI/ISO to indicate their acceptance as international standards. Most of these standards are in the area of photography and micrographics. Figure 1-2 provides an example of how 35mm film containers have become standardized so that all manufacturers produce them in the same size.

Some countries actually identify degrees of conformity between their national standards and the corresponding international equivalents. The British Standards Institution, for example, designates conforming standards as "identical," "technically equivalent," or "related."

European Standards Come to the Fore

Because of the creation of the European Union in the early 1990s and the desire to unite disparate nations under one economy, Europeans have been among the most prolific standards creators in the world. Moreover, European industry has a long history of participation and support of international standards efforts. The reasons are twofold:

Figure 1-2. Standardization of 35mm film containers.

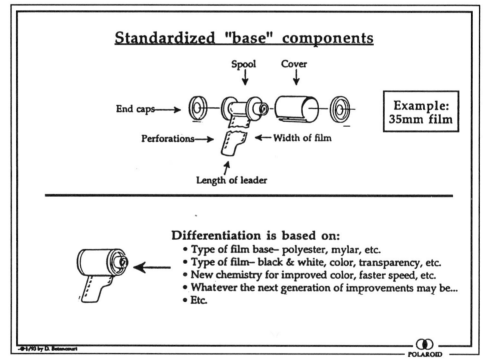

Source: © D. Betancourt, 1993.

1. European nations and the United Kingdom have a long history of worldwide trading.
2. Until the 1990s, European companies had to cross borders within their own region to do business.

Although representatives of American industry have long served on international standards technical committees, Europeans reportedly dominated those committees up to the early 1970s. It was often Europeans who handled the intricacies of harmonizing standards for the rest of the world. The other major industrial powers—Japan and the United States—displayed far less interest in international standards creation until recently, Japan's having been a member of ISO since 1952 and the United States since 1947.

Tracking Standards Developments Internationally

Europeans are not the only ones focusing more attention on standards development. As examined in later chapters, major U.S. trading partners in Latin America, as well as Southeast Asia, are also becoming standards players.

As more and more U.S. industries are involved in international trade, more and more industries will encounter international standards, making it prudent for them to become familiar with those standards. In the late 1970s, for example, standards activities affected an estimated $69 billion of U.S. exports.

U.S. exports grew at a rapid rate as a percentage of gross domestic product (GDP) over the past decade. Total U.S. exports more than doubled from 1985 to 1993, from $218 billion to $464 billion. Goods and services exports rose from 7.5 percent of GDP in 1986 to approximately 13 percent in 1993. Merchandise exports alone rose from 5 percent of GDP in 1984 to 8 percent in 1993. Exports of advanced technology products also rose sharply and now constitute a large percentage of U.S. exports. Many of these exports—from semiconductors to software—are subject to international standards, as well as technical government regulations.

The days when American standards served as worldwide models have been waning. A noted European standards official points out that "It's the U.S. habit to write standards and impose them on the rest of the world. Look at what we [Europeans] did to IBM in the mid-1980s. We obliged them to open their standards and make them compatible [with other computer standards]."

With the 1994 Uruguay Round of the General Agreement on Tariffs and Trade (GATT) and the efforts to lower trade barriers, standards, conformity assessment, and testing certification became tools for protecting markets. No nation wants other countries or markets to dictate to it how to make a product, how its companies should operate, or how it should test its products.

Given the high economic and social stakes attached to standards, how standards are developed and implemented in this emerging global order is becoming a matter of major concern to American industry. The standards development process must be fair to prevent any single interest from dictating the outcome—an outcome that may mean overhauling a company, reorienting how products are produced, how employees work, and how customers are treated. Such an outcome could be very costly if a business operating under one set of standards or testing criteria found itself having to meet another set of standards.

Example: JIS Z9901

A major battle between the United States and Japan over specialized software registration criteria was narrowly averted in the summer of 1995. That spring the Japanese Accreditation Board (JAB) announced creation of JIS Z9901, a variant of the ISO 9000 standard to be applied specifically to software manufacturers. As originally designed, JIS Z9901 affected manufacturers of all types of software—including pre-existing or mass-market "shrink-wrap" software—who wanted to sell their products in Japan, as well as manufacturers of products that include software. The clincher was that the standard mandated certification through registrars accredited and trained under this system.

Upon learning that JIS Z9901 contained special registration criteria, American electronics and software giants, as well the U.S. government, actively lobbied worldwide to force the Japanese to back off implementing JIS Z9901 in October 1995.

The American Electronics Association (AEA) and the Information Technology Industry Council (ITIC) were especially active in mobilizing industry support against the controversial JIS Z9901. These groups and their constituents considered JIS Z9901 a potential trade barrier, a possible effort to steal trade secrets, and not applicable to software manufacture.

American multinationals involved in this battle represented the crème de la crème of the computer industry. Apple Computer, IBM, Microsoft, Sun Microsystems, Motorola, and Hewlett-Packard, among others, were involved. These companies claimed JIS Z9901 could affect U.S. software sales to Japan, which totaled $504 million in 1994, making Japan the second-largest market for U.S. software in the world.

JIS Z9901 meant not only potential market loss, but also that software manufacturers worldwide with business in Europe, as well as those supplying major U.S. auto manufacturers, would have to meet three different types of ISO 9000 registration criteria: to enable them to transact business in Europe, in Japan, and for the Big Three automakers. This was a costly proposition given that earning an ISO 9000 certificate can cost an estimated $250,000 to $1 million, depending on the size and complexity of a company.

In August 1995, ANSI entered the picture and began negotiations with the Japanese over JIS Z9901. The JAB and ANSI agreed that both would conform to ISO/IEC norms for the application of ISO 9000 rather than impose special JIS Z9901 registration requirements on software manufacturers—a major victory for the industry worldwide. The agreement document is set forth in the Appendix at the end of this chapter.

The JIS Z9901 controversy backed up the contention of U.S. government experts—from the National Academy of Sciences (NAS), the Office of Technology Assessment (OTA), and the National Institute of Standards and Technology (NIST)—who had issued warnings that standards and conformity assessment practices are potent weapons in the worldwide economic arsenal. Reports from all these agencies suggest that U.S. government and industry should be striving for harmonization of standards worldwide, as well as encouraging mutual recognition agreements in the conformity assessment arena, as a means of avoiding another crisis like JIS Z9901.

Some Basic Terms

Explanations of some terms commonly used by the standards-setting community are given below.

Accreditation   The role of accreditation is similar to the role of certification. Accreditation schemes—which mainly operate on the national level—monitor the structures and working procedures of testing laboratories as well as inspect and certify bodies for both products and quality assurance. They provide customers confidence that goods and services being offered on the marketplace match recognized standards.

Conformity Assessment   Conformity assessment is the comprehensive term for the system by which products and processes are evaluated and determined to conform to particular standards. Testing, inspection, auditing, and related procedures are the tools of conformity assessment.

Laboratories   In the last decade or so many national accreditation bodies have established their own testing laboratories. Many of these laboratories, especially those existing in developed countries, operate under the auspices of standards organizations.

Metrology   The role of metrology, or measurement, is a crucial factor in setting many standards because measurement and calibration are necessary adjuncts to the testing process.

Mutual Recognition   The aim of mutual recognition is to dismantle technical obstacles and barriers to trade that relate to testing and certification and to promote worldwide harmonization of standards.

Second-Party Auditing and/or Certification   An audit by customers or large-scale buyers of their manufacturing or service suppliers. This is called second-party auditing. When these entities can offer certificates to show the suppliers are in compliance, this is called second-party certification.

Supplier's Declaration or First-Party Declaration of Conformity   A declaration by a manufacturer or service operator declaring that its product or service conforms to a certain standard—whether a national, industrial, or company standard. This is called supplier's (or first-party) declaration of conformity. Buyers are often satisfied with a declaration of conformity, believing that few companies want to risk losing face in the marketplace with false declarations.

Testing   Testing research is a necessary component of standards creation and also serves as the basis for conformity assessment. A certain amount of research testing is required to identify a product's properties and to establish criteria for follow-up testing. Industry, sometimes in collaboration with government and often with government financial backing, conducts testing in special laboratories. Once standards are written and accepted, manufacturers, users, and traders agree on routine testing procedures.

Testing plays an important role in national and international trade. Products, especially sophisticated products, require some form of testing for compliance with specifications and safety regulations before release into the world market. Even simple products and commodities are now traded on the basis of test results.

Third-Party Certification   Specialized certification bodies also offer third-party certification to buyers or suppliers who want assurance that products or services they buy or sell conform to certain standards. In this case, a specialized or independent party conducts the actual certification, and the cost is passed on to the supplier, which may then pass the cost on to the customer.

Since the release of the ISO 9000 international quality assurance standards series in 1987, quality assurance is commonly certified as well. Quality assurance tests the process of producing a product or delivering a service, or how a company operates. Third parties, or registrars, award certificates if they deem the company to be conforming to the criteria spelled out in the ISO 9000 standards series, or what is called the ISO 9000 quality assurance model.

As addressed in later chapters, the preferability of third-party certification to second-party certification is currently in dispute. Although independent bodies provide largely unbiased proof that all is functioning as it should be, third-party certification can be a costly proposition for small, midsize, and even some large companies, as has been the case with ISO 9000. Whether major customers actually save money through third-party certification is also questionable.

Example

A major-industry executive estimated that it would cost roughly $8 million a year to conduct second-party auditing of its supply base. By contrast, he estimated that third-party certification was costing this multinational approximately $20 million as suppliers increased the cost of their products to cover certification expenditures.

Resources

Eicher, Lawrence D., Secretary-General and CEO of the ISO, "The Scope of Standardization Technology, Standards Development and the Role of International Standards Organizations."

Garcia, Linda, *Global Standards: Building Blocks for the Future.*

International Organization for Standardization, Memento 1995.

National Institute of Standards and Technology, *U.S. Participation in International Standards.*

National Research Council, *Standards, Conformity Assessment and Trade into the 21st Century.*

Nicolas, Florence, with the cooperation of Jacques Repussard, a European Union publication, *Common Standards for Enterprises.*

Appendix

ANSI-JAB Agreement Establishing a Common Set of Principles and Procedures to Address Issues Involving the Development of Quality System Conformity Assessment Programs

In order to work in cooperation and resolve issues that may arise with regard to development and implementation of standards relating to quality management, and, in particular, conformity assessment for such quality management standards, the American National Standards Institute ("ANSI") and the Japan Accreditation Board for Quality System Registration ("JAB") have determined that it would be appropriate to agree on a common understanding of the role of international standards in the development of quality management system conformity assessment programs by individual standard setting organizations and accreditation bodies. The principles and guidelines that will be followed by ANSI and JAB are those that have been established by the International Standards Organization ("ISO"), the International Electrotechnical Commission ("IEC"), the World Trade Organization ("WTO"), International Accreditation Forum ("IAF"), and other related organizations, including Technical Committee 176 of the ISO, which has been assigned the role of developing international standards for quality management. Attached to this agreement as Appendix 1 is a description of certain principles and guidelines that relate to these issues.

ANSI and JAB hereby agree that they will adhere to the principles and guidelines established by ISO/IEC and related organizations in their mutual efforts to address conformity assessment issues that have arisen or may arise between them. JAB and ANSI further agree that they will work together in the context of these principles and guidelines and within the framework of the ISO/IEC to develop, agree upon, and implement any standards and any conformity assessment programs for quality management.

Dr. Takashi Ohtsubo
Executive Director
Japan Accreditation Board
for Quality System
Registration

Sergio Mazza
President
American National Standards
Institute

August 19, 1995
Dated

August 22, 1995
Dated

Part I
The American Standards System

2

The U.S. Standards System: Who's Who in Standards Institutes, Certification Bodies, Registrars, and Government Entities and How the System Works

Questions the Reader Will Find Addressed in This Chapter

1. Why start with the U.S. standards system?
2. How is the American system pluralistic?
3. How did U.S. standards develop?
4. What is the current system?
5. How does the U.S. government control standards today?
6. What are NIST services and programs?
7. What are the private-sector standards entities?
8. Who are standards organizers/coordinators?
9. What are other government activities relating to standards? International outreach?
10. What are other major American standards and quality organizations?
11. Why is the U.S. standards system criticized?

Introduction

Our exploration of world standards starts at home because American standards have often served as the basis for international standards. For many years the government and the American business sector have combined forces to create some of the most respected standards in the world. American testing and certification practices have also been emulated worldwide.

Example

The U.S. Department of Defense quality procedures, designated as MIL Q9858, served as the basis for the ISO 9000 international quality assurance standard series.

Today the United States faces competition on the standards front, especially from Europe. The European Union through contracts with private standards bodies is not only busy creating standards and testing practices to unite its disparate economies, it is also imposing those practices on any business entering its market (see Chapter 6). Other regional blocks in South America and Southeast Asia are also starting to exert pressure on the standards and testing fronts, together known as conformity assessment.

The U.S. standards system differs quite a bit from other national or regional systems. Government plays a more hands-off role than in many countries, and no single standards body dominates standards creation. Whether this system serves American business well is a matter of debate within U.S. standards circles. Therefore, it is important for businesses to understand how the U.S. system operates and determine whether the current system is serving industry needs. Becoming a standards player, or at the very least advising trade associations and legislators about concerns surrounding standards and conformity assessment practices, may very well mean survival in this new economic order.

The following are three reasons the American system bears studying at this juncture:

1. National standards bodies play major roles in international standards developments. When government and industry standards efforts are combined, the United States is one of the prime movers and shakers in the worldwide standards arena.

2. American standards, especially industry standards, are respected worldwide and form the basis for a number of international standards, if not the majority.

3. A number of American industry standards and standards programs are the international pacesetters, especially in electronics and more

recently in automotives with the Big Three automakers' common quality program QS-9000.

The Pluralistic American System

What sets the U.S. standards system apart from other countries' is its pluralistic nature. All other countries operate monolithic standards organizations, meaning one entity runs standards for that nation or national bloc.

The American National Standards Institute (ANSI) now has official government sanction to represent American standards interests overseas. ANSI coordinates standards activities for many American standards bodies, but it does not develop standards. As discussed later in this chapter, other standards developers have resisted allowing ANSI the role of premier standards institution.

That means that no single standards body predominates, allowing for a competitive approach to standards development. Because there is no public funding of standards creation and dissemination, the word *competitive* cannot be overstressed. Most American standards institutions depend on standards sales and memberships to survive.

There are about 275 private-sector standards developers maintaining ongoing standardization programs in the United States. About 150 additional organizations are occasionally involved in standards creation, while many groups or agencies review standards that concern their personal interests. This pluralistic system reflects American individualism and a market-driven economy.

See Appendix A to this chapter for a listing of industry-related standards organizations in the United States.

Although American standards proliferate, critics of the system point out that there is also a great deal of overlap and redundancy. Also, because record keeping is so hard to maintain in such a diverse system, it is almost impossible to know how many of the 94,000 private- and public-sector standards published in the United States are current. A 1991 National Institute of Standards and Technology (NIST) report listed 41,500 private-sector standards in existence. However, the author also warned that many standards developers rarely inactivate standards once they have been published.

Another factor that distinguishes the United States from other governments is its generally hands-off approach to standards organizations. Although government and industry commonly work together to develop standards, the U.S. government does not directly fund standards institutions, which means that standards development and dissemination generally take place in one of the following four ways:

1. The government promotes voluntary or mandatory standards. Mandatory standards are known as regulations.
2. The private sector develops standards for industry or service sector use.
3. The government and the private sector cooperate on standards development.
4. Government standards are placed in contracts as a condition of sale of products to government agencies, or as work conditions to the same.

A Short History of U.S. Standards Development

The United States Pharmacopeial Convention was the first American standards organization. It was organized in 1829 to establish uniform standards for drugs. Other standards organizations soon followed, generally emerging to deal with specific problems as they arose on an industry-by-industry basis. For many years these institutions operated separately without much interaction. All were private sector, setting the tone for the U.S. standards system as it exists today.

The American Iron and Steel Institute, established in 1855, was the first trade association to develop standards. The American Society of Civil Engineers, which was formed in 1852, was the first scientific standards organization.

The following is a list* of major U.S. standards-setting bodies and their founding dates. Many are still in existence today.

American Society of Mechanical Engineers (ASME)	1880
Underwriters Laboratories (UL)	1894
National Fire Protection Association (NFPA)	1896
American Society for Testing and Materials (ASTM)	1898
Building Officials and Code Administrators International (BOCA)	1915
American Gas Association Labs (AGA Labs)	1918
American National Standards Institute (ANSI)	1918
American Conference of Government Industrial Hygienists (ACGIH)	1938
Southern Building Code Congress (SBCC)	1940

---

*This list is from the U.S. Department of Commerce, National Bureau of Standards, *Standards Activities of Organizations in the United States,* NGS Special Publication 681 (Washington, D.C.: U.S. Government Printing Office, August 1984).

The federal Office of Weights and Measures was created at the end of the nineteenth century. During this period, industrialists discouraged government involvement in standards creation, but scientists and engineers began to agitate for national standards to govern measurements, precision instruments, specialized tools, and electricity. The National Bureau of Standards was established in 1901 to meet these needs.

When the United States entered World War I, it became evident that there was a need to standardize products for the war effort. The Commercial Economy Board of the Council of National Defense came into being and eventually supervised the production of over thirty thousand commercial items. This was part of a campaign to simplify the use of labor, capital, and equipment for all industries.

By the 1920s, there was additional call to introduce government into the standards process. Then Secretary of Commerce Herbert Hoover waged his standardization crusade of 1921 to reduce waste in industry and the economy as a whole. The Commerce Department eventually established the Division of Simplified Practice to supply government guidance, information, and assistance to business in the standards arena. All participation was strictly voluntary.

The pattern for the rest of the century was set during the 1920s as consumers started to press for more government intervention in standards development and regulation and the business community resisted this approach. Industry complained that the National Bureau of Standards was meddling in its affairs.

During the Depression, the Division of Simplified Practice lost most of its staff and funding. Much of its work in the area of commercial standards was transferred to the private-sector American Standards Association (ASA). ASA, in the meantime, proposed a stronger role as de facto national standards coordinator. These proposals were rebuffed by government and industry alike. No national charter for ASA was issued, but the organization was allowed to rename itself the American National Standards Institute (ANSI). As discussed later, ANSI continues its efforts to serve as the prime U.S. standards body, with other standards organizations resisting this approach.

Thanks to Ralph Nader and other consumer and safety activists, the 1960s and 1970s saw a rekindling of government involvement in standards. Nader particularly targeted the automobile industry. In 1967 Congress set up the National Commission on Product Safety to analyze the effectiveness of consumer product standards. The conclusion was that many standards created under the voluntary system were not adequate to protect the health and safety of the public.

As a result of commission findings, a Federal Trade Commission (FTC) investigation into the U.S. standards system, and other studies, there was a general push for additional regulation and a major increase in the number of federal agencies issuing standards. A large body of environmental, health, and safety legislation was passed, and agencies were created to administer these laws. They include the Consumer Product Safety Commission (CPSC), the Environmental Protection Agency (EPA), and the Occupational, Safety and Health Administration (OSHA).

Moving Into the Current System

Throughout the 1960s and 1970s, there was a continued government push for a unified, national standards policy with government playing a major role. As it had since the nineteenth century, the business community successfully resisted government control of standards creation and implementation. By the late 1960s, though, there was some agreement that additional coordination of standards activities should take place on a federal level, and Congress directed the Commerce Department to set up an interagency mechanism to better advise federal agency chiefs on implementing standards policy.

A major recognition of standards' growing economic importance came in 1968 with the formation of the Interagency Committee on Standards Policy (ICSP) to act as a coordinator and liaison between federal agencies that deal with standards. The Office of Management and Budget (OMB) Circular A-119 specified ICSP's makeup and function. Under this circular it was decreed that the ICSP be made up of policy-level representatives of the thirteen federal cabinet departments, twelve independent federal agencies, and two offices in the Executive Office of the President, including the OMB. The National Institute of Standards and Technology—which had long assumed the duties of the former Bureau of Standards—was to provide the chairman and general direction for the committee, with overall direction resting with the OMB. The committee was required to report back to the OMB on a triennial basis.

In its early years, the ICSP focused on encouraging federal agency use of voluntary standards. The committee also set standards for agency participation in voluntary standards bodies and laid out guidelines for public-sector use of private certification bodies. Recommendations were generally in the form of guideline documents transmitted to the secretary of commerce for distribution to the heads of agencies and departments represented on the committee, and they might also be published in the *Federal Register*. Over the years, the ICSP has focused little on evaluating U.S. standards policy or identifying future standards issues.

During this same period, an interagency task force was also set up under the auspices of the Office of the U.S. Trade Representative (USTR) in conjunction with the 1979 Trade Act. Although somewhat more active than the NIST Interagency Committee on Standards Policy, its focus is more limited. Agency members meet when necessary to try to reconcile trade and other agency policies. In terms of standards, the committee is reputed to be reactive, responding only when the need arises.

The Trade Act of 1979 continued the government's ambivalent approach to directing U.S. standards activities, with government officials eager to take a more proactive role yet holding back for lack of industry approval. The act required the secretaries of commerce and agriculture to monitor the standards process to ensure that U.S. interests were adequately represented, but it provided no guidelines by which to make those determinations.

Although the Trade Act of 1979 lacked clout, it has resulted in a great deal of government participation in private-sector standards development. For example, the Nuclear Regulatory Commission (NRC) works closely with the American Society for Manufacturing Engineers (ASME) on nuclear-related standards. The EPA advises on private efforts to produce and promote environmental standards.

The Department of Defense (DOD) remains one of the largest promulgators of standards in the world. Also prolific is the General Services Administration (GSA), which produces federal specifications and standards for federal and state agencies to procure many common products. GSA test methods are used in many industries.

Of late, both the DOD and the GSA are moving away from standards creation. Industry standards, including the ISO 9000 series, are increasingly being accepted in lieu of military specifications to such an extent that both agencies are currently canceling out more standards than they are creating (see Appendix B at end of chapter).

Example

From 1981 to 1990, the DOD canceled seventy-six hundred of its specifications and standards, created three thousand new ones, and adopted two thousand industry standards. The three thousand new standards fell into the commercial-item-description category, which provides procurement specifications for off-the-shelf products.

The U.S. Government and Standards Today

In terms of domestic policy, the U.S. government's approach to standards has not changed much since the late 1970s. In the last twenty years, NIST and other government agencies have still actively participated in private-sector standards development while maintaining a hands-off approach to standards implementation. The government has focused most of its attention on ensuring that the standards-development process is carried out in a fair and effective fashion while retaining the right to assume a greater role in this area when necessary.

Some government agencies are set up to respond to business concerns about standards, but to date there is no formal government body established to educate the public about the use of standards in global trade. The government does sponsor National Standards Week as one of its premier efforts to promote public awareness of standards and their economic importance.

More recently, government spending cutbacks also have affected NIST outreach in the standards arena. Congress has even considered eliminating the Commerce Department, of which NIST is a part.

Critics of the U.S. standards system believe interagency task forces like the ICSP are largely ineffective because they lack focus and clout in the standards arena. None of these task forces or committees has adequate staffing or is directed to act strategically. In fact, it is generally conceded that interagency committees tend to be weak in policy coordination.

It is largely on the international front that the government's involvement in standards is changing most. Information on this subject is outlined later in this chapter and more fully in Chapter 3.

Standards Figures

The huge numbers of U.S. standards in print can be deceiving. Many standards are never used. Standards developers report that 80 percent of orders they receive for standards sales are for about 15 to 20 percent of the standards published. Furthermore, NIST studies indicate that despite five-year reviews, many U.S. standards document obsolete technology that is not relevant to new designs. As much as 25 to 30 percent of national standards—both industry and government—may fall into this category.

Moreover, redundancy is rife in this system of overlapping standards activity. For example, more than two hundred government and private-sector organizations generate eleven thousand standards that fall in the category of building and construction. Studies indicate that as many as five hundred or six hundred standards defining the same processes may be in existence.

By the early 1990s, NIST had started to address the issue of redundancy. The agency also started to sort out defunct standards bodies such as the Fragrance Materials Association and drop them from rosters of U.S. standards organizations. At the same time, the agency discovered at least forty new standards producers, many in the fields of new technology. These included the following:

- Automated Imaging Association
- Corporation for Open Systems International

- Home Automation Association
- Laser Institute of America
- Robotic Industries Association

Summary of Government Players

The Commerce Department is the main government body involved in standards activities both in the United States and abroad. Within Commerce, standards activities are largely divided between the National Institute of Standards and Technology (NIST) and the International Trade Administration (ITA).

National Institute of Standards and Technology

NIST handles much of the technical and educational side of standards, as well as provides technical assistance to developing countries. Although NIST is quite active in attempts to harmonize standards worldwide and to assist developing countries with their standards efforts, much of its current domestic standards role is limited to educational programs and publication of standards directories and reports. NIST also serves as the U.S. inquiry point under the General Agreement on Tariffs and Trade (GATT) Agreement on Technical Barriers to Trade.

NIST Programs and Services. NIST offers a wide variety of services and programs to help U.S. industry improve its international competitiveness through proper use of new technology and emphasis on quality processes and conformity assessment. The following are some of the sectors where NIST provides services and programming that relate to standards and conformity assessment:

Standards Code and Information Program. The Standards Code and Information (SCI) Program staff assist federal agencies and industry with specific technically based trade issues related to standards and conformity assessment. SCI serves as the secretariat for the U.S. Interagency Committee on Standards Policy (ICSP) and has published guidelines on U.S. government participation in international standards bodies, federal use of third-party and self-certification, and federal use of laboratory accreditation. It has formed various working groups to deal with issues of multiagency concern related to standards and conformity assessment issues.
  In addition, the SCI staff

- Develop technical positions for U.S. negotiators in bilateral and multilateral discussions

- Monitor and report on the adequacy of U.S. participation in international standardization efforts
- Handle complaints from U.S. industry representatives concerning foreign standards and certification practices
- Review and transmit U.S. comments on proposed foreign regulations, especially under its cooperative government-industry program with the Saudi Arabian Standards Organization
- Monitor national and international developments related to standards and conformity assessment activities
- Hold voting membership in various national and international standards committees
- Participate in interagency task forces and working groups to develop government positions on major international standards-related developments, such as the formation of the European Single Market, the North American Free Trade Agreement (NAFTA), and negotiations under the Standards Code
- Publish information detailing the standards and conformity assessment activities of U.S. private and government organizations as well as international and regional organizations
- Publish other reports related to the ISO 9000 standards series, U.S. participation in international standardization, formation of the European Single Market, and other topics

National Center for Standards and Certification Information. Not to be confused in name or intent with the aforementioned Standards Code and Information Program, the NIST National Center for Standards and Certification Information is strictly information based. It serves as the U.S. focal point for information on standardization programs and related activities at home and abroad.

Center staff provide information on U.S., foreign, regional, and international voluntary standards bodies, as well as on mandatory government regulations and conformity assessment procedures for nonagricultural products.

The center maintains an extensive collection of reference materials, including U.S. military and other federal government specifications, U.S. industry and national standards, international standards, and selected foreign national standards.

As the U.S. member of the International Organization for Standardization Information Network (ISONET), the center has access to foreign national standards information through approximately sixty other ISONET members and the ISO information center in Geneva, Switzerland.

Weights and Measures Program. One of NIST's longest-running programs, Weights and Measures helps federal, state, and local governments ensure equity in marketplace measurements. It includes an accreditation program for state weights and measures laboratories in the areas of mass, length, and volume, as well as provides test protocols, training, and ongoing laboratory assistance.

Through this program NIST sponsors the National Conference on Weights and Measures, a standards development organization that involves over three thousand industry and regulatory agency representatives. Program staff also manage the National Type Evaluation Program, which, at manufacturers' expense, evaluates commercial measuring devices against national and international standards. The staff also produce numerous training manuals, handbooks, and other publications, and they operate an electronic bulletin board to provide the weights and measures community with a mechanism for rapidly exchanging information.

Standards Management. NIST manages U.S. technical representation and participation in the International Organization of Legal Metrology (OIML). OIML is a treaty organization with a membership of fifty-one voting and thirty-seven nonvoting nations. OIML's objective is to enhance trade through harmonization of national regulations governing performance requirements for measuring instruments. These are instruments used for equity in commerce, for ensuring public and worker health and safety, and for protecting the environment.

NIST also administers the U.S. Department of Commerce's Voluntary Product Standards (VPS) program. Under the VPS program, NIST provides the secretariat for the development and maintenance of voluntary standards for selected products. Trade associations help fund this program, with current emphasis on softwood lumber, construction and industrial plywood, wood-based structural-use panels, and glass bottles for carbonated soft drinks.

National Voluntary Laboratory Accreditation Program. The NIST National Voluntary Laboratory Accreditation Program (NVLAP) evaluates the competencies and technical qualifications of public and private laboratories that provide testing and calibration services. A NIST-accredited laboratory must meet all requirements of national consensus standards, as well as international accreditation requirements of the International Standards Organization (ISO Guide 25 and related standards).

For a fee, NVLAP offers current accreditation to qualified laboratories that offer services in the following testing areas: product testing (acoustics, carpets, paints, paper, plumbing, seals, sealants, insulation), computer networks, construction products (cement, concrete), electromagnetic compatibility, energy-efficient lighting, fasteners and metals (chemical, dimensional, metallurgical), telecommunications, and others. Accreditation is also available in the following calibration areas: dimensional, electrical, radiation, mechanical, thermodynamics, and time and frequency.

Any interested laboratory, organization, or agency can apply for accreditation in these and other areas. Requests for expanded program services are evaluated on a case-by-case basis.

Calibration Services. NIST provides more than five hundred different services to ensure that manufacturers and other users of precision instruments achieve measurements of the highest possible quality, a major component of quality assurance programs such as ISO 9000. These services, which satisfy the most demanding and explicit requirements, link a customer's precision equipment or in-house standards to national standards.

For calibrations and special tests, NIST personnel check, adjust, or characterize an instrument, device, or set of in-house or transfer standards. Customers are assured that measurements are consistent with national standards and adequate for their intended use. Besides individual equipment items, NIST measurement assurance programs calibrate entire measurement systems.

The services, available for a fee, encompass seven major areas: dimensional measurements; mechanical, including flow, acoustic, and ultrasonic; thermodynamics; optical radiation; ionizing radiation; electromagnetics, including direct current, alternating current, radio frequency, and microwave; and time and frequency.

National Voluntary Conformity Assessment Systems Evaluation Program. The National Voluntary Conformity Assessment Systems Evaluation (NVCASE) program provides government assurance to foreign competitors that U.S.-accredited testing laboratories are providing credible service. NIST has already achieved recognition of the laboratories it accredits through agreements with several countries, but NVCASE addresses all aspects of conformity assessment (e.g., product certification, quality assurance, type approval).

Malcolm Baldrige National Quality Award. First presented in 1988, the Malcolm Baldrige National Quality Award is the U.S. national award of excellence for achievement in industry and a comprehensive guide to quality improvement. Congress established the award to raise awareness about quality management and to recognize U.S. companies that have successful quality management systems. NIST develops and manages the award program with the assistance of the American Society for Quality Control (ASQC). In recent years European and Japanese standards officials have emulated the Baldrige, setting up indigenous awards to promote quality.

Information Hot Lines. NIST provides information about foreign standards and certification requirements and maintains a GATT hot line with a recording that reports on the latest technical developments that could affect trade. The agency also helps exporters identify European standards and directives so they can correctly market products to the EU. An EU hot line provides information on directives and draft standards of the European Committee for Standardization (CEN) and the European Committee for Electrotechnical Standardization (CENELEC).

The following are NIST numbers to contact for standards information:

- National Center for Standards and Certification Information: 301-975-4040
- GATT hot line: 301-975-4041
- EU hot line: 301-921-4164
- Interagency Committee on Standards Policy (ICSP): 301-975-2396

International Trade Administration

ITA staffers offer the following standards-related services help to U.S. exporters:

- The Interagency Federal Advisory Committee (IFAC) answers general business concerns about standards.

- The Office of Multilateral Affairs serves as a contact point for U.S. multilateral trade policy issues related to the General Agreement on Tariffs and Trade (GATT), now the World Trade Organization (WTO), and other international organizations.

- International Economic Policy (IEP) country desk officers provide information on trade potential for U.S. products in specific countries. Specialists are organized by the following regions: Western Hemisphere, Europe, Africa, the Near East, South Asia, East Asia and the Pacific, and Japan.

- Trade development industry officers work with manufacturing and service industry associations, as well as individual companies, to identify trade opportunities and obstacles by product, service, industry sector, and market.

- The Office of European Union and Regional Affairs (OEURA), part of the ITA, works to ensure that U.S. exporters maintain access to European markets and to improve market access wherever possible. In carrying out this mission, OEURA develops policy, participates in negotiations, and provides information to U.S. businesses regarding legislative, regulatory, and policy matters in western Europe that might have an impact on U.S. exports to that region.

Additional Government Players

United States Trade Representative. The United States Trade Representative's (USTR) office also becomes a player when there are concerns that foreign governments are manipulating standards and conformity assessment practices to their competitive advantage. The USTR maintains an inter-agency task force to address conflicts that arise when standards affect trade issues. It does not set standards policy or act strategically in this area. The USTR also responds to business inquiries about standards, but is not set up to offer standards education.

National Academy of Sciences. At the request of Congress or other government agencies, the National Academy of Sciences has written extensive reports, booklets, and policy statements on standards issues. The academy also issues reports on standards topics.

Other. Quite a few government agencies are active participants in private-sector standards creation. This is especially true in health, safety, environment, food and drugs, as well as energy and nuclear power. The number of standards that government agencies set is small in comparison to private-sector standards efforts. Many agencies rely on standards created by the private sector.

The Private Sector

As noted, the private sector contributes heavily to standards creation. There are five major types of private-sector standards organizations actively involved in standards development:

1. Trade associations
2. Science and professional societies
3. General membership organizations
4. Third-party certifiers
5. Consortia

Trade Associations. Standards developed by trade associations reflect industry needs and market forces and are designed to promote individual industries and their products. Some develop standards only at the request of individual members, while others create standards for the industry as a whole. Although some trade associations sell standards, most are supported through membership dues. Participation is generally high. The following are some major trade association players in the standards arena:

- National Electrical Manufacturers Association (NEMA)
- American Petroleum Institute (API)
- Information Technology Industry Council (ITIC)
- Aerospace Industries Association (AIA)

Science and Professional Societies. Professional societies tend to create standards to advance theory and practice in a technical field. Most have a strong engineering bent. Members participate as individuals, not as industry or company representatives. For this reason, industry groups often complain that the standards set by professional societies do not adequately represent market forces.

Many professional societies rely on sales of standards for funding. This free-market approach makes them competitive and jealous of other standards bodies, creating tension within the U.S. standards community. The following are five professional societies known for their standards:

1. American Society of Agricultural Engineers (ASAE)
2. American Society of Automotive Engineers (ASAE)
3. Institute of Electrical and Electronics Engineers (IEEE)
4. American Association of Cereal Chemists
5. Society of Photographic Scientists and Engineers

General Membership Organizations. General membership organizations are the most broad-based of all standards development organizations, meaning participants represent a variety of backgrounds and interests. Standards sales often make up as much as 80 percent of their income. One example of an association in this category is the National Fire Protection Association (NFPA).

Third-Party Certifiers. Third-party certifiers are independent product-testing organizations. Most have a strong engineering bent. Some groups double as standards writers. Two major certifiers that participate in standards creation are the Underwriters Laboratories and the American Gas Association.

Consortia. Consortia are relatively new to the U.S. standards community. These groups have emerged to deal with the rapidly developing information and communication technologies and tend to be exclusive, operating in a relatively closed membership environment.

There are currently about four hundred consortia operating in the United States. Very much the mavericks of the U.S. standards community, some consortia are known to ignore regular standards channels and directly lobby international bodies such as ISO and IEC, which has raised alarm among the more established standards organizations. Consortia ignore such concerns. Their members complain to U.S. government officials that the current system is too cumbersome to adequately handle standards issues in the fast-moving high-tech sector.

Note: Organizations founded specifically to develop standards are often called standards-developing organizations, or SDOs. The American Society for Testing and Materials (ASTM) is often classified as an SDO.

The growth of international standards is depicted in Figure 2-1.

Figure 2-1. The growing trend toward the use of international standards.

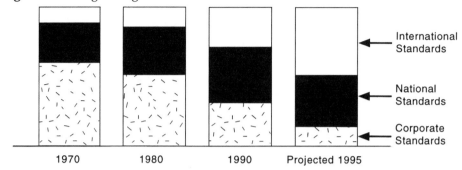

Standards Organizers and Coordinators
==========

In addition to organizations involved in developing standards, there are those that sell or promote standards, as well as coordinate such standards activities as seminars and conferences and standards dissemination. Some serve various purposes—promotion of quality, for example—while maintaining an active presence in the U.S. standards community. The American National Standards Institute (ANSI) is by far the most prominent of these sorts of organizations.

American National Standards Institute

Based in New York, the American National Standards Institute (ANSI) is a private, nonprofit federation of some 285 technical, professional and trade standards, labor, educational, and consumer organizations, 1,300 private companies, and government representatives whose main purpose is to act as a clearinghouse for voluntary national standards. Although functioning independently, many major U.S. standards bodies take advantage of ANSI's wide outreach and coordinate the technical content of their activities with the organization. (ANSI officials consider the diversity and expertise of its broad membership to be a major organizational strength.)

ANSI does not develop standards and it does not act as judge or overseer of the standards its member organizations create. These bodies develop standards on a decentralized, committee basis, whereas ANSI helps coordinate those efforts. ANSI certifies that these voluntary standards bodies have arrived at standards through one of three ANSI-accredited procedures that ensure due process and consensus have been achieved.

Once a standard meets ANSI's approval, it is considered an American national standard. An estimated 25 percent of all nongovernmental standards—close to ten thousand—have gone through the ANSI process. Only

ANSI-accredited standards developers can submit standards for consideration as American national standards. The process for achieving status as an American national standard is laid out in ANSI's *Procedures for the Development and Coordination of American National Standards*.

ANSI is also a source of technical and nontechnical standards-related information. The institute publishes several publications to provide information on the initiation of standards projects, as well as domestic and international standards-related information.

ANSI's Main Functions. ANSI officials consider the following to be the institute's five main functions and purposes:

1. Serving as the national body for voluntary standardization activities in the United States through which standards-developing groups may cooperate in establishing, approving, and improving standards based on a consensus of all interested parties
2. Promoting the voluntary standardization system as a means of advancing the national economy; benefiting the public health, safety, and welfare; and facilitating domestic and international trade and commerce
3. Establishing, promulgating, and administering procedures and criteria for the recognition and approval of American national standards
4. Encouraging existing organizations to develop and submit standards for approval
5. Representing the interests of the U.S. voluntary standards system in international nontreaty standardization organizations

ANSI Governance. A board of directors manages and controls the institute's activities, affairs, and property. The board reflects ANSI's membership and is made up of senior-level representatives from industry, government, trade associations, professional societies, and academia.

A chairman and three vice chairmen are elected from the board. All board members are expected to participate in ANSI's governance through representation in one or more board committees. These are the Executive Committee, the Finance Committee, the Audit Committee, the International Advisory Committee, the Compensation Committee, the Strategic Planning Committee, the Board Committee on Conformity Assessment, the Accreditation Committee, the Membership Committee, and the Education Committee.

In addition, ANSI has four member councils that represent the concerns and interests of various elements of its membership: the Company Member Council, the Consumer Interest Council, the Government

Member Council, and the Organizational Member Council. The chairman of each member council sits on both the board of directors and the executive committee of the board to ensure that members' interests reach the ANSI hierarchy. Council activities range from advising the board of directors on policy matters to assisting in program implementation.

There are also the following councils, boards, planning panels, and coordinating committees: the United States National Committee of the International Electrotechnical Commission (USNC), the Information Technology Consultative Committee, the Standards and Data Services Committee, the Executive Standards Council, and the Board of Standards Review. There are also appeals boards, standards boards, and standards-planning panels.

Publication of American National Standards. Developers of standards that are accepted as American National Standards have the right to publish the final approved standard themselves or have ANSI do so. The ANSI Publications Department prepares manuscripts for publication according to the IEC/ISO format and style to provide for international consistency and availability of U.S. standards for international use.

Relationship With U.S. Government. As noted, the U.S. government only occasionally offers direct funding to ANSI in the form of grants and government agency memberships. Most of ANSI's income is derived from publication sales, membership dues, and private-sector support. To survive, ANSI must meet the needs of its diverse and sometimes contentious membership.

There are several ways the U.S. government directly participates in ANSI, including the following:

• Members of government agencies—including the Department of Defense (DOD) and Occupational Safety and Health Administration (OSHA)—serve on ANSI's board.

• In the summer of 1995, ANSI and NIST signed a memorandum of understanding (MOU) that granted ANSI government recognition and support as the leading U.S. standards organization and official representative of U.S. standards interests abroad. The decision to grant ANSI government backing—which was many years in the making—revolved around awareness that U.S. competitiveness abroad was weakened because of fragmented representation in foreign standards activities. (See Appendix C to this chapter for a copy of the actual document.)

In granting the MOU, NIST officials cited support of U.S. competitiveness, economic growth, health, safety, and the protection of the environment as main reasons for their support of ANSI. There was agreement that a national approach to creating an international standards policy was proving necessary to U.S. interests abroad.

The MOU cites the need for better communications within and between the private sector and the federal government to ensure the timely flow of information and the need for improved liaison to facilitate decision making and implement actions on standards at the national and international levels. According to both ANSI and NIST, it is critical that affected U.S. regulatory agencies have the opportunity to contribute to the development and implementation of national and international voluntary standards. The MOU is expected to achieve the following four objectives:

1. Strengthen the recognition of ANSI and the entire U.S. voluntary standards community at the international and national levels.
2. Ensure that international players recognize ANSI's representation of U.S. interests.
3. Increase the effectiveness of federal agency participation in the international voluntary standards-setting process.
4. Improve domestic communication among both private- and public-sector parties in the United States on voluntary standards issues.

Note: The MOU does not alter NIST's involvement in standards activities or remove federal government authority to regulate standards and conformity assessment practices where it now does so. Both NIST and ANSI under this new relationship provide for greater involvement of government agencies in standards development and implementation while promoting continued growth of public- and private-sector cooperation.

ANSI had made numerous requests for an MOU prior to 1995 but was always rebuffed. Major players in the U.S. standards community were not willing to cede the primary U.S. standards role to ANSI. Not only do a number of organizations act independently of ANSI in their international standards dealings, but some standards bodies refuse to defer to ANSI leadership when it comes to domestic standards activities. Sometimes, rather than work through ANSI, these organizations have called on the government to take charge.

It is still too soon to tell how the ANSI-NIST memorandum of understanding will affect U.S. standards development, standards policy, and standards posture in the world. Despite the MOU, the U.S. standards system is still pluralistic. Whether other leading U.S. standards developers will consider ANSI their leading body or go their own way is uncertain.

Other Government Activities. Even before the memorandum of understanding signing, ANSI was involved with NIST in the following sort of government-related activities:

• ANSI and NIST are creating the National Standards System Network (NSSN) to electronically link the standards systems of hundreds of organizations involved in the development, production, distribution, and use of technical standards. NSSN will provide cataloging, indexing, searching, and routing capabilities to the entire range of national, regional, and international standards and standards-related information bases. Development is projected over a five-year period.

• ANSI and the Environmental Protection Agency (EPA) are working on an outreach and education project for environmental management standards.

• In 1995, ANSI's government relations activities focused on building stronger, bipartisan relationships with Congress.

• ANSI operates coordinating committees with both the Occupational Safety and Health Administration (OSHA) and the Consumer Product Safety Commission (CPSC). Both these joint coordinating committees provide for policy-level dialogues on voluntary standards activities.

• ANSI representatives testified before congressional committees and subcommittees on numerous occasions in 1995 on issues ranging from the proposed dismantling of the Commerce Department to proposed regulatory reform, U.S. competitiveness, and economic growth.

Note. ANSI has been a staunch defender of NIST, its backer as the leading U.S. standards organization. During the legendary 1995 budget battles, ANSI members argued in favor of maintaining NIST and all its activities, especially its test laboratories. In addition, ANSI members and staff have met with other congressional committee staff to educate them about NIST's importance to U.S. industry and the U.S. voluntary standardization community.

• In April 1995, ANSI and the Defense Department cosponsored a conference on DOD's efforts to reduce reliance on military specifications and standards and increase reliance on private-sector standards.

International Outreach. ANSI's international role is discussed more fully in later chapters. Besides serving as the recognized U.S. member body to ISO and as the U.S. National Committee to the IEC, ANSI is also the U.S. member body of the Pacific Area Standards Congress (PASC) and the Pan-American Standards Commission (COPANT), among others.

Other international activities include:

• Promoting international standards that reflect U.S. interests through development of an international distribution network for American National Standards.

- Facilitating and promoting U.S. interests in international standards arenas.
- Serving the United States as representative to the two major non-treaty standards organizations, the Geneva-based ISO and IEC.
- Acting as partner to the U.S. Registrar Accreditation Board (RAB), which accredits registrars to offer ISO 9000 certificates. In this arrangement, ANSI sets policy and the RAB acts as the operational arm.

Other Major American Standards and Quality Organizations

Through its partnership with the U.S. Registrar Accreditation Board (RAB), ANSI is an active participant in conformity assessment issues relating to quality and quality assurance. However, it is not the only influential American standards body operating in this and other realms. Following are some other institutions of note.

United States National Committee of the International Electrotechnical Commission (USNC/IEC). USNC/IEC is the U.S. representative to IEC. Technically, USNC is an independent organization, although it is attached to ANSI through its Electrical and Electronics Standards Board.

American Society for Quality Control (ASQC). Headquartered in Milwaukee, Wisconsin, ASQC is a leading promoter and seller of quality-related standards. This nonprofit organization both administers the Malcolm Baldrige Award for the Commerce Department and serves as "parent" organization to the RAB, which accredits ISO 9000 registrars. ASQC also administers the U.S. technical advisory group to the ISO's quality management Technical Committee (TC) 176 on behalf of ANSI. TC 176 is the developer of the ISO 9000 standards series (see Chapter 8).

According to the ASQC, its members include individuals and organizations dedicated to the ongoing development, advancement, and promotion of quality concepts, principles, and technologies, with the aim of facilitating continuous improvement and increased customer satisfaction by identifying, communicating, and promoting the use of quality principles, concepts, and technologies.

ASQC has 130,000 individual and 1,000 "sustaining" members worldwide. Divided into 248 sections of local chapters, its concerns range over twenty-one technical divisions, from chemical and process industries to design and construction, education, defense, automotive, electronics, textiles, and many others.

United States Registrar Accreditation Board. The RAB oversees accreditation of third-party certifiers that assess suppliers of goods and services. A nonprofit organization, it is known especially for accrediting ISO 9000 registrars through the American National Accreditation Program for Registrars of Quality Systems, which it runs in partnership with ANSI. ISO 9000 registrars are the independent parties that issue ISO 9000 certificates.

The RAB is the sole operator of the Certification Program for Auditors of Quality Systems. Auditors who pass through this process are considered qualified to audit quality systems against recognized quality standards series such as ISO 9000. The RAB also accredits training courses for ISO 9000.

International Association of Accredited Registrars. The International Association of Accredited Registrars (IAAR) has been in existence since 1993 and represents the interests of registrars accredited to work with companies on their ISO 9000 certification. Its main purpose is to promote consistency, credibility, and integrity in the accreditation process. IAAR members also provide input to international organizations such as the International Accreditation Forum on proposed standards and operating procedures.

IAAR has about thirty-six members. To be eligible for joining, registrars must be accredited by a worldwide recognized accreditation body, such as the U.S. RAB.

Government-Industry Standards Forums. Given the rise of standards and conformity assessment as nontariff trade barriers, industry has been concerned that standards—whether product-oriented or quality-related—do not turn into trade barriers inadvertently. There is also an effort to ensure that standards programs are implemented properly on an international level without undue coercion and undue government regulation.

Several government-industry forums have been created in recent years to gather industry input, especially in the area of international standards. These include the following:

- *National Industries Competitiveness Information Technology Forum.* The Commerce Department runs this forum, which gathers industry input into international standards issues.
- *Industry Coalition on Standards and Trade.* A relatively new forum that represents multinationals and trade associations, this group has been discussing ways for U.S. industry to become more involved in international standards development.
- *Government Quality Liaison Panel (GQLP).* The GQLP is made up of representatives from government and industry working together to

rethink the policies, practices, and procedures that have been the cornerstone of government acquisition. As part of this process, the GQLP has developed a plan to move the government toward adoption of commercial and industrial quality practices. ISO 9000 is recommended as the base quality system.

U.S. Standards System Under Attack

As the United States becomes increasingly involved in the global market, there is growing criticism that the country lacks a national standards policy. Moreover, on the government side, standards activities abroad are divided generally between NIST and the United States Trade Representative (USTR). NIST focuses primarily on mutual recognition and harmonization efforts, along with helping developing countries with their standardization efforts. The USTR gets involved when standards pose a possible barrier to trade.

Standards experts, especially those involved on the government side, decry this divided approach to representing American standards efforts in the international economic and political arena. There is concern that the country lacks leadership on the standards front just at a time when it is becoming obvious that standards of other countries have a major impact on costs to U.S. producers trying to export to foreign countries. (The issue of standards as trade barriers is discussed further in Chapter 12.)

Many standards experts—especially government experts—would like to see the U.S. standards community either unite or allow more government intervention. Industry continues to resist these sorts of proposals, as it has historically resisted government control of standards activities. As the NIST/ANSI memorandum of understanding indicates, there is a movement toward more public- and private-sector cooperation in this arena.

That the U.S. government offers very little direct funding of standards activities can be considered both a strength and a weakness. On the one hand, control of standards development and dissemination remains within the private sector. On the other, standards organizations are often dependent on sale of standards and standards-related publications for their financial survival. Under the worst-case scenario, unproven standards may be pushed onto the market and hyped beyond their worth.

Example

Many businesspeople in the United States and Europe believed the ISO 9000 standards series became so popular in part because it provided income for standards institutions, seminar holders, consultants, and registrars. ISO 9000 gained the reputation in some circles as the "cash cow" of quality buzzwords. In fact, a reputed $10-billion-a-year business has grown up around ISO 9000. The hype around ISO 9000 often obscured its usefulness as both a quality and a communications tool.

Advice for Companies

With standards emerging as a major pocketbook item, companies cannot afford to ignore the debate surrounding the U.S. standards system. Working with and improving the U.S. standards system should be a major agenda item for businesses and their trade associations. Here are some recommendations that companies can consider for internal discussion and bring to the attention of the lobbying arm of their trade association, or even to legislators:

- Strike a better balance between the public and private sectors on the standards front.
- Unite private-sector standards bodies for better coordination with government and present a stronger front overseas.
- Improve coordination of government standards efforts, as well as institute some system for conflict resolution.
- Create a government organization capable of identifying standards problems, setting goals, and evaluating system performance—although some major companies still oppose this type of action.

Resources

American National Standards Institute Public Relations Office (ANSI reports and releases), 11 West 42nd Street, New York, N.Y. 10036.

Defense System Management College, *Standards and Trade in the 1990s: A Source Book for Department of Defense Acquisition and Standardization Management and Their Industrial Counterparts.*

Global Standards: Building Blocks for the Future.

National Institute of Standards and Technology, *A Review of U.S. Participation in International Standards Activities.*

Toth, Robert B., ed., *Standards Activities of Organizations in the United States*, NIST Special Publication 806.

Appendix A

Directory of U.S. Industry-Related Standards Organizations (by Acronym)

AREA
American Railway Engineering
  Association

ARI
Air-Conditioning & Refrigeration
  Institute

ARINC
Aeronautical Radio Inc.

ARM
Asphalt Roofing Manufacturers
  Association

ARMA
ARMA International

ARTBA
American Road & Transportation
  Builders Association

ASA
Acoustical Society of America

ASAE
American Society of Agricultural
  Engineers

ASBC
American Society of Brewing
  Chemists

ASCE
American Society of Civil
  Engineers

ASEP
American Society of Electroplated
  Plastics Inc.

ASHRAE
American Society of Heating,
  Refrigerating & Air-
  Conditioning Engineers Inc.

ASME
American Society of Mechanical
  Engineers

ASNT
American Society for
  Nondestructive Testing Inc.

ASPA
American Sod Producers
  Association

ASPRS
American Society for
  Photogrammetry & Remote
  Sensing

ASRS
Automated Storage/Retrieval
  Systems Association

ASSE
American Society of Safety
  Engineers

ASSE
American Society of Sanitary
    Engineering

ASTA
American Spice Trade Association
    Inc.

ASTM
American Society for Testing &
    Materials

ATA
Air Transport Association of
    America

ATMA
American Textile Machinery
    Association

ATMI
American Textile Manufacturers
    Institute Inc.

AVS
American Vacuum Society

AWCI
Association of the Wall & Ceilings
    Industries International

AWI
Architectural Woodwork Institute

AWIRA
American Wax Importers and
    Refiners Association

AWP
American Wire Producers
    Association

AWPA
American Wood-Preservers'
    Association

AWPB
American Wood Preservers
    Bureau

AWPI
American Wood Preservers
    Institute

AWS
American Welding Society Inc.

AWWA
American Water Works
    Association

A2LA
American Association for
    Laboratory Accreditation

BCA
Billiard Congress of America

BCI
Battery Council International

BGA
Barre Granite Association

BHMA
Builders Hardware Manufacturers
    Association Inc.

BIA
Binding Industries of America

BIFMA
Business & Institutional Furniture
    Manufacturers Association

BISSC
Baking Industry Sanitation
    Standards Committee

BOCA
Building Officials &
    Code Administrators
    International Inc.

BOMA
Building Owners & Managers
    Association International

BSC
Biological Stain Commission

CABO
Council of American Building
    Officials

CAGI
Compressed Air & Gas Institute

CAMI
Coated Abrasives Manufacturers
   Institute Inc.

CAM-I
Computer Aided Manufacturing
   International

CAPPA
Crusher and Portable Plant
   Association

CARF
Commission on Accreditation of
   Rehabilitation Facilities

CCTI
Composite Can & Tube Institute

CDA
Copper Development Association
   Inc.

CED
Civil Engineering Data

CEMA
Conveyor Equipment
   Manufacturers Association

CFFA
Chemical Fabrics & Film
   Association Inc.

CFTMA
Caster and Floor Truck
   Manufacturers Association

CGA
Compressed Gas Association Inc.

CHI
Chlorine Institute Inc.

CI
Cordage Institute

CIMA
Construction Industry
   Manufacturers Association

CINS, also CI
Composites Institute

CISP
Cast Iron Soil Pipe Institute

CLFMI
Chain Link Fence Manufacturers
   Institute

CLPCA
California Lathing and Plastering
   Contractors Association

CMA
Chemical Manufacturers
   Association

CMA
Cookware Manufacturers
   Association

CMAA
Crane Manufacturers Association
   of America Inc.

CMI
Can Manufacturers Institute

CPB
Contractors Pump Bureau

CPMB
Concrete Plant Manufacturers
   Bureau

CR
Corn Refiners Association Inc.

CRA
California Redwood Association

CRI
Carpet & Rug Institute Inc.

CRMA
Commercial Refrigerator
   Manufacturers Association

CRSI
Concrete Reinforcing Steel
   Institute

CSDA
Concrete Sawing & Drilling
   Association

CSI
Construction Specifications
  Institute Inc.

CSMA
Chemical Specialties
  Manufacturers Association

CSSB
Cedar Shake & Shingle Bureau

CTFA
Cosmetic, Toiletry & Fragrance
  Association Inc.

CTI
Cooling Tower Institute

DCDMA
Diamond Core Drill
  Manufacturers Association

DEMA
Diesel Engine Manufacturers
  Association

DFI
Deep Foundation Institute

DFISA
Diary and Food Industries Supply
  Association

DHI
Door & Hardware Institute

DISA (see EDIA)
Data Interchange Standards
  Association

DSAC
Diaper Service Accreditation
  Council

ECSA
Exchange Carriers Standards
  Association

EDIA
Electronic Data Interchange
  Association

EGSA
Electrical Generating Systems
  Association

EIA
Electronic Industries Association

EJMA
Expansion Joint Manufacturers
  Association

ESCSI
Expanded Shale, Clay & Slate
  Institute

ETI
Equipment and Tool Institute

FACT
Federation of Automated Coding
  Technologies

FASB
Financial Accounting Standards
  Board

FBA
Fibre Box Association

FCI
Fluid Controls Institute Inc.

FGMA
Flat Glass Marketing Association

FIA
Footwear Industries of America
  Inc.

FIAS
Forging Industry Association

FMERC
Factory Mutual Engineering &
  Research Corp.

FPA
Flexible Packaging Association

FPI
Fiberglass Pipe Institute

FTI
Facing Tile Institute

GA
Gypsum Association

GAMA
General Aviation Manufacturers
  Association

GCA
Graphic Communications
  Association

GIA
Gummed Industries Association
  Inc.

GMA
Grocery Manufacturers of
  America Inc.

GPA
Gas Processors Association

GTA
Glass Tempering Association

GTA
Gravure Technical Association

GWI
Grinding Wheel Institute

HEI
Heat Exchange Institute Inc.

HFS
Human Factors Society

HI
Hydraulic Institute

HI
Hydronics Institute Inc.

HIMA
Health Industry Manufacturers
  Association

HPMA
Hardwood Plywood
  Manufacturers Association

HPSSC
Health Physics Society Standards
  Committee

HTMA
Hydraulic Tool Manufacturers
  Association

HVI
Air Movement & Control
  Association /Home Ventilation
  Institute Division

IA
Irrigation Association

IAI
International Association for
  Identification

IAPMO
International Association of
  Plumbing & Mechanical
  Officials

IAR
Institute of Ammonia
  Refrigeration

IAWCM
International Association of
  Wiping Cloth Manufacturers

ICBO
International Conference of
  Building Officials

ICEA
Insulated Cable Engineers
  Association Inc.

ICI
Investment Casting Institute

ICM
Institute of Caster Manufacturers

ICRU
International Commission on
  Radiation Units and
  Measurements

IEEE
Institute of Electrical &
  Electronics Engineers

I.E.S.
Institute of Environmental
  Sciences

IES
Illuminating Engineering Society
  of North America

IFAI
Industrial Fabrics Association
  International

IFI
Industrial Fasteners Institute

IGCC
Insulating Glass Certification
  Council

IGCI
Industrial Gas Cleaning Institute
  Inc.

IIAR
International Institute of
  Ammonia Refrigeration

IIE
Institute of Industrial Engineers

ILIA
Indiana Limestone Institute of
  America Inc.

IMAC
International Mobile Air
  Conditioning Association Inc.

IME
Institute of Makers of Explosives

IMI
International Masonry Institute

IMSA
International Municipal Signal
  Association

INDA
Association of The Nonwoven
  Fabrics Industry

IPA
Industrial Perforators Association
  Inc.

IPC
Institute for Interconnecting and
  Packaging Electronic Circuits

IRI
Industrial Risk Insurers

ISA
Instrument Society of America

ISAN
International Silo Association

ISANTA
International Staple, Nail & Tool
  Association

ISDSI
Insulated Steel Door Systems
  Institute

ISHM
International Society for Hybrid
  Microelectronics

ISRI
Institute of Scrap Recycling
  Industries

ISWA
Insect Screening Weavers
  Association

ITE
Institute of Transportation
  Engineers

MLA
Metal Lath/Steel Framing
  Association
  A Division NAAMM

MPTA
Mechanical Power Transmission
    Association

NABADA, also NABDA
Association of Container
    Reconditioners (formerly
    National Barrel and Drum
    Association)

NARM
National Association of Relay
    Manufacturers

NFI
National Fisheries Institute

NSC
National Safety Council

NWHA
National Wholesale Hardware
    Association

NWPCA
National Wooden Pallet &
    Container Association

NWWDA
National Wood Window & Door
    Association

OPEI
Outdoor Power Equipment
    Institute

PAD
Pitless Adapter Division

PBI
Plastic Bottle Institute

PCI
Precast/Prestressed Concrete
    Institute

PD
Plastic Drum Institute

PDCA
Painting & Decorating Contractors
    of America

PDI
Plumbing & Drainage Institute

PFI
Pipe Fabrication Institute

PGMC
Primary Glass Manufacturers
    Council

PI
Perlite Institute Inc.

PLASTEC
Plastics Technical Evaluation
    Center

PLA
Pulverized Limestone Association

PPI
Plastic Pipe Institute

PSA
Photographic Society of America

PSTC
Pressure Sensitive Tape Council

PTI
Post Tensioning Institute

RAC
Reliability Analysis Center
    Radc/Rac

RESNA

RFCI
Resilient Floor Covering Institute

RIA
Robotic Industries Association

RMA
Rubber Manufacturers
    Association

RMI
Rack Manufacturers Institute

RTA
Railway Tie Association

RTCA
RTCA Inc.

RVIA
Recreation Vehicle Industry
    Association

RWMA
Resistance Welder Manufacturers
    Association

SAAMI
Sporting Arms & Ammunition
    Manufacturers Institute

SACMA
Suppliers of Advanced Composite
    Materials Association

SAE
SAE International

SBCCI
Southern Building Code Congress
    International Inc.

SCMA
Southern Cypress Manufacturers
    Association

SDI
Steel Deck Institute

SDI
Steel Door Institute

SEM
Society for Experimental
    Mechanicals

SEMI
Semiconductor Equipment and
    Materials International

SFSA
Steel Founders Society of America

SI
Salt Institute

SIA
Scaffold Industry Association

SIGMA
Sealed Insulating Glass
    Manufacturers Association

SJI
Steel Joist Institute

SM
Scale Manufacturers Association

SMA
Screen Manufacturers Association

SMACNA
Sheet Metal & Air Conditioning
    Contractors National
    Association Inc.

SMF
Snell Memorial Foundation

SMMA
Small Motor Manufacturers
    Association

SMPTE
Society of Motion Picture &
    Television Engineers

SNAME
Society of Naval Architects &
    Marine Engineers

SPIB
Southern Pine Inspection Bureau

SPII
Society of The Plastics Industry
    Inc.

SPRI
Single-Ply Roofing Institute

SSCC
Snowmobile Safety & Certification
    Committee Inc.

SSFI
Scaffolding & Shoring & Forming
    Institute Inc.

SSPC
Steel Structures Painting Council

SSPMA
Sump & Sewage Pump
  Manufacturers Association

STI
Steel Tank Institute

SWI
Steel Window Institute

SWRI
Sealant /Waterproofing &
  Restoration Institute

TAPPI

TCA
Tile Council of America Inc.

TEMA
Tubular Exchanger Manufacturers
  Association

TFI
The Fertilizer Institute

TI
Thermoforming Institute

TIMA
Tima Inc.

TMC-ATA
The Maintenance Council of
  American Trucking
  Associations

TMMB
Truck Mixer Manufacturers
  Bureau

TPI
Truss Plate Institute Inc.

TRA
Tire & Rim Association Inc.

TRI
The Refractories Institute

TTMA
Truck Trailer Manufacturers
  Association

UL
Underwriters Laboratories Inc.

USGA
United States Golf Association

Appendix B

Federal Departments, Agencies, and Other Organizations That Are Among Major U.S. Standards Developers

Department of Agriculture/Agricultural Marketing Service/Federal Grain Inspection Service/Food Safety and Inspection Service/Foreign Agricultural Service
  Forest Service
  Information Resources Management
  Packers and Stockyards Administration
  Rural Electrification Administration
Department of Commerce
  Bureau of the Census
  General Coordinator for Meteorology
  International Trade Administration
  National Institute of Standards and Technology
  National Computer Systems Laboratory
  National Engineering Laboratory and Law Enforcement Standards Laboratory
  Technology Services
  National Oceanic and Atmospheric Administration
  National Marine Fisheries Service
  National Environmental Satellite, Data, and Information Service
  National Weather Service
  National Telecommunications and Information Administration
U.S. Patent and Trademark Office
  Assistant Commissioner for Information Systems

Assistant Commissioner for Patents
International Patent Documentation
Trademark Examining Operation
Consumer Product Safety Commission
Department of Defense
Department of Energy
Building Technologies
Building Systems and Materials Division
Building Equipment Division
Energy Information Administration
Environment, Safety, and Health
Environmental Protection Agency
Executive Office of the President
U.S. Trade Representative
Federal Communications Commission
Federal Trade Commission
General Services Administration
Information Resources Management
Federal Supply Service
Public Building Service
Health and Human Services
Centers for Disease Control and Prevention
Food and Drug Administration
Health Care Financing Administration
Department of Housing and Urban Development
Interdepartmental Screw Thread Committee
Department of the Interior
Minerals Management Service
U.S. Geological Survey
Information Systems Division
National Mapping Division/Water Resources Division
Department of Justice
Department of Labor
Mine Safety and Health Administration
Occupational Safety and Health Administration
Library of Congress
Collection Services
Information Technology Service
National Library Service for the Blind and Physically Handicapped
Photoduplication Services
National Aeronautics and Space Administration
Occupational Health Office

Safety, Reliability, Maintainability and Quality
   Assurance Division
National Archives and Records Administration
Nuclear Regulatory Commission
Department of State
Department of Transportation
Federal Aviation Administration
Federal Highway Administration
   Engineering
   Environmental Policy
   Highway Operations
   Bureau of Motor Carriers
   Traffic Operations
Maritime Administration
National Highway Traffic Safety Administration
Research and Special Program Administration
United States Coast Guard
   Marine Safety, Security and Environmental Protection
   Auxiliary, Boating, and Consumer Affairs Division
Department of the Treasury
   Bureau of Alcohol, Tobacco, and Firearms
   Internal Revenue Service
   U.S. Customs Service
   Commercial Operations
Office of Laboratories and Scientific Services
Bureau of the Mint
Department of Veterans Affairs
U.S. Postal Service

Appendix C

Memorandum of Understanding Between ANSI and NIST

1.0 Purpose

1.1 The underlying purpose of this Memorandum of Understanding (MOU) is to enhance and strengthen the national voluntary consensus standards system of the United States and to support continued U.S. competitiveness, economic growth, health, safety, and the protection of the environment.

1.2 The National Institute of Standards and Technology (NIST) of the Department of Commerce (DOC) and the American National Standards Institute (ANSI) agree on the need for a unified national approach to develop the best possible international standards. This approach requires the best technical efforts of the United States in standards to ensure that our needs and interests are considered as international standards are developed, and that our international competitiveness is strengthened.

1.3 ANSI and NIST agree on the need for better communication within and between the private sector and federal government on voluntary standards. There is a need to ensure the timely flow of relevant information about developments that affect those interests, and for improved liaison to facilitate decision making and implement actions on standards at the national and international levels. It is also critical that affected U.S. regulatory agencies have the opportunity to contribute to the development and implementation of national and international voluntary standards.

1.4 This MOU is intended to facilitate and strengthen the recognition of ANSI and the entire U.S. standards community at the international level; improve domestic communication among both private- and public-sector parties in the United States on voluntary standards issues; increase the effectiveness of federal agency participation in the international voluntary standards-setting process; and ensure that ANSI's representation of U.S. interests is recognized by the other players on the international scene.

2.0 Agreement

2.1 NIST and ANSI agree jointly that ANSI is the recognized U.S. member body to the International Organization for Standardization (ISO), and through the U.S. National Committee to the International Electrotechnical Commission (IEC). It is also the U.S. member body to the Pacific Area Standards Congress (PASC) and to the Pan American Standards Commission (COPANT). As the U.S. representative to these bodies, ANSI shall convene delegations and appoint technical groups of a broad spectrum of experts, to represent the United States in all deliberations, of relevant Boards, individual Technical Committees, and Working Groups.

2.2 ANSI and NIST agree to provide a communications axis between the voluntary, private sector, and the federal government standards interests. They will work together to ensure the flow of relevant information about developments that affect those interests, and provide a liaison service to facilitate decision making and implementation of needed actions at the national and international levels.

3.0 ANSI Responsibilities

3.1 ANSI is responsible for ensuring that U.S. interests are represented at all levels within ISO and IEC. It must convene accountable and competent delegations to develop and present U.S. positions for all ISO and IEC committees for which the U.S. holds technical advisory groups (TAGS), including Board committees. ANSI will facilitate the building of consensus on standards issues and provide information about international standardization activities. ANSI is responsible for ensuring that the various standards-developing organizations are informed about ISO and IEC activities and given every opportunity to participate. ANSI shall take into account the positions of all affected interests and shall work with them to develop and promote a single, coordinated U.S. message at international voluntary standards bodies.

3.2 This MOU recognizes the desirability of direct cooperation between ANSI or a particular Standards Developing Organization (SDO) and any given federal agency. In fact, such cooperation is highly desirable—as is cooperation among federal agencies. Cooperation among domestic entities responsible for standards is essential to ensure international competitiveness and effective representation of U.S. interests internationally. The intent of this MOU is to develop focal points for the exchange of information and development of representative U.S. positions for consideration at international nontreaty voluntary standards bodies.

4.0 NIST Responsibilities

4.1 NIST's role, as delegated by the Secretary of Commerce under OMB Circular A-119 and the Trade Agreements Act of 1979 (P.L. 96-39), is to coordinate federal activities in voluntary standards. NIST coordinates standards activities with responsible government agencies to ensure that they are aware of private voluntary activities and that the private sector is cognizant of regulatory agency responsibilities. This MOU recognizes the regulatory responsibilities of individual agencies and does not preempt the statutory regulatory responsibility of any federal agency nor take away any authority from any federal agency to pursue its legislated regulatory programs.

4.2 NIST is responsible for developing and implementing means for facilitating, coordinating, and communicating information on voluntary standards activities among government agencies. NIST is also responsible for ensuring that federal agencies are aware of ANSI activities within ISO, IEC, or other private-sector, international standards bodies such as COPANT or PASC.

4.3 NIST is responsible for facilitating information exchange between federal agencies and the private sector on voluntary standards activities. It must work with these entities to ensure that U.S. interests can participate appropriately in international standards activities to enhance U.S. international competitiveness.

5.0 Other Agreements

This MOU does not take precedence over any other MOUs that ANSI may have with individual government agencies such as the Occupational Safety and Health Administration (OSHA); or that NIST may have with other private-sector bodies.

Sergio Mazza
President, American National Standards Director

Arati Prabhakar
National Institute of Standards and Technology

3

U.S. Involvement in World Standards Bodies, Standards Development, Standards Activities

Questions the Reader Will Find Addressed in This Chapter

1. What are the tangible benefits of standards participation?
2. How does the United States participate in worldwide standards activities?
3. What is government involvement in standards? Private sector?
4. How is the nature of U.S. standards involvement worldwide changing?
5. What is the degree of U.S. participation in ISO/IEC?
6. What is the exports-standards correlation?
7. What is the U.S. government involvement in worldwide standards activities?
8. What are ongoing mutual recognition efforts?
9. What does the MRA case study of the United States and Europe reveal?
10. What does the MRA case study of the United States and Asia reveal? What is APEC?
11. What is the private-sector involvement with the international standards system?
12. How does ANSI globally outreach in the private sector?
13. What are some foreign uses of U.S. standards?
14. How have international standards been adopted in the United States?
15. How has the United States become involved in international quality assurance?

> In terms of economic development, market size, and access to [the international] market, the United States ranks in the forefront among the world's industrialized nations. But in the areas of export of manufactured goods and the resulting trade balances, the United States has not kept pace with other developed countries, and is further threatened by newly industrializing countries. . . . Much of the reason for this decline in U.S. exports has been attributed to economic factors (e.g., the strength of the U.S. dollar vs. other currencies, the lure of low-cost labor, and government subsidies overseas), but some of the loss may well be due to limited participation and a decline of U.S. influence in the development of international standards.
>
> —NIST, "A Review of U.S. Participation
> in International Standards Activities"

Until recently, the American private sector championed U.S. involvement in world standards development with the government playing a supporting role. Industry representatives not only developed American standards that were adopted worldwide, but actively participated on international technical committees and advisory groups that developed standards. Individual American companies—especially those in the electronics industry—have been known to help other countries and regions create standards and conformity assessment practices simply because they were the frontrunners in those foreign markets.

While private-sector standards work continues and even accelerates internationally, the government is now taking a more active role in international standards. This is especially true regarding efforts to harmonize standards and testing procedures on a worldwide basis. The memorandum of understanding between the National Institute of Standards and Technology (NIST) and the American National Standards Institute (ANSI) also increases U.S. government participation in international standards.

Tangible Benefits of Standards Participation

NIST officials actively involved in promoting U.S. standards activities abroad find that standards participation provides the following tangible benefits:

- Development of a broader market base for exports
- A source of state-of-the-art knowledge on foreign technology
- Development of higher-quality standards benefiting U.S. products
- A basis for defensive actions to counter foreign competition

- Promotion of product or test method standards to enhance economies in manufacturing operations
- A vehicle for professional growth and face-to-face contact with authorities from foreign product-approval agencies
- Minimization of possible foreign regulatory surprises

U.S. Participation in Worldwide Standards Activities

In several reports published over the last decade, NIST officials have come
up with two major findings about the impact of U.S. involvement in world
standards activities, whether the representatives come from government
or the private sector:

1. U.S. involvement in international standards activities seems to correlate more directly with the sustained growth of world trade overall rather
than with the level of U.S. exports.

2. U.S. multinationals, whose operations are increasingly global, appear to be the prime beneficiaries of an increased U.S. presence on the international standards scene.

As more and more small and midsize companies venture abroad and
encounter international standards, they too will benefit from government
and private-sector efforts in this arena. To become active participants in international standards arenas, American managers and employees must be
aware of ongoing efforts in the U.S. government and private sectors to promote American standards-related interests abroad.

What Are the Roles of Government and the Private Sector?

When it comes to standards creation and development, there exists a fine
line in the United States between the role of government and that of the
private sector because both entities often cooperate in this realm. Now that
ANSI has the backing of NIST to represent the United States abroad in
standards forums, that line is blurring. Moreover, there is a great deal
of standards activity that involves direct cooperation between the private and public sectors. Government agencies are members of ANSI, and
private companies participate in NIST standards delegations to foreign
countries.

In addition, there is one major area where the government and private
sector meet: the working groups and technical committees of international
standards bodies.

Example

A recent NIST delegation to Argentina included representatives from the following public- and private-sector organizations: the U.S. Food and Drug Administration, NSF International, the Institute of Electrical and Electronics Engineers (IEEE), the National Fire Protection Association, Merck Co., MET Laboratories, the U.S. Pharmacopeial Convention, the American Society of Mechanical Engineers (ASME), Entela Inc., Amp Inc., NIST, ANSI, Underwriters Laboratories, Xerox Corp., SIMCOM, and Inchcape Testing Services.

Example

The U.S. Geological Survey supervises the development of the U.S. viewpoint for ISO work on measurement of liquid flow in open channels. The National Bureau of Standards administers the TAG for a subcommittee of the ISO committee on industrial automation systems.

Even so, distinctions still exist between the government and private-sector roles in this arena. The government clearly represents U.S. interests abroad during trade disputes that require standards. The government does not fund standards creation unless the work emanates from a government agency, and the government does not control or administer private-sector standards bodies.

Changing Nature of U.S. Standards Involvement Worldwide

Examination of American participation in international standards committees—both government and private sector—can help to illustrate the changing nature of U.S. involvement in the international standards-setting arena, which generally correlates with U.S. trade activity. For the most part, industry specialists, scientists, and engineers from throughout the world voluntarily staff ISO and IEC committees. About 75 percent of the delegates to ISO conventions are drawn from private companies. The rest come from government, trade associations, and academia. International standards creation involves travel and time commitment. Those involved may require approval from companies or the organizations and agencies that employ them. U.S. industries tend to participate in standards creation in part from a defensive posture—to keep foreign competitors from writing in standards elements that will be detrimental to their products. Some other industries and nations act offensively, attempting to write standards that benefit their products. Those industries actively involved in international trade have a natural predilection to protect or enhance their market position through standards creation.

U.S. Participation in ISO/IEC

The level of U.S. participation in ISO/IEC technical committees is considered to be a barometer of U.S. government and industry commitment to the standards process. NIST staffers have been tracking U.S. participation in ISO and IEC for a number of years, specifically focusing on the number of U.S.-held secretariats—or chairmanships—of key ISO and IEC technical committees.

NIST records on the twenty-year span from 1966 to 1986 show American participation in international standards on the rise. These figures correlate with higher levels of overseas trade, indicating an increasing level of U.S. industry and government commitment to international standards development. Although hardly scientific, this compilation of ISO/IEC activity—when compared with import/export levels—indicates that U.S. participation in international standards activities does correlate with trade figures.

Where standards activity is the greatest—high-tech product groups, for example—the export values are the highest. For example, U.S. participation has been greater in IEC than in ISO, reflecting the fact that U.S. electronics companies are major exporters. Conversely, U.S. representation in international standards forums is lower in basic product groups, which is also reflected in lower U.S. exports in those categories.

ISO Participation Since 1966. ISO's technical committee system is explained in Chapter 8. In short, technical committees are the bodies that develop ISO standards. Secretariats are held by an ISO member body, which is usually a country's main standards institution. Secretariats fund and administer technical committees.

In 1966, the United States held ISO secretariats on the following 10 of the 118 technical committees (TCs) that then existed. Those followed by an asterisk were still held by the United States in 1987.

TC 11   Unification of Boiler Code*
TC 28   Petroleum Products*
TC 36   Cinematography*
TC 42   Photography*
TC 61   Plastics*
TC 66   Determination of Viscosity (This TC has been dissolved.)
TC 85   Nuclear Energy (The Federal Republic of Germany held this
        secretariat in 1987.)
TC 97   Computers and Information Processing*
TC 104 Freight Containers*
TC 108 Mechanical Shock and Vibration*

As this list reflects, U.S. industries with strong domestic markets, such as building construction, concrete, mining, rivets, fire safety tests, and textile machinery, had little interest in participating in ISO technical committees thirty years ago. In 1966, the United States ranked fourth behind the United Kingdom, Germany, and France in the number of ISO secretariats. The percentage of U.S.-held ISO secretariats remained fairly constant over the twenty years from 1966 to 1986.

ISO Participation in 1986. By 1986 the United States also held secretariats for the following committees:

TC 20	Aircraft and space vehicles (since 1976)
TC 31	Tires, rims, and valves (since 1966)
TC 68	Banking (since 1972)
TC 127	Earthmoving machinery (since 1968)
TC 131	Fluid power systems (since 1969)
TC 153	Valves (since 1984)
TC 161	Control and safety devices for heat-generating systems (since 1985)
TB 189	Ceramic tile (since 1986)

The United States also held 12.6 percent of other available ISO leadership positions—whether subcommittee secretariats or conveners of technical committees—in 1986. In addition, the United States was represented in a majority of the technical committees—113 of the 164 then in existence—and had "observer" status for an additional 48. Only three ISO technical committees—Glass Containers, Tobacco and Tobacco Products, and Jewelry—had no U.S. representation at all.

By the late 1980s, much of the U.S. international standards focus was in the areas of the newer technologies and those products with the highest export value. These included electrical products or those with electronic components, the purview of the IEC. That means that overall U.S. standards emphasis, as noted, is stronger at the IEC than at the more diverse ISO.

Exports-Standards Correlation. As stated, NIST reports a strong correlation between standards participation and U.S. export dollars. It turns out that the following product areas, in which the United States has strong influence, also happen to be the areas in which exports are high: plastics, automobiles, petroleum, fuels and lubricants, electric machinery, and telecommunications.

However, exports of some of the more basic product groups had fallen by 1986 compared to earlier performance records. Not surprisingly, NIST staffers found there also existed an apparent underrepresentation of U.S. interests in ISO-related international standardization activities for those product areas, including wood manufactured goods, footwear, furniture, and toys.

ISO Participation in 1991. By 1991, the United States through ANSI held participating or observer status on 95 percent of ISO's technical committees and 100 percent of IEC's. Although the United States still did not hold the greatest number of international technical committee secretariats, its standards product skills were widely recognized. ANSI secretariats have been widely recognized for their strong standards development skills by the ISO community. In fact, they hold the efficiency record for ISO standards development.

IEC Participation. For many years U.S. standards relating to electricity and electronics pretty much dominated world trade, sometimes superseding international standards. A shift started after World War II with the emergence of other players, particularly the Japanese and Germans.

The American electrical industry, which had maintained a largely passive role in IEC activities, started to become more involved in international electrical standards development. Participation increased dramatically in the late 1960s and early 1970s.

This larger-scale American emersion into the international standards scene proved somewhat shocking. American delegates to the IEC met language barriers and displayed limited understanding of European culture, history, and traditions, all of which reduced their effectiveness in European-dominated forums. In IEC committees they met delegates from other countries, especially Europeans, who were schooled in the American market and understood the American standards scene. The European delegates of this era were far more dedicated to international standards development than their U.S. counterparts.

IEC Participation on the Rise. As with ISO, industry provides the majority of delegates to IEC meetings and conventions (85 percent), with the rest coming from trade associations and government agencies.

NIST registered increased U.S. participation in IEC as reflected in the growth in U.S. IEC secretariats from 1966 to 1986. In 1966, the United States held 9 percent of the leadership posts; it held 16 percent in 1986. In 1966, the United States ranked fourth in leadership, behind the United Kingdom, France, and Germany. By 1986, it had moved into the second slot behind France.

Historically, many U.S. and IEC standards shared similar elements, especially relating to safety criteria. Both sets of standards, however, contained arbitrary "design" requirements that neither party was particularly willing to relinquish. To break this sort of deadlock over design requirements—a deadlock that could lead to trade barriers—both parties adopted a new approach to "harmonizing" standards. IEC standards committees moved from the old "design" criteria to "performance-based" criteria, allowing each side to maintain its own product designs.

Once this deadlock was broken in the 1970s, the United States began to participate in IEC activities on a much greater and more enthusiastic level. U.S. delegate participation was expanded to include all levels of standards development, delegates were asked for a three-year commitment to IEC committees and subcommittees to guarantee continuity, and U.S. technical advisory groups were enlarged.

U.S. National Committee of IEC. The U.S. National Committee of the International Electrotechnical Commission (USNC/IEC) manages U.S. participation in the technical work of the IEC. In this role the USNC takes part in the commission's entire technical program.

The USNC begins its work with a particular committee by first appointing a technical adviser and a technical advisory group to develop the U.S. viewpoint. These advisers to IEC committees are selected from U.S. professional and technical societies, trade associations, companies, government agencies, and testing laboratories concerned with national electrotechnical standards development. ANSI also provides secretariat services to the USNC and its executive committee, technical advisers, and technical advisory groups.

The technical adviser is then responsible for presenting the U.S. position to the appropriate IEC technical committee and in turn consulting with IEC advisory groups to put forward the U.S. position on IEC committee issues. The technical adviser also selects knowledgeable delegates and secures the financial support necessary to ensure their attendance at IEC meetings. Delegates are selected from U.S. professional and technical societies, trade associations, industrial companies, government agencies, and testing laboratories that are also involved in the development of national electrotechnical standards.

In the past, the system has helped the United States to develop international recommendations for solar photovoltaic energy systems; safety of data processing equipment and office machines; cables, wires, and wave guides for telecommunication equipment; and safety of household and similar electrical appliances.

Note: Despite a growing U.S. presence in international standards arenas, there are many in the public and private sector who believe the United States still lags behind Europe in international standards efforts. As noted in Chapter 2, as a result of past and present policies and attitudes the United States is playing catch-up on the international standards front. There is hope that the recent cooperation between NIST and ANSI will shore up U.S. representation in worldwide standards activities.

U.S. Government Involvement
in Worldwide Standards Activities

Until the 1980s the U.S. government played more of a supportive role in international standards activities than did other governments worldwide.

Overview

U.S. industry has historically led American standards development and recommended a restricted government role. Moreover, U.S. industry and the service sector had not ventured abroad in great numbers until the last decade or so. Lack of overseas trade translated into a certain amount of apathy on the part of Americans to international standards development.

As noted in Chapter 2, the Trade Act of 1979 redirected the government's role in standards, setting the tone for much of the interplay between the public and private sectors that exists today. The recent signing of a memorandum of understanding between NIST and ANSI may change the way the U.S. government approaches standards.

Besides being the official U.S. representative to ISO/IEC, ANSI has long been involved in efforts to integrate private- and public-sector standards activities. Through ANSI, some federal agencies are already actively involved in ISO technical advisory groups.

U.S. Government Outreach

Throughout the last decade American presidents have firmly committed to expanding international trade. In all administrations, international standards and measurement issues were identified as major concerns. For this reason, NIST was authorized to push standards harmonization and development efforts in developing countries. Of prime concern was helping developing countries create standards infrastructures that matched the U.S. model.

NIST administrators work directly with standards creators in those other countries helping to develop standards that will unite markets rather than create additional trade barriers. Pilot standards programs have been operating in a number of countries under NIST auspices.

Following are some of the places worldwide where NIST is focusing much of its attention on the standards programs under development there. These are parts of the world where U.S. trade interests are strong and where conflicting standards or conformity assessment practices could hinder U.S. interests. Most of the work described below is ongoing. (More detail is provided in Chapter 11.)

- *Former Soviet Union.* In the mid-1990s, the President's Business Development Mission to Russia, led by then Commerce Secretary Ron Brown (now deceased), and the Joint Business Development Committee, established by the Gore-Chernomyrdin Commission, began to explore harmonization of U.S. and Russian standards.

The ultimate goal was to ensure mutual acceptance of private-sector certifications, quality assurance measures, and so forth, from standards and conformity assessment entities that both the U.S. and Russian governments could recognize. In the United States, these included the National Recognized Testing Laboratories (NRTL) program of the Occupational Safety and Health Administration (OSHA) and government-recognized programs under the National Voluntary Conformity Assessment Systems Evaluation (NVCASE) arm of NIST.

- *Chile and Argentina.* Chile and Argentina have fast-developing economies. Argentina is part of the Mercosur economic block, which includes Brazil, Paraguay, and Uruguay. Both Chile and Argentina are developing private-sector economies that could benefit U.S. trading efforts, which is a main reason for offering assistance on the standards front. Chile and Argentina are both in the process of creating quality assessment certification bodies, so the opportunity to build mutually acceptable systems exists right now. They are also signatories to the Uruguay Round of the General Agreement on Tariffs and Trade (GATT) and its predecessor standards code.

Moreover, both countries are active participants within ISO and have adopted the ISO 9000 standards series (see Chapter 9). Companies within each country are currently pursuing ISO 9000 certification. NIST and other government agencies are focusing a great deal of time, energy, and funding in this region to help these countries develop standards bodies, as well as create a testing and certification infrastructure that is compatible with the preexisting U.S. model.

Example

A recent NIST delegation to Argentina covered a wide area of standards and conformity assessment concerns, with special attention given to electrical, food, pharmaceutical, and medical device standards. As a first step toward creating mutual confidence between U.S. and Argentine inspection programs, there is discussion of establishing a mutual exchange training program between the U.S. Food and Drug Administration and its Argentine counterpart.

In this region there is concern that standards initiatives by Japan and European Union countries, especially Germany, will supersede U.S. standards efforts. If so, the impact on U.S. trade could be highly detrimental, with different standards and conformity assessment practices serving as possible trade barriers. These are not specious concerns. Both countries are receiving help from European Union nations, particularly the United Kingdom, France, and Germany, in efforts to upgrade their industrial base. To increase its influence, NIST officials are actively pursuing increased communication, technology transfers, and standardization and harmonization efforts with both Argentina and Chile.

Ongoing Mutual Recognition Efforts

As discussed in more detail in Chapter 12, there is growing concern in government and private-sector circles about the misuse of standards and conformity assessment practices as trade barriers. Efforts are taking place internationally to unify these practices through mutual recognition agreements (MRAs). MRAs establish a basis by which trading partners can accept each other's conformity assessment practices. Under the terms of these agreements, regulators do not have to inspect all foreign plants to be confident that an imported product meets local requirements.

Trade experts consider MRAs desirable because they accept differences between countries while reducing costs for regulators and manufacturers by eliminating the need for compliance with two standards systems. Manufacturers, in turn, can export without paying redundant certification costs.

Example

Consider the costs one company must incur to sell its products worldwide. A computer manufacturing company recently sought six regulatory approvals worldwide—two (from the Federal Communications Commission and Underwriters Laboratories) in the United States, another in Canada, and three in Europe, for all or most of its products. In 1996, the company must meet Mexican, Czech, European Union, German, Japanese, and seventeen other international requirements.

Some of these requirements are nothing more than what is necessary to protect consumer interests in those countries. Necessary or no, these sorts of additional requirements are costly and stifle trade. (See Chapters 7, 9, and 12 for examples of how meeting standards translates into costs for companies.)

MRA Case Study: The United States and Europe

Because Europe is the largest U.S. trading partner, both American and European Union (EU) officials are spearheading efforts to come to accord on conformity assessment practices, the basis for many standards.

At present, there is no mechanism for any non-European organization to gain access to EU decision making as a participating body. Under an MRA with the EU, U.S. organizations could become notified bodies and perform testing and certification of exports to the EU. However, the EU has indicated that any mutual recognition will require some form of U.S. government involvement in guaranteeing the competence of private U.S. conformity assessment organizations before they will be accepted by EU regulatory authorities.

Creation of the National Voluntary Conformity Assessment Systems Evaluation (NVCASE) program in 1994 was in direct response to EU conformity assessment concerns. NVCASE provides government assurance that a given testing lab, or other conformity assessment organization, is operating at levels acceptable to other countries.

The EU, in turn, wants to gain greater access to the U.S. market for European exports. European negotiators are concerned about the complex U.S. conformity assessment system, with public components at the national, state, and local levels and a variety of private certification systems. U.S. product liability law is another concern.

At the beginning of 1995, the United States and the EU began ongoing mutual recognition talks relating to test laboratories—the basis for product certification and product acceptance in both markets. Although Canada was not directly involved, Canadian officials were keeping an eye on developments with the understanding that they might directly affect their industry. High-level EU officials met with representatives from NIST, the FCC, and other government agencies. What emerged from the first round of these talks was awareness that the U.S. and European political systems were very different. EU officials, for example, had more authority to act than individual U.S. government agencies. They also presented a more united front than U.S. agencies. U.S. government agencies, autonomous by structure, were more turf conscious than ever in the face of possible budget cuts.

The EU wants the United States to adopt the sort of blanket product certification—CE Mark—that exists in Europe (see Chapter 7 for a thorough discussion of CE Marking). The advantage of the CE Mark is that it will ideally eliminate national product standards and allow for more freeflowing trade within the EU. U.S. officials believe that this sort of product certification system would be impossible to implement in the United States at this time. The U.S. laboratory testing system is a mixture of government labs and private testing laboratories. There is no movement in the United States—or expressed desire—to dismantle this private/public certification system in favor of a European-style system that would involve a greater government role in the testing certification process.

In July 1995, the United States came up with a proposal that appeared to break the stalemate between the United States and Europe over product testing and certification. Rather than force either side to accept foreign systems, the aim was to build confidence between the U.S. and European conformity assessment systems over a three- or four-year period.

Discussions focused on the market access for trade in products subject to the testing, inspection, and certification requirements for electrical safety, electromagnetic compatibility, telecommunications attachment, machinery safety, medical devices and drugs, and biologics for human and veterinary use. Other sectors and requirements were also discussed.

After much discussion, a senior Commerce Department official noted, "It finally became clear that the only way to satisfy the stakeholders in the MRAs that labs, inspectors, certifiers, surveillance and enforcement agents, and regulators were competent for the broad range of products and technologies covered was to start to actually exchange test packs, documents, inspection reports and build confidence that engineering procedures and judgment were competently carried out."

Analysis of test results was identified as the starting area. Ultimately, individual testing laboratories in both regions would have to pass new requirements to be included in a U.S./EU MRA. In an effort to build mutual trust between the United States and the EU, the United States proposed the following agenda:

1. Test results are the primary concern, because this is the most rudimentary aspect of product conformance. A product is tested in a lab for engineering results. It either passes or fails.

2. Once mutual recognition of test results is achieved, the United States and Europe will move on to testing reports, which involve engineering judgment.

3. Next comes mutual recognition of evaluative judgment. For example, there are seven model types and those seven model types have thirty product variations. Evaluative judgment is a method for sorting out similarities to allow for selective testing. If evaluative judgment is successfully applied, then only seven models must be tested out of the thirty.

4. The final stage relates to issues surrounding the actual certification and inspection process.*

---

*The source of some material in this case study is "The Essential Guide to U.S.-EU Mutual Recognition Agreements (MRAs)" by Dr. Charles M. Ludolph, International Trade Administration, U.S. Department of Commerce.

MRA Case Study: The United States and APEC

Asia and Latin America have been cited also as priority regions where streamlined conformity assessment through MRAs would benefit U.S. trade. Asia is of particular concern because the U.S. Trade Representative's office has noted a significant number of technical barriers to trade in this region. In an effort to remove trade barriers, there have been ongoing talks in the Asian region through the Asia Pacific Economic Cooperation Forum (APEC) since 1994.

APEC consists of most of the principal economies bordering the Pacific Ocean: the United States, Canada, Japan, South Korea, Taiwan, Hong Kong, Singapore, China, Australia, New Zealand, and the members of the Association of Southeast Asian Nations (Malaysia, Indonesia, the Philippines, Thailand, Brunei, and Myanmar). Chile joined APEC in 1994. Together, these countries account for approximately 40 percent of global economic activity, and that share is increasing rapidly.

In November 1994, APEC leaders in Jakarta, Indonesia, agreed to a broad endorsement of MRAs among APEC members. This was considered part of a long-term process to open the region to trade by the year 2020. Two key principles for mutual recognition were outlined: (1) reducing trade barriers in the region and (2) reducing redundant testing and certification.

A year later, APEC announced wide-ranging plans to lower barriers to one another's products as part of a plan to form the world's largest free-trade area. Among the steps outlined was reduction of import tariffs with most APEC countries agreeing to an accelerated tariff reduction program.

Need for a Stronger U.S. Government Presence to Benefit Industry

While recognizing industry's reluctance to create a government-run U.S. standards system, U.S. government officials say there are ways that the government could better assist industry. Most of these efforts involve an increased U.S. presence in the world and would require a commitment from American business as well as the general public to recognize the need for international outreach. Here are some suggestions from members of the U.S. Mission to the European Union for an increased government role:

- There's a necessity for increased public relations around standards and conformity assessment issues to educate the American populace as to their importance. These sorts of campaigns are waged regularly in European countries such as Germany and Spain, and consequently the population supports standards activities.

- Small and medium-size companies need to be encouraged to partici-pate in international standards activities. The government could as-sist by making videotapes of international standards conferences or forums available regionally, and through tools such as newsletters.
- NIST's Washington-based information center should be replicated in district offices throughout the United States to offer easier access to information for small and midsize companies.
- The United States needs to establish standards offices throughout the developing world to help local industry and businesses with their standards and conformity assessment practices. At this time, NIST conducts missions to various regions of the world but does not offer a permanent presence.

The Private Sector

As noted, U.S. participation in nontreaty international standardization ac-tivities is voluntary. Industry, standards bodies, trade associations, and in-dividuals fund participation according to perceived market-based needs.

Not surprisingly, some U.S. industries have been more active in inter-national standards activities than others, while some industries have never been involved at all. Participation almost always correlates directly with an industry's commitment to international trade.

Besides NIST and other U.S. government agencies, the American Na-tional Standards Institute (ANSI) is one of the main U.S. conduits between the private sector and the international standards arena. As noted, ANSI fulfills this role as U.S. representative to ISO and IEC, which together form the world's largest international, nongovernmental open forum for volun-tary industrial and technical standards collaboration and development.

ANSI is one of the few private-sector members of ISO. As of this writ-ing, the U.S. is the only major industrialized nation that does not provide direct government representation to ISO. Moreover, the U.S. government does not fund ANSI's domestic or international standards activities. ANSI raises revenues through standards and publication sales, subscriptions, and membership fees and services.

ANSI as a Global Player

With the drive toward global standardization and in response to member needs, ANSI has allocated more and more of its resources to international outreach. International standardization programs now receive 64 percent of ANSI's funds; they were allocated 25 percent ten years ago (from the 1995 Annual ANSI Report).

Increasingly, ANSI and NIST are starting to combine forces under the terms of their recent memorandum of understanding. NIST is recommending that ANSI study the current process of distributing ANSI standards to ISO members and get more involved with standards dissemination in Argentina, for example.

How ANSI Interacts With ISO

In ISO, the ANSI federation holds participant or observer status on 95 percent of the technical committees or subcommittees. The U.S. National Committee (USNC) is a participant or observing member in almost all IEC technical committees and subcommittees. Through this participation, the United States produces over 38 percent of all ISO and IEC standards (ANSI, *The U.S. Voluntary Standardization System: Meeting the Global Challenge,* February 1993, p. 27).

There is interplay between ISO and ANSI whereby international standards are adopted and then harmonized as American National Standards. On occasion, American National Standards are adopted as international standards.

ANSI is committed to increasing U.S. participation in international standardization. One of the organization's main concerns is addressing needs as they arise within the U.S. industrial sector for creation of international standards, which subsequently become American National Standards. The relationship between ANSI and ISO is illustrated in Figure 3-1, which provides an overview of the functions of the groups and bodies involved.

Example

In 1989, ISO set up TC 198 on Sterilization of Health Care Products to respond to public- and private-sector concerns regarding the regulatory role of standards in the integration of western European markets.

Under the auspices of ANSI, a number of American government agencies and industry groups and associations met to discuss the impact of standardization in this area. Following this session, ANSI submitted a request to ISO to create a committee to address health care technology. ISO responded by assigning the secretariat of ISO/TC 198 to ANSI, which delegated administration of TC 198 to the Association for the Advancement of Medical Instrumentation (AAMI). As administrator of the secretariat, AAMI coordinates international standards development.

Example

In response to a request from the National Solid Wastes Management Association (NSWMA), ANSI submitted a proposal for creation of a

Figure 3-1. Overview of ISO-ANSI process.

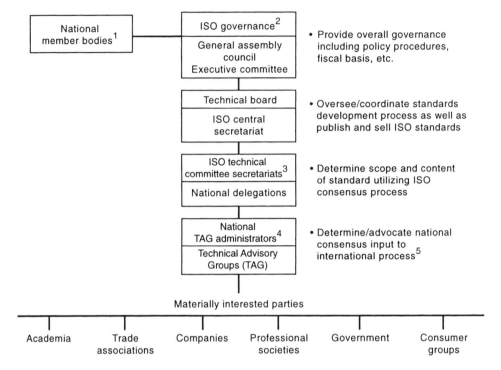

Notes:
[1]ANSI, AFNOR, BSI, DIN, JISC, SCC, etc.
[2]Includes ISO Secretary-General and Treasurer
[3]Generally ISO national member body except in U.S. *Typically* delegated to TAG administrator
[4]ANSI-*Accredited* U.S. administrators include: AAMI, ASME, ASTM, CBEMA, NEMA, etc.
[5]In U.S. involves advancing either consensus standard or position as determined by TAG

Source: American National Standards Institute.

new ISO technical committee on solid wastes. ISO approved this proposal and ISO/TC 200 was formed in 1992 with ANSI as the secretariat. ANSI delegated administration of the secretariat to NSWMA.

ANSI and TAGs

In the United States, members of trade associations, technical or professional societies, and government agencies all participate in and administer
technical advisory groups or TAGs. TAGs work in conjunction with technical committees (TCs) to create international standards, a topic that will be
addressed more fully in Chapter 8.

The work of developing technical positions and assuming responsibility for selecting qualified people to represent U.S. interests at international standardization meetings takes place within the TAGs. U.S. positions in ISO technical committees and subcommittees are formulated by U.S. TAGs. ANSI plays a major role in the staffing and development of U.S. TAGs.

Example

ANSI has accredited the Information Technology Industry Council's (ITIC's) Accredited Standards Committee X3 (ASC X3) on Information Technology to develop and maintain domestic standards for information technology. ANSI has also accredited ITIC to serve as the TAG administrator to JTC 1, as well as serving as the accredited secretariat to Accredited Standards Committee X3.

Information technology standards are developed through Joint Technical Committee 1 (JTC 1) on Information Technology through a joint technical committee of ISO/IEC. ANSI represents the United States on JTC 1 and accredits standards developers, or standards organizations, to represent the information technology community within JTC 1.

Example

In 1992 ISO formed a new technical committee on Building Environment Design, designated ISO/TC 205. ANSI was assigned the secretariat, which it delegated to the American Society of Heating, Refrigerating and Air-Conditioning Engineers.

To support the efforts of U.S. TAGs, ANSI provides them with

- Guidance regarding criteria and procedures to help them reach consensus on positions for international standards activities
- Advice from staff
- Communication on matters pertinent to ISO technical committees and subcommittees, especially when ANSI is seeking recommendations from the TAG(s) in question
- Guidance from ANSI standards boards when there is an attempt to coordinate parallel national and ISO international standards

ANSI's International Outreach

Although best known for its work with ISO and IEC, ANSI is also reaching out globally to represent U.S. standards-related interests. In recent years, ANSI representatives have been developing relationships with the Pacific Area Standards Congress (PASC) in the Pacific Ocean area and the Pan

American Standards Commission (COPANT) in Latin America, among other global standards groups.

In Europe, ANSI has established an ongoing cooperative relationship with the Europeans to broaden U.S. access to the three major European standards bodies: the European Committee for Standardization (CEN); the European Committee for Electrotechnical Standardization (CENELEC); and the European Telecommunications Standards Institute (ETSI). As discussed in Chapter 6, these bodies are the key sources of European recommendations to ISO, IEC, and other technical groups. U.S. input and access to these organizations is limited because they are not completely open to outside standards bodies. However, a survey conducted by the defense industry in early 1995 of U.S. international standards participants—both private sector and government—indicated that access to European standards bodies is improving and that it was not difficult to communicate concerns to European groups. In some cases, direct participation is allowed. Many U.S. standards officials credit ANSI outreach efforts for these improvements.

There is widespread U.S. support for ANSI to continue increased interaction with EU standards bodies. Of specific interest is future participation in EU standards development at working levels. Ultimately, there is a desire to see all regional bodies that develop standards work under ISO, IEC, or under their procedural guidelines to better harmonize U.S. and EU standards.

Problems do persist with some subsets of major EU standards bodies. Government surveys conclude that, while cooperation and accord with CEN and CENELEC are improving and the United States is strengthening its overall position in Europe, it would be misleading to assume that there are no existing programs that are, in fact, creating technical trade barriers, either through standards or conformity assessment requirements.

Note: Government agencies and private companies have no official right under EU law to participate directly in CEN/CENELEC activities, or even act as observers. In practice, many U.S. companies offer input to CEN/CENELEC standards activities because non-European experts are allowed to sit on technical committees in member states that feed into the CEN/CENELEC system. It is also well known in standards communities that observer status is granted on occasion when a representative of a foreign business or government has an "in" with CEN/CENELEC officials.

Foreign Use of U.S. Standards

In some instances, U.S. standards are so widely accepted that they have become de facto international standards. Professional societies with large international memberships have managed to create wide acceptance of U.S. standards. For example,

- The American Society of Mechanical Engineers (ASME) codes and standards, particularly the ASME Boiler and Pressure Vessel Code, enjoy broad recognition and acceptance around the world.
- The American Society for Testing and Materials (ASTM) is also recognized worldwide for its high-quality test methods and material specifications, especially in the areas of petroleum, metals, coal, concrete, and plastics.
- Many ASTM standards, especially for petroleum products and plastics, form the basis for ISO standards, as well as for those that regional standards bodies issue.

In general, U.S. government officials report a decline in the use of U.S. standards worldwide. They warn that if U.S. industry and government do not become more involved in standards development on an international basis, American companies will have to adapt more and more to the standards of other countries and regions at increasing cost.

Example

In areas where there is no significant American participation in international standards development there are reports that standards and conformity assessment practices are being derived from European models. This is particularly true in South America.

Adoption of International Standards in the United States

There are occasions when ANSI adopts international standards for use in the United States. The ISO 9000 standards series is a well-known example of an international standard that ANSI sponsors in this country.

Following approval at the international level, a standard may be submitted to ANSI for approval as an American National Standard. International standards may also serve as the basis of national standards.

As with American-based standards, ANSI will not accept an international standard and offer it the designation of American National Standard without consensus from all known and affected parties. In certain high-tech fields, a standard may be submitted for national review. In these cases, it is important to determine the degree of equivalency between the current specific U.S. standard and the ISO/IEC, or other international standard being considered for designation as an American National Standard. This factor is especially critical if the international standard(s) will be used for military acquisition purposes. The following are international (ISO) definitions of categories of equivalency between national and international standards:

- *Identical.* The U.S. standard corresponds to the international standard exactly as an authentic translation with identical content and presentation.
- *Technically equivalent.* The U.S. standard corresponds to the international standard so that what is acceptable to one standard is acceptable to the other, and vice versa.
- *Partially equivalent.* The U.S. standard is technically equivalent in part to the international standard.
- *Related.* The U.S. standard is related, but not equivalent to the corresponding international standard.

In the early 1990s, ANSI analyzed approximately seventy-eight hundred ISO and IEC standards. This study was not complete, but netted some interesting results:

- Twenty-two percent of international standards were identical or technically equivalent to U.S. standards.
- Thirty-three percent were partially equivalent or related to U.S. standards.
- Forty-five percent were not equivalent.

The study's authors predict that U.S. and international standards will edge toward equivalency—and become closer to those of other highly industrialized countries—as international standards become more universally accepted. As noted, the United States is involved in harmonization efforts that could affect these percentages.

Quality Assurance Activities

The U.S. private sector—both ANSI-RAB and individual companies—is very active in quality assurance activities worldwide, a topic that receives more scrutiny in Chapter 9. Here are some of the ways Americans are involved in international quality assurance efforts.

International Accreditation Forum

The International Accreditation Forum (IAF) was formed in the early 1990s to harmonize worldwide accreditation practices and is rapidly becoming the forum that could serve as a nongovernmental regulatory arm for international standards.

Reuben Autrey, president of the Gas Appliance Manufacturers Association and chairman of the International Accreditation Forum at this writing, is generally credited with getting IAF off the ground. ANSI was a founding member.

Note: Autrey is expected to step down from his role as IAF chairman in 1996 and become the first chairman of ISO's Quality System Assessment Regulation (QSAR) program. QSAR is discussed further later in this section.

IAF members include accreditation bodies, regional accreditation bodies, and associate members, which can be international industrial organizations or international organizations representing registrars. Members include accreditation bodies from Australia, Brazil, China, Japan, the Netherlands, Sweden, the United Kingdom, and the United States.

In 1995, the IAF issued a memorandum of understanding among its members, stating the group's goals and tasks. These include:

- Defining the scope of accreditation
- Harmonizing accreditation body operating procedures, certification and registration procedures and their implementation, and the contents of certificates of conformance and competence
- Participation in an evaluation and reevaluation program based on peer review of accreditation body members or regional groups with the aim of creating a worldwide multilateral agreement
- Maintaining this multilateral agreement through peer review among accreditation body members
- Opening and maintaining channels for the exchange of information between accreditation body members and other relevant organizations

The IAF also created a partnership with ISO to assist the ISO's Quality System Assessment Recognition (QSAR) program. QSAR is a relatively new ISO committee that is working on developing worldwide accreditation practices with an emphasis on spelling out registration criteria for implementation of the ISO 9000 standard series.

ISO has given the IAF the green light to create international rules binding national and regional accreditation bodies. If all goes as planned, ISO will serve as the administrative arm of QSAR, and IAF will set up a structure whereby multilateral agreements can be made to unite ISO 9000 on a worldwide basis.

Sector-Specific Conformity Assessment Schemes

In related activities, the IAF is exploring limiting the proliferation of sector-specific conformity assessment schemes worldwide, especially in the area of management systems standards. The ISO 9000 series and ISO 14000 are two examples of management system standards. The IAF's concern is to limit sector, or industry-specific registration variants applied to these sorts of standards to save industry the cost of meeting multiple registrations.

In a January 1996 resolution, IAF members supported the development of management systems standards through the ISO/IEC process that are subsequently used for conformity assessment purposes. The organization issued "Resolution of the International Accreditation Forum Sector Specific Conformity Assessment Schemes," which states the following:

> IAF recognizes that the act of certification/registration of suppliers requires relevant competence in each scope area utilizing both expertise and guidance documentation as necessary. The accreditation body has the responsibility to satisfy itself that the certification body/registrar has an effective management system in place to ensure the provision of the appropriate skills and competence.
>
> IAF recognizes the existence of conformity assessment schemes for management system standards which are sector-specific. However, IAF does not promote the future development of national, regional, sector-specific (including discipline-specific) programs which are outside the supplier/customer relationship. Such programs can lead to multiple audits, expanded resource requirements, barriers to trade, and extensive duplication without noticeable benefit.
>
> IAF will support the development of future national, regional, or sector-specific programs only when they are driven by the customers and actively supported by the suppliers in the relevant market, and aim to:
>
> - Avoid adding to, or subtracting from, the relevant ISO/IEC standards either explicitly or through interpretation,
> - Have a defined process for fair and open representation by all affected parties in the participating countries,
> - Discourage national, industry, sector, or other specific marks or identifiers on third-party management system certificates which imply that the certificate represents something other than conformance to the relevant ISO/IEC standard,
> - Allow for the inclusions of accredited certificates issued under an equivalent process which ensures the integrity of the audit.
>
> IAF requests that any organization that is considering the development of a sector-specific program should seek the involvement of IAF at the earliest opportunity.

At an earlier IAF meeting, the members agreed that the Supplier Audit Confirmation (SAC) effort to streamline the registration process of management system programs is not sector-specific. It was decided to establish a task force to monitor pilot SAC efforts, and the following position statement was released:

Supplier Audit Confirmation—IAF Position

1. At its June 1995 meeting, IAF agreed that "SAC is not a sector-specific program" and "that there is room for moving all or part of the way to SAC subject to conditions to ensure that confidence is not misplaced."
2. Consequently, IAF aims to establish a system that will enable a certificate to be issued, regardless of the conformity assessment methodology used, without compromising confidence or credibility.
3. ISO/IEC Guides 61 and 62 and the draft IAF guidance provide sufficient flexibility to enable recognition, where appropriate, of an organization's history of good performance, within the existing arrangements for accredition and registration.
4. IAF believes therefore that the options for giving appropriate credit for mature management systems and good consistent performance should be examined by means of pilot projects.
5. IAF will establish a task force which will monitor the progress of the pilot projects and will draft the criteria for implementation based on the results of the pilot projects. The criteria will address issues such as the competence and independence of internal auditors, accreditation registration body competence, and the degree of flexibility in approach that should be permitted.

Note: There is resistance to the IAF's proposed limiting of sector-specific schemes for conformity assessment, especially in the United Kingdom, where any restrictions on registration are viewed as possible limitations to specific British certification schemes such as TickIT for the software industry.

Advice to Companies

Learning about standards activities and developments in export markets is a first step to protecting a company's economic interests abroad. As is evident from the activities of IAF and other international standards-related organizations, this is a dynamic field with many ongoing developments that will affect both a company's finances and operating procedures. Alerting trade associations or legislators about standards-related concerns as they arise is a good second step to ensuring that these markets stay open to American businesses.

Example

So many American companies raised concerns about CE Marking (see Chapter 7) that the International Trade Administration (ITA) produced explanatory materials to help companies cope with meeting this European product performance standard. Companies also notified government officials that CE Marking could prove a potential trade barrier. For this reason CE Marking is now included in the United States Trade Representative's (USTR's) list of potential trade barriers, which means the USTR is watchdogging the process for signs that it will restrict U.S. products in European markets.

Resources

American National Standards Institute, "The U.S. Voluntary Standardization System: Meeting the Global Challenge," pp. 5–11, 17, 25–27, 30–31.

American Society for Testing and Materials, "The Use of ASTM Standards in International Trade," Parts 1 and 2, *ASTM Standardization News*, May–June 1984.

Ludolph, Charles M., "Standards and Trade in the 1990s: The Essential Guide to the U.S.-EU Mutual Recognition Agreements," International Trade Administration, U.S. Department of Commerce, July 10–13, 1995.

National Institute of Standards and Technology, *A Review of U.S. Participation in International Standards Activities.*

Warshaw, Stanley I., "Background: Fundacion Chile," International Trade Administration, U.S. Department of Commerce.

———, "Standards and Technology Policy Trends in Chile and Argentina," International Trade Administration, U.S. Department of Commerce.

———, "The Standardization and Balance of Nations With Economies in Transition," International Trade Administration, U.S. Department of Commerce.

4

Quality Assurance Programs in QS-9000: The Big Three Quality Standard

Questions the Reader Will Find Addressed in This Chapter

1. What is ISO 9000 in relation to QS-9000?
2. What are some ISO 9000 basics?
3. What are the elements of ISO 9000?
4. What are the answers to commonly asked questions about ISO 9000?
   - How are the standards applied?
   - Who offers the ISO 9000 certification?
   - Why pursue ISO 9000 certification?
   - What do I seek in an ISO registrar and consultant?
   - What are the benefits of ISO 9000 certification?
   - Are there any disadvantages to ISO 9000?
5. Why did the automobile industry form QS-9000?
6. How are QS-9000 rules in flux?
7. What are four major differences between ISO and QS-9000?
8. What is advanced quality planning?
9. To what degree may a supplier have a quality system in place?
10. What are some tips on implementing QS-9000?
11. What are the steps in QS-9000 implementation?
12. What Big Three automaker quality elements serve as the second basis for QS-9000?
13. How do you organize management and employees to work under a QS-9000 team system?
14. What steps should be added to the Big Three process that are specific to QS-9000?

15. What are the steps in designing a quality manual?
16. Why conduct preassessment audits?
17. How is QS-9000 fine-tuned?
18. How does IASG field inquiries?
19. What are commonly asked questions about QS-9000 from automobile industry suppliers?

QS-9000—the Big Three automakers' first ever common quality program—was unleashed in the fall of 1994. Major truck manufacturers like Freightliner, Mack, Navistar, Paccar, and Volvo/GM have adopted QS-9000. Other industries, specifically steel and metal tooling, are reportedly spinning off their versions of QS-9000.

QS-9000 utilizes an ISO 9000 quality assurance base coupled with industry-specific guidelines drawn from the former auto industry quality programs: GM's North American Operations Targets for Excellence, Ford's Q101 Quality System Standard, Chrysler's Supplier Quality Assurance Manual, and GM Europe's General Quality Standard for Purchased Materials.

General Motors was the first to mandate QS-9000 for its North American suppliers; Chrysler followed suit, and Ford is holding back on mandating third-party registration until QS-9000 is more established. However, Ford does require compliance with QS-9000 requirements, as described below. General Motors and Chrysler have introduced QS-9000 to their European suppliers and will introduce them to their worldwide operations in the future. Ford is also considering introducing QS-9000 to its European suppliers.

QS-9000 deadlines were set as follows:

• *June 1995.* Ford's North American suppliers should have conducted a self-assessment audit, addressed nonconformance issues between existing specifications and QS-9000, and put in place a work plan to address these issues. Third-party registration was not yet required, but Ford was to check directly with suppliers to ensure these measures were carried out. The only exception is Ford Australia, where QS-9000 registration is in fact required because of ongoing business practices in that region.

• *January 1, 1996.* Potential GM North American suppliers must comply with QS-9000.

• *July 31, 1997.* Chrysler suppliers must have earned QS-9000 certificates.

• *December 31, 1997.* Longtime GM suppliers must comply.

European suppliers to General Motors and Ford are working under the same deadlines for either registration or compliance as their American counterparts. GM, for example, mailed QS-9000 manuals to its European supply base in July 1995. Chrysler, which has only two plants on the continent, mandated QS-9000 certification for European suppliers at the same time as the company did for its American supply base.

ISO 9000 Base

To truly comprehend QS-9000, it helps to have some awareness of ISO 9000, ISO's international quality assurance program, which is discussed in full in Chapter 9.

Although a standards series, ISO 9000 fits under the umbrella of quality assurance, which measures a company's quality level in terms of process rather than end result. ISO 9000 is the first attempt to create an international quality assurance standard to cover all industries worldwide and the service sector. It combines a Total Quality Management (TQM) employee involvement approach with use of documentation to create an internal auditing system. This combination of efforts becomes the company's quality system.

ISO 9000 Basics

ISO released the first generation of the ISO 9000 standards in 1987. The original series is actually comprised of five subdivisions:

1. ISO 9000 is a description of the standards series.
2. ISO 9001 is for companies that research, design, build, ship, install, and service their products.
3. ISO 9002 is for companies that produce and install products.
4. ISO 9003 is designed for warehousing and distribution companies.
5. ISO 9004 serves mainly as a guidance document.

All of these standards include a set of models and guidelines for quality assurance and quality management.

Note: Revisions to this basic series were issued in 1994. Details can be found in Chapter 9.

ISO 9000 Elements

ISO/TC 176 is the technical committee on quality management and quality assurance; it is responsible for developing and maintaining the ISO 9000 standards. National delegations from fifty-two countries participate in its work, with another fifteen countries present as observers.

Under the original ISO 9000 systems, ISO 9001 is the most comprehensive standard, with twenty elements or functional clauses that companies must implement to pass registration. In 1994, ISO/TC 176 issued substantial revisions to the original ISO 9000 series. In general, the revisions call for the rest of the series to follow the ISO 9001 elements more closely.

Note that the elements themselves generally follow the course that a company would take to audit all of its internal, and some external, work processes. The elements stress process in the same way that ISO 9000 as a quality assurance program stresses process. ISO 9004 offers guidelines and recommendations for the implementation of the ISO 9000 elements. However, each registrar may interpret those guidelines as it sees fit before issuing an ISO 9000 certificate.

Element No. 1: Management Responsibility. Defines the role management must play for a company to earn ISO 9000 registration.

Element No. 2: The Quality System. Asks a company to set up a quality system that coordinates the functional activities of the organization in a documented form. Included are all aspects of the organization that affect quality.

Element No. 3: Contract Review. A holdover from the period when ISO 9000 was used to control specific manufacturing contracts, this element forces a review of ways that companies deal with customers on a contractual basis.

Element No. 4: Design Control. This element has been unique to ISO 9001 and asks a company to review the means in which it has undertaken its own product design and development. Both tangible products or services are included.

Element No. 5: Document Control. Forces a company to prove it is doing what it claims through controlled documentation.

Element No. 6: Purchasing. Designed originally with suppliers in mind, it highlights the vendor-customer relationship and asks a company to review policies that affect that relationship. When the relationship is between a supplier or subcontractor and the company, it may require that suppliers or subcontractors be brought in for quality review.

Element No. 7: Purchaser-Supplied Product. Refers to the process applied to anything supplied to a customer and the control a company exerts over that process.

Element No. 8: Product Identification and Traceability. The ability to identify and trace the history of a product or service at each stage of its production or process cycle is the focus of this element.

Element No. 9: Process Control. Establishing and maintaining standards of workmanship, supervision, control of special procedures, and means of monitoring all procedures is the aim of this element.

Element No. 10: Inspection and Testing. Quality control, or the physical testing of a product, is addressed by this element.

Element No. 11: Inspecting, Measuring, and Testing Equipment. Inspection, especially instrument calibration, is a major concern of ISO 9000 and is covered by this element.

Element No. 12: Inspection and Test Status. Forces a company to determine the accuracy and viability of its inspection processes.

Element No. 13: Control of Nonconforming Products. Addresses areas in which products or services do not conform to specification.

Element No. 14: Corrective Action. Addresses correction of immediate problems and offers guidelines for ensuring that all runs smoothly and efficiently in the long run.

Element No. 15: Handling, Storage, Packaging, Preservation, and Delivery. Forces a company to move beyond the production process and review how products are treated through delivery.

Element No. 16: Quality Records. A company must provide objective evidence that the quality system is in place and functioning.

Element No. 17: Internal Audits. Requires that quality audits be conducted throughout an organization.

Element No. 18: Training. Recommends that all staff be involved in the quality assurance process and be properly trained for this role.

Element No. 19: Servicing. Refers to companies that service products sold. It states that procedures related to servicing must be documented.

Element No. 20: Statistical Control. Can be applied to any company activity where statistical techniques can be of assistance in monitoring quality.

Commonly Asked Questions About ISO 9000

How are the standards applied?

Unlike most industry standards, ISO 9000 standards are applied throughout a company. The aim is to increase quality performance and awareness in all company operations, not just in manufacturing divisions. ISO 9000 standards can also be applied to service companies, with the main goal being quality service.

The key to this level of quality control is creation of an "internal auditing" system whereby *all* company functions—even office functions—are constantly monitored. Application of the standards is flexible and will vary from company to company. Only the results matter when it comes to that crucial audit by an outside registrar.

Who offers ISO 9000 certification?

ISO 9000 certification is offered by companies who have been certified by the registration accreditation boards of thirty-two countries. Numbers of registrars fluctuate as companies enter or leave the business of ISO 9000 registration.

Why pursue ISO 9000 certification?

The pressure to pursue ISO 9000 certification usually comes from industry majors to suppliers. As noted, some corporate leaders are urging—and sometimes pressuring—their suppliers to comply with ISO 9000. General Motors, Ford, and Chrysler have mandated QS-9000, as have major truck manufacturers. Ford is requiring conformity to the new standard.

Companies with local or regional operations, and no contact with multinationals or exporting, may find little or no pressure to pursue ISO 9000 certification. Many companies are seeking certification anyway, to increase acceptability in overseas markets, as a marketing tool, and as a means of improving their products and internal performance.

What qualities should be sought in an ISO 9000 registrar and consultant?

Registrars are the arbiters of a company's ISO 9000 destiny. They have the authority to withhold or grant ISO 9000 certificates. When selecting a registrar, companies should seek the following:

- A registrar that is compatible with their corporate culture.
- A registrar that is accredited to issue ISO 9000 certificates in the countries where they do business, or could do business in the future.
- A registrar that is willing to negotiate a fair price.
- A registrar that is properly accredited for the ISO 9000 program they are pursuing. For example, only registrars that pass the Big Three's QS-9000 accreditation criteria can issue QS-9000 certificates. The Japanese have considered similar restrictions for JIS Z9901.

Consultants can be of great assistance or hindrance to a company's ISO 9000 effort. Here is what to look for in a consultant:

- An emphasis on training, not taking over the process
- Understanding of the company's corporate culture
- A willingness to bow out when a particular job is complete
- Willingness to negotiate a fair price

What are the benefits of ISO 9000 certification?

Companies that stick to the process rather than rushing to earn an ISO 9000 certificate report many ISO 9000 benefits. Better awareness of customer needs and the advantage of running a tighter ship are most commonly cited as reasons for continuing with the ISO 9000 process, not to mention marketing advantages. The following are among the most commonly cited benefits of ISO 9000:

- Better control of an operation
- Ability to identify inconsistencies
- The ability to offer quality service to customers with the assurance that the company can deliver
- Creation of a more comprehensive, formalized quality system
- Increased employee input into the decision-making process
- Improved ability to follow up on procedures
- Increased ability to determine the root causes of errors
- Its use as a top-notch marketing tool
- Improved communication of customer specifications—removing the guesswork
- Improved tracking of employee skills

Are there any disadvantages to ISO 9000?

No holder of an ISO 9000 certificate is claiming the certificate has harmed its business. However, there are problems with how the standards are implemented in the United States. So-called ISO 9000 consultants are not regulated, the American Registrar Accreditation Board does not have sufficient funding to maintain its own records, and U.S. registrars are not always considered acceptable overseas. Cost is also a major drawback, especially for small companies. Certification costs start at about $15,000 and range into the hundreds of thousands of dollars, depending on a company's size and organization.

QS-9000

In 1988, the Big Three automakers formed the QS-9000 Task Force, which in December 1992 was sanctioned to create a quality program that would satisfy ISO 9000 requirements while meeting auto industry quality criteria. Meetings were held with suppliers, ISO 9000 registrars, and other interested parties. What emerged by the summer of 1994 was a base of ISO 9000 quality assurance coupled with sector-specific guidelines drawn from the former auto industry quality programs.

Note: The Big Three are working on a variant of QS-9000 called TE-9000. TE refers to Tooling and Equipment, and TE-9000 will be directed at that end of the industry if implemented.

Rules in Flux

Because QS-9000 is still very much in its infancy, the rules governing the program are in flux. For this reason, any auto supplier or related-industry supplier should be aware of a number of factors when pursuing QS-9000:

- ISO 9000 certificates alone will not be accepted by the Big Three.
- The Big Three are pursuing acceptance for QS-9000 outside the United States. At least eleven national accreditation bodies have agreed to accept QS-9000 certificates in lieu of ISO 9000 certificates. They are the United Kingdom, the Netherlands, Australia, New Zealand, Canada, Italy, Sweden, Switzerland, Germany, Spain, and Finland. Negotiations are underway with several other countries, and blanket European acceptance of QS-9000 is being sought.
- So-called hybrid or transplant companies—specifically Honda North American, Toyota, and Nissan North American—are not adopting QS-9000 for their suppliers; however, the Australian divisions of Toyota and Mitsubishi have adopted QS-9000.
- ISO 9000 registrars must comply with the Big Three Code of Practice of Quality Systems Registrars to issue QS-9000 certificates. Training of registrars is ongoing, and Big Three representatives have been in Europe scouting reinforcements. Only registrars that prove they can comply with specialized QS-9000 registration criteria can issue QS-9000 certificates.

Note: GM officials are exploring slightly altering the mandated registration process to allow suppliers to train internal auditors to augment registrar efforts. All such efforts are in the investigatory phases. Suppliers are expected to comply with registration requirements as currently designed.

Differences Between QS-9000 and ISO 9000

Companies must always bear in mind that QS-9000 has ISO 9000 as its base. Setting up a long-running, low-maintenance internal auditing system based on documentation will be just as important to earning a QS-9000 certificate as passing ISO 9000 certification. But in many ways the two standards are quite different.

Here are four major differences between ISO and QS-9000:

1. ISO 9000 is nonprescriptive, while QS-9000 is highly prescriptive.
2. QS-9000 entails a whole list of skills that ISO 9000 does not address at all. These include qualifications in usage of geometric tolerances and design of experiments.

3. QS-9000 is product oriented, with concern for failure rates, while ISO is not.
4. Borrowing from the Malcolm Baldrige Quality Award criteria, QS-9000 takes customer satisfaction and continuous improvement into account, along with an emphasis on key company information, trend data, and performance metrics.

Advanced Quality Planning

When auto and truck suppliers have completed a QS-9000 system, they will have redirected their resources to be more customer specific and commodity specific. To accomplish this goal, suppliers must practice what auto experts call "advanced quality planning" under a specific product control plan. Here are some of the factors that go into advanced quality planning:

- Market research
- Customer input
- Establishing a cross-functional, multidisciplinary team
- Establishing benchmarking data
- Creating a control plan, of which there are three types: prototype, prelaunch, or production
- Identifying design goals
- Identifying key safety characteristics that need to be controlled in the product
- Setting up a preventative system to identify the ways systems and system characteristics can fail to ensure that failures do not happen or to mitigate the effect of failures
- Conducting feasibility reviews to make sure the facility is capable of producing parts at quantities required

Supplier Knowledge Base

Many of these quality-planning factors feature prominently in preexisting Big Three quality programs such as Q1 and Targets for Excellence. And many, if not all, Big Three suppliers will be familiar with the auto industry quality programs that form the sector-specific basis for QS-9000. Because the Big Three recommended suppliers hold off implementing ISO 9000, fewer suppliers may be familiar with the specifics of that process. Three basic types of suppliers will face QS-9000:

1. Those with highly evolved quality systems in place (some may hold ISO 9000 certificates). For suppliers in this group who already hold ISO

9000 certificates, QS-9000 should be very simple, or in the parlance of the auto industry, "10 to 15 percent tweaking systems." In most of these cases improved documentation is the major issue.

2. Those with no quality system in place.

3. Suppliers who fall somewhere between these categories and maintain a "loose" quality system.

Example

A former Ford Motor Company engineer designed a type of airbag that Ford wanted. Being "the only game in town," this supplier proceeded to manufacture the product in quantity without concern for the quality process. This entrepreneur knew how to manufacture in quantity, but was overlooking the necessity of producing consistent, high-quality results.

Tips on Pursuing QS-9000

Most of this chapter addresses concerns of those suppliers that face creating a QS-9000 quality system from scratch. More advanced companies can still benefit from the cost-saving advice and recommendations for hiring a registrar and maintaining a long-term documentation system. QS-9000 must be approached in a two-pronged fashion. Companies pursuing this process must

1. Build an ISO 9000–style quality system involving employees and management in documenting work procedures and training to form part of the QS-9000 internal auditing system
2. Make sure that the right staffing, materials, machines, environmental variables, resources, equipment, and QS-9000 control plans are established to meet special sector-specific criteria

QS-9000 Implementation Steps

As with ISO 9000, the order and fashion in which a company pursues QS-9000 certification will have a direct bearing on savings. QS-9000 presents different demands from ISO 9000 and quite a few additional steps. QS-9000 is also a detailed process with heavy emphasis on engineering. The following steps include advice from auto industry experts on meeting QS-9000 criteria. Company leaders should always keep in mind that, as with ISO 9000, QS-9000 has danger zones, or stages in the process that lead to increased spending. Initial panic, lack of information about ISO 9000 and QS-9000, internal disorganization, and reaching out for help unnecessarily all contribute to waste of time and resources.

1. *Do not embark on QS-9000 certification in a hurry.* General Motors and Chrysler have set deadlines for QS-9000 implementation. That does not mean that suppliers cannot approach these customers to negotiate a time-table that is realistic for their company. Whether or not there is any leeway in the implementation schedule, companies must dig into the process as soon as possible. Always recognize that facing a major quality program deadline while running a company can seem overwhelming. Companies should work through the process, design an employee-driven, customized system, and have employees and management run that system internally. The best way to stave off panic is to be systematic, focus in on the task, and get to work.

2. *Learn about Big Three quality elements that serve as the second basis for QS-9000.* Although QS-9000 is a common quality program—the first under the Big Three banner—it is not entirely harmonized. Each company has retained some individual requirements. Those pursuing QS-9000 should take care to contact their customers, or members of the Automotive Industry Action Group, to ensure they are covering all individual company requirements. Those who have not implemented one of the Big Three quality programs should take special care to learn as much as possible about those requirements. Areas that may present problems include the following:

- Statistical process control
- Process capabilities studies
- Measurement system analysis, including gauge variation studies, effective use of failure mode and effective analysis and prevention strategies, and production part approval
- Engineering change control
- Root cause analysis, including problem-solving methodology, unique math data, and transportation

Note: The Automotive Industry Action Group (AIAG) can supply some task force manuals on some of these topics. Write to: AIAG, 26200 Lahser Road, Suite 200, Southfield, MI 48034. Also use *ISO 9004-1* and other related guidance documents.

3. *Focus on calibration, control plans, subcontractors, inventory management, and other issues of this nature.* Because of the exacting nature of manufacturing vehicles and the desire to eliminate failures of all sorts, QS-9000 relies heavily on providing consistent quality and delivery, as well as avoiding failures. Here are some main areas of concern suppliers will encounter when implementing QS-9000:

Calibration. Calibration is extremely important to the QS-9000 process. Companies pursuing QS-9000 must implement a top-flight measurement or calibration system capable of measuring in mils, not in inches or feet.

Control plans. Control plans are key elements of QS-9000 and resemble the quality planning element added to the 1994 ISO 9000 standard revisions. The plans are designed to address product specifics such as the thickness of walls or graphic art design. The aim is to control these critical characteristics respective of the product, as well as to be concerned with process.

Subcontractors. QS-9000 requires auto suppliers to involve their subcontractors in the quality process. Suppliers are required to track their subcontractors' performance.

Inventory management. Those familiar with GM's former Targets for Excellence will recognize the inventory management system that QS-9000 requires for GM suppliers. Those unfamiliar with Targets for Excellence would do well to study this system, although QS-9000 goes well beyond Targets for Excellence.

Product Quality Planning. Product Quality Planning is a structured method of defining and establishing the steps necessary to assure customer satisfaction with a product while meeting production schedules. Top management commitment is a key component of this process, which offers the following benefits:

- Directs resources to satisfy the customer
- Promotes early identification of required changes
- Avoids late changes
- Provides a quality product on time at the lowest cost

Product material identification/traceability. This process involves identifying materials at all phases of production. To determine whether the end product is good or not—a good versus a bad muffler, for example—it is necessary to be able to track the materials that went into producing each part.

The product quality planning cycle depicted in Figure 4-1 represents a typical cycle. The purpose of the cycle as QS-9000 experts have outlined it is to emphasize

- *Up-front planning.* The first three quarters of the cycle (labeled *Plan, Do,* and *Study* in Figure 4-1) are devoted to up-front product quality planning through product-process validation.
- *The actual act of implementation.* The fourth quarter is the stage where the output is evaluated to serve two functions: (1) to determine if customers are satisfied and (2) to support the pursuit of continual improvement.

4. *Rely on employees to run the process.* As in implementing ISO 9000, companies should appoint someone in-house to oversee the certification

process. This individual should be aware of all aspects of the business operation. As much as possible, QS-9000 should be a homegrown process involving employees throughout the company. They offer the advantage of knowing the most about the company, its operating procedures, and its culture, and can be assisted by consultants on a piecemeal basis.

The supplier's first step in product quality planning is to assign responsibility to a cross-functional team. Effective product quality planning requires the involvement of more than just the quality department. The initial team should include representatives from engineering, manufacturing, material control, purchasing, quality, sales, field service, and subcontractors and customers, if appropriate.

5. *Shop around for a registrar that meets the company's bureaucratic style.* Do this early in the process and negotiate the best price possible. Registrars

Figure 4-1. Typical product quality planning cycle.

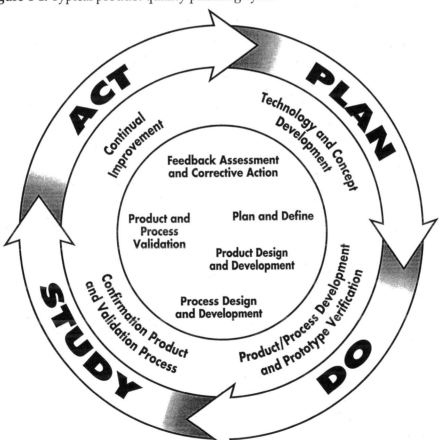

are free-market entities and are facing tough competition in the United States, Canada, Europe, and will eventually do so in South America. Make sure the registrar is qualified to handle QS-9000.

Many of the issues companies face when choosing an ISO 9000 registrar are equally pertinent when selecting a registrar for QS-9000. Although QS-9000 is far more prescriptive than ISO 9000 and registrars are far more regulated, they do have some leeway in "interpreting" the standard. Companies should bear in mind the following when hiring a QS-9000 registrar:

- Registrars have the right to define the acceptance criteria for the QS-9000 audit that will lead to issuing a certificate within the bounds of the standards in question.
- Registrars should be qualified by a QS-9000 recognized accreditation body.
- The QS-9000 registrar should suit the needs of overseas customers, European Union directives, and criteria of individual national accreditation bodies where a company is doing business or plans to do business. This is especially important in Europe, where not all national accreditation bodies have yet accepted QS-9000 certification.
- A registrar should match your company's operating style if possible.
- Companies should interview as many registrars as time permits and conduct random reference checks. They can use these interviews as a means of learning more about the QS-9000 certification process. Companies should not hire a registrar until they are ready to start the QS-9000 process.
- Companies should be aware that there may be a waiting period for a registrar. Although registrars and national accreditation bodies involved with QS-9000 are being added almost daily, the QS-9000 program is still gearing up. The Big Three are working to meet that demand.

ISO 9000 registrars have been training since the summer of 1994 to conduct third-party auditing of auto company suppliers. Specifically, registrars must comply with Appendices B, G, and H of the Code of Practices of Quality Systems Registrars, and the International Automotive Section Group (IASG) QS-9000 Sanctioned Interpretations (see "Fine-Tuning QS-9000" later in this chapter) to issue QS-9000 certificates.

Note: It is very important to test a registrar's automobile experience. The more experience with the automobile industry, the better. Many registrars work internationally and maintain several offices in countries as large as the United States. For this reason, it is important to note not only whether a registrar is authorized to practice under the QS-9000 system, but which of its offices is able to do so.

6. *Organize management and employees to work under a QS-9000 team system.* As with ISO 9000, QS-9000 is employee-intensive, meaning that it encourages involvement by as many employees as possible. Although employee input may be extremely positive and beneficial to a company in the long run, involving employees in unfamiliar tasks can prove difficult, confusing, and costly in the short run.

Companies that have succeeded in earning ISO 9000 certificates did so because management was firmly behind the process and led the process through employee training programs that allowed the employees to assume charge of internal auditing. Management assisted in the creation of a team system that involved employees as ISO 9000 coordinators, data collectors, and ultimately as informal in-house auditors. The person chosen to oversee ISO 9000 or QS-9000 certification must be qualified in the process and well respected by employees at all levels.

Note: The idea of utilizing employees to informally "audit" or inspect their company should not be confused with the Supplier Confirmation Audit (SAC) process, whereby employees become qualified ISO 9000 lead auditors and work directly with a registrar.

7. *Recognize steps that are specific to QS-9000.* The steps that follow are specific to the Big Three process as outlined in the Automotive Industry Action Group manual *Advanced Product Quality Planning and Control Plan.*

Product quality planning timing plan. The product quality planning team's first order of business following organizational activities should be the development of a timing chart (see Figure 4-2). The type and complexity of product and customer expectations should be considered in selecting the timing elements that must be planned and charted. All team members should agree with each event, action, and schedule. A well-organized timing chart should list tasks, assignments, and other events. The chart also provides the planning team with a consistent format for tracking progress and preparing meeting agendas. To facilitate status reporting, each event must have a "start" and a "completion" date with the actual point of progress recorded. Effective status reporting supports program monitoring with a focus on identifying items that require special attention.

Product quality planning cycle plans relative to the timing chart. The success of any program depends on meeting customer needs and expectations in a timely manner at a cost that represents value. The product quality planning timing chart and the product quality planning cycle require a planning team to concentrate its efforts on defect prevention. Defect prevention is driven by simultaneous engineering performed by product and manufacturing engineering activities working concurrently. Planning

Figure 4-2. Product quality planning timing chart.

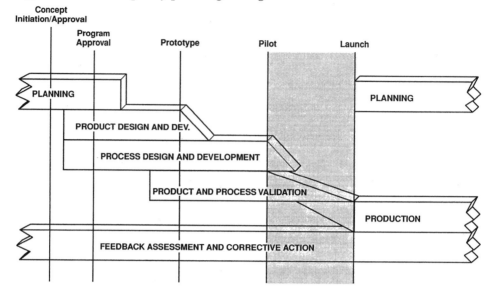

teams must be prepared to modify product quality plans to meet customer expectations. The product quality planning team is responsible for ensuring that timing meets or exceeds the customer timing plan.

Defining the scope. It is important for the product quality planning team in the earliest stage of the product program to identify customer needs, expectations, and requirements. At a minimum, the team must meet to

- Select a project team leader responsible for overseeing the planning process. (In some cases it may be advantageous to rotate the team leader during the planning cycle.)
- Define the roles and responsibilities of each area represented.
- Identify the customers—internal and external.
- Define customer requirements. Use QFD if applicable, as referenced in Appendix B of the *Advanced Product Quality Planning and Control Plan (APQP)*, published by the Automotive Industry Action Group (AIAG).
- Select the disciplines, individuals, and subcontractors that must be added to the team, and determine which are not required.
- Understand customer expectations (e.g., design, number of tests, math data requirements, and program timing).
- Identify costs, timing, and constraints that must be considered.
- Conduct a team feasibility study (see the *APQP*).
- Determine assistance required from the customer.
- Identify documentation process or method.

Team-to-team. The product quality planning team must establish lines of communication with other customer and supplier teams. This may include regular meetings with other teams. The extent of team-to-team contact is dependent upon the number of issues requiring resolution.

Training. The success of a product quality plan depends on an effective training program that communicates job descriptions and defines training requirements and training records needed to fulfill customer needs and expectations.

Customer and supplier involvement. The primary customer may initiate the quality planning process with a supplier. However, the supplier has an obligation to establish a cross-functional team within its company to manage the product quality planning process. Suppliers must expect the same performance from their subcontractors.

Simultaneous engineering. Simultaneous engineering is a process where cross-functional teams strive for a common goal of defect prevention. It replaces the sequential series of phases where results are transmitted to the next area for execution. The purpose is to expedite the introduction of quality products sooner. The product quality planning team assures that other areas/teams plan and execute activities that support the common goal or goals.

Control plans. Control plans are written descriptions of the systems for controlling parts and processes. Separate control plans cover these distinct phases:

- *Prototype.* A description of the dimensional measurements and material and performance tests that will occur during prototype build (where prototype material is being supplied).
- *Pre-launch.* A description of the dimensional measurements and material and performance tests that will occur after prototype for production launch.
- *Production.* A comprehensive documentation of product or process characteristics, process controls, tests, and measurement systems that will occur during mass production.

Concern resolution. During the planning process, the team will encounter product design or processing concerns. These concerns should be documented on a matrix with assigned responsibility and timing. Disciplined problem-solving methods are recommended, and may be required, in difficult situations.

8. *Determine a system for collecting, processing, and formatting documentation of operating procedures before embarking on meeting a registrar's QS-9000*

demands. Lack of in-house preparation and coordination may cost a company thousands of extra dollars.

Because of the sector-specific nature of QS-9000, documentation requirements will be far more specific than those of ISO 9000. QS-9000 provides documentation requirements and copies can be obtained through the AIAG.

At the heart of a long-running, efficient, low-maintenance documentation system is solid interviewing. Only the right questions lead to the right answers. And the key to the right answers is solid employee-management communication.

The key to running a system over a period of time—which both ISO and QS-9000 require—is customization. Templates, graphs, and pre-designed manuals are fine as models, but they may not reflect the corporate culture or temperament of a particular workplace. Over the long haul, if not streamlined and realistic, they will fail.

ISO 9000 and QS-9000 are both heavily oriented toward documentation of procedures. Companies that lack quality control manuals altogether will find that they must devise a means of culling information from employees, recording that information, and formatting it, while continuing to operate their business. Even those with quality control departments and manuals may find their systems require an overhaul.

Because few manufacturers or service companies involve employees in reporting and documenting their functions, ISO 9000 can seem bewildering and even overwhelming. Organizing the work that leads to certification, while staying in business, can seem daunting. Rather than pause and create a system, many companies will hire outsiders to move the process along for them.

Up-front organization and creation of a documentation system that suits the company may save countless hours of confusion in the long run, and savings of hours almost always equals saving dollars.

Follow these steps for the best coordination, and most efficient operation, of a data collection and formatting system:

- Organize management and employees into teams for the collection and processing of data. In the process, develop project plans with time frames to accomplish work.
- Management should establish a framework for data collection and processing based on the ISO 9000 requirements and the company's organization.
- Uniform methods of data collection should be established up front, along with formats—graphs, tables, listings, headings—under which to organize information (QS-9000 4.20).
- Set up all formats in the company's network first, if such a network

exists. In the absence of a computer system, establish typists who will sort and format material employees gather.
- Ensure that employees receive ample instruction in data collection before starting. Make sure those in charge of sorting data, formatting, and producing the manual receive instruction in editing and formatting.
- Be flexible within the formats established. Allow the process to dictate where additional topic areas may need to be added and others deleted.
- Take QS-9000 requirements into consideration while deciding coverage zones, but make sure that all data collection and processing systems are in place and tested before starting the actual documentation process.

Requirements for QS-9000 documentation progression are shown in Figure 4-3.

9. *Design a quality manual (level one quality system documentation).* Once a functioning documentation system is in place, or even in trial phase, it is time to design a customized company quality plan and procedures. Here is a process to consider:

- Information can be gathered from the manufacturing floor about product specifications, work procedures, and general concerns utilizing the newly created documentation system.
- The individual or team charged with designing the quality manual will analyze data and make recommendations based on what is really taking place in-house, rather than guessing.
- Criteria that emerge from this process become the basic elements of the quality manual.
- Employees and management can review the draft manual and provide fine-tuning.

10. *Hire a qualified registrar/select a qualified consultant.* Once employees are trained and organized and have set up a system for collecting and processing data, hire the selected registrar. Use outside consulting help sparingly.

Companies may need outside assistance. When selecting a consultant, search for one who is experienced in automotive auditing procedures and offers means of saving costs and streamlining the company's QS-9000 quality system.

A quality consultant can help interpret QS-9000, determine where the company ranks vis-à-vis QS-9000, conduct mock preassessment audits, train employees in internal auditing, and assist in creation of a quality manual that meets QS-9000 requirements.

Figure 4-3. Quality system documentation progression.

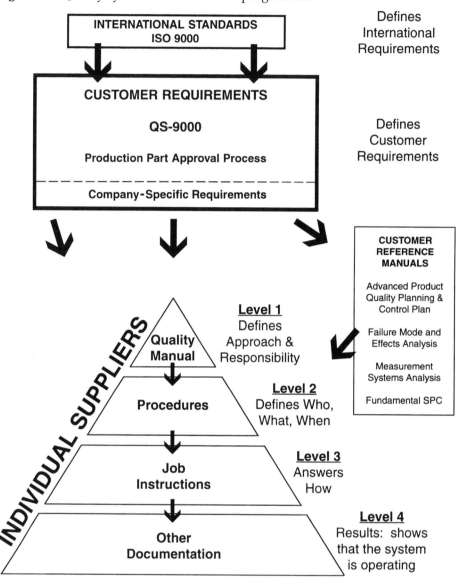

11. *Have a registrar conduct a preassessment audit.* Because of the exacting, detailed nature of QS-9000, companies embarked on this process highly recommend having registrars conduct preassessment audits. It is best to pick up system failures or system problems before attempting a final audit for a QS-9000 certificate.

Case Study

A Pittsburgh-based tubing manufacturer and Tier 1 auto industry sup-plier faced the QS-9000 process after earning ISO 9002. One of the first companies in the United States to embark on QS-9000, the company ended up serving as the accreditation site for its registrar, Steel Related In-dustries (SRI), so the two companies walked through the process together.

Luckily for this company, SRI was its ISO 9000 registrar. That meant the tubing manufacturer faced few changes in its implementation of the ISO 9000 aspects of QS-9000 and could focus mainly on the special sector-specific criteria. With lots of hard work and determination, this company had also passed Ford Q1 audits and was familiar with auto industry requirements.

The tubing manufacturer earned QS-9000 certification in tandem with its registrar earning QS-9000 accreditation from the Big Three. Because the company was already involved in ISO 9000 and had implemented Q1, it found it relatively easy to earn QS-9000 certification.

Fine-Tuning QS-9000

The QS-9000 Task Force has been working with the International Automo-tive Section Group (IASG) on fine-tuning the program, with special atten-tion devoted to improving registrar criteria and interpretation issues. The IASG meets regularly to discuss and resolve interpretation issues relative to the QS-9000 criteria and third-party registration of auto suppliers to QS-9000. This is an international ad hoc working group composed of rep-resentatives from:

- Big Three-recognized accreditation bodies
- QS-9000 qualified registrars
- Representatives of the Chrysler/Ford/General Motors Supplier Re-quirements Task Force
- Tier 1 automotive suppliers (raw materials and parts suppliers only)

How the IASG Fields Inquiries

When the Big Three embarked on QS-9000, it was decided to make this as open and accessible a program as possible. Therefore, the IASG willingly fields inquiries and recommendations from interested parties. There are three steps for queries within the IASG. Only the "agreed" category re-sponses are released to the public. The order in which requests and in-quiries are entertained is as follows:

1. New written requests
2. Draft interpretations
3. "Agreed" (interpretations the IASG has decided are ready for publication)

Agreed responses are labeled by the year and month they were addressed. Following this numerical sequence is a dash and a sequential letter and number for permanent reference. The answers are considered valid as of the date they were agreed upon. Subsequent changes in the answer to an interpretation will show the same category-sequential number, but a new "agreed" date.

Note: To reach the IASG with requests or questions, fax inquiries in English to IASG Fax Voice Mail Box (614-847-8556). For the latest updates of IASG Sanctioned QS-9000 Interpretations, call the American Society for Quality Control (1-800-248-1946) or contact its Web site at http://www.asqc.org/qs-9000.

Commonly Asked Questions About QS-9000
From the IASG Sanctioned QS-9000 Interpretations

The following are questions from the "agreed"-upon interpretations that the Chrysler/Ford/General Motors Supplier Quality Requirements Task Force has sanctioned, along with participating ISO 9000 accreditation bodies and QS-9000 qualified registrars. These "IASG Sanctioned QS-9000 Interpretations" were issued during the summer of 1995. The document was directed at Chrysler/Ford/General Motors recognized accreditation bodies, QS-9000 qualified registrars, suppliers, and interested parties.

These questions offer real-life examples of how the Big Three, the IASG, and others are grappling with issues that have arisen around QS-9000 implementation.

DRAFT OF 6/28/95

1. Appendix B: Code of Conduct (B)
   (Regarding registrars who also maintain consulting services)
   9504-B03

Question
It is our understanding from our meeting with the Big Three Task Force on November 18, 1994, that the implementation date of the requirements of Clause 9 of QS-9000 Appendix B, "Code of Practice," is from the date of

first issue of the QS-9000 document itself (August 1994). Does "two year rule" for defining consultancy apply?

Answer
No. Consultancy to the company by a registrar or related body is allowed two years before the registration audit. Because this is a new (8/94) requirement, consultancy before August 1994 is waived.

2. Database (D)
   9503-D02

Question
Customers need to know which registrars have been qualified and which suppliers have been certified to QS-9000. Who will keep the information and how will it be disseminated?

Answer
The IASG will publish this list each time it releases or revises the QS-9000 Sanctioned Interpretations.

3. 9503-D03

Question
Will a database exist for QS-9000 certified companies? Can anyone use it for searches, etc.?

Answer
Yes. The IASG is currently exploring this issue with several potential service providers. The intent is to stimulate and support a worldwide database, easily accessible by everyone.

4. 9506-01 (R)

Question
I am a Tier 1 Supplier, with five bids from QS-9000 registrars. Three violate the (5/1/95) Appendix H Chart minimums with man-days that are 20–30 percent below the 80 percent level for ISO 9002.
    The two registrars not violating the (5/1/95) Appendix H minimums indicate my registration or accreditation is at risk if I go with one of the other three.
    The low three explain that their bids reflect the application of a "shift factor" to the minimums, allowing a lower man-day count for three shift operations.
    The two non-violator registrars indicate that the man-days were constructed using the (5/1/95) Appendix H Chart with "total" employees.

I'm confused and await a copy of the latest IASG Interpretations before I make my choice. How can your suppliers make a good selection if the registrars don't operate under the same rules?

Answer
The definition of how to apply the Appendix H table has been amended to clarify this situation. See the 6/15/95 revised answer to 9503-R131.

5. 9506-02 (C)

Question
When a subcontractor performs a final operation, such as painting, what is required of the supplier to meet the intent of 4.10.4? Is this requirement altered if the subcontractor is on an approved list?

Answer
The supplier must assure all quality system requirements and final inspection and testing are met by the supplier and subcontractor. The requirements of 4.10.4 are not altered if a subcontractor is on an approved list.

6. 9506-04 (A)

Question
Can the assessment of a Tier 1 supplier to a truck manufacturer listed in QS-9000 Section III be an acceptable witness audit for registrar qualification?

Answer
Yes.

7. 9506-06 (R)

Question
QS-9000 Section 1 is ISO 9001 *plus the additional automotive requirements*. Does using a registered third party to achieve QS-9000 certification also result in attainment of ISO 9001 certification? Since all requirements of ISO are included in QS-9000 and the certifying third party our company will use is an ISO 9000 and QS-9000 registered certification body, it would seem logical our company would be recognized as achieving ISO 9001 and QS-9000 certification by successfully completing the QS-9000 audit. Our company is strictly automotive and has achieved VDA certification in Europe, and we see no need to achieve a separate ISO 9001 certification if QS-9000 is attained.

Answer
Yes. Registration to QS-9000 includes registration to either ISO 9001 or 9002. QS-9000 registration can only be attained once the firm has been audited

and found to be in conformance with both ISO 9000 and QS-9000. Both references to conformance with ISO 9000 and QS-9000 will appear on the registration certificate.

8. 9506-10 (C)

Question
Would like interpretation on the following scenario:
A supplier has been told by a certified ISO auditor and it has been published in an ISO reference book that, "gauges must have calibration stickers," and "the operator must know the status of a gauge (meaning the date it is due for re-calibration)." Other certified lead assessors have stated that neither is required by ISO. The supplier's current system includes a process of etching a serial number on each gauge. A computer program is maintained with all required information for each gauge, and re-calibration is done based on computer printouts prior to due dates. This system has passed both GM and Ford audits in previous years. Does this system meet the requirements of 4.11.2d?

Answer
Yes, it appears to. Address this with your registrar during his pre-audit visit(s).

9. 9506-11 (B)

Question
I recently attended a QS-9000 course, where the requirements of Appendix B and G were explained as understood by the trainer. Unfortunately, our understanding is different and will present us with considerable difficulties unless we can resolve them.

The problem is as follows: From the information available to me and following a discussion with the NACCB assessor, I understood that an audit team comprising a QS-9000 trained assessor plus an automotive industry expert would satisfy the requirements covering the audit team. On this basis I attended the course. I do not have automotive experience. It would now appear that we sent the wrong person to the course.

Answer
All audit team members must be QS-9000 certified. At least one team member must have relevant automotive industry experience.

Question
Does this same requirement apply to surveillance? This appears very restrictive and not necessary. Nowhere in the appendices is this specified.

Answer
All audit team members must be QS-9000 certified. It is not restrictive and is considered necessary.

10. 9506-12 (B)

Question
I fully agree with these requirements but I do not understand why every member of the audit team needs to be QS-9000 trained and why the team member with automotive experience needs to be ISO 9000 *and* QS-9000 trained. We would currently cover these requirements by using a team with "combined" qualifications, covering all areas but not necessarily all trained assessors, QS-9000 trained, etc. We would be accompanied by technical experts if necessary.

Answer
Not acceptable. See previous question.

Question
In addition, our surveillance visits would include an automotive expert only when necessary, possibly every other visit. It would appear counterproductive to take an automotive expert or even possibly a QS-9000 assessor, if the surveillance visit was only to cover ISO 9000 elements without any specific QS-9000 additions.

Answer
All surveillance audits will cover elements of ISO 9000 and QS-9000. Therefore, all audit and surveillance team members must be QS-9000 certificated: No exceptions!

11. 9506-33

Question
We [OEM] supply a valve that has two plastic rectangular plastic covers placed on both ends of the valve. [OEM's] employees, after unpacking and removing the plastic covers, collect them in a box and send them back to us to be sorted, washed, and reused if determined good. Where would we address this issue in the QS-9000? Would this be considered OEM-owned parts (4.7)?

Answer and Status: Draft 6/19/95
Valve is a product supplied with plastic covers to OEM. Plastic covers are procurement issues depending on ownership changes in the use cycle. If OEM owns, it would be covered under 4.7; if you provide and own returned parts, then it is a 4.6 issue.

Resources

Automotive Industry Action Group, *Advanced Product and Quality Planning and Control Plan* [manual], 1994–1995.

Automotive Industry Action Group, *Quality System Requirements: QS-9000* [manual].

International Automotive Section Group, "The IASG Sanctioned QS-9000 Interpretations," 1995. [Permission is given to QS-9000 recognized accreditation bodies, accredited ISO 9000 registrars, automotive OEM customers and suppliers, and industry media to reproduce this document for the purposes of improving the understanding and communication of QS-9000 interpretations.]

Appendix A

Acronyms

AIAG	Automotive Industry Action Group
CFT	Cross Functional Team
DCP	Dynamic Control Plan (Dimensional Control Plan)
DFMEA	Design Failure Mode and Effects Analysis
DOE	Design of Experiments
DVP&R	Design Verification Plan and Report
FMA	Failure Mode Analysis
FMEA	Failure Mode and Effects Analysis
FTC	First Time Capability
GR&R	Gauge Repeatability and Reproducibility
PFMEA	Process Failure Mode and Effects Analysis
PQP	Product Quality Planning
PQPT	Product Quality Planning Team
QFD	Quality Function Deployment
QS-9000	Quality System Requirements
SFMEA	System Failure Mode and Effects Analysis
TGR	Things Gone Right
TGW	Things Gone Wrong
VE/VA	Value Engineering/Value Analysis

Appendix B

International Registrars Approved to Issue QS-9000 Certificates

The offices of international registrars listed below are approved as of March 22, 1996, to issue QS-9000 certificates.

Registrar	Office Qualified	Accrediting Body		
ABS	Texas	RvA	RAB	
A.G.A. Quality	Ohio	RvA	RAB	
AQA	South Carolina		RAB	
AT&T QR	New Jersey		RAB	
BSI	U.K.	RvA		UKAS
BSI	Virginia	RvA		
BVQI	Netherlands	RvA		
BVQI	New York		RAB	
CRS	Ohio		RAB	
DNVI	Netherlands	RvA		
DNV	Texas		RAB	
DQS	Germany			TGA
DRS	Pennsylvania		RAB	
Entela	Michigan	RvA	RAB	
Intertek	Virginia	RvA	RAB	
JQA	Japan	RvA		
KPMG	New Jersey	RvA	RAB	
LRQA	New Jersey		RAB	
LRQA	U.K.	RvA		
NQA	U.K.			UKAS
NSF	Michigan	RvA		
OMNEX	Michigan		RAB	

Registrar	Office Qualified	Accrediting Body		
QMI	Canada	RvA	RAB	
QSR	Virginia	RvA	RAB	
SGS	New Jersey		RAB	
SGS	U.K.			UKAS
Smithers	Ohio	RvA		
SRI	Pennsylvania	RvA	RAB	
TUV America, Inc.	Massachusetts		RAB	
TUV Essen	California		RAB	
TUV Rheinland	Connecticut	RvA	RAB	
UL	New York	RvA	RAB	

5

Quality Assurance Programs in the U.S. Military: Q 9000

Questions the Reader Will Find Addressed in This Chapter

1. What is the defense standards system?
2. What is the history of standards at the Department of Defense?
3. How are military standards in transition?
4. Why and how might military specifications be maintained?
5. What is a strategic quality plan?
6. How does the Q 9000 system relate to the military?
7. How is Q 9000 implemented?
8. How is Q 9000 audited?
9. How do individual branches of the military handle Q 9000?
10. What is the *Mil Handbook 9000*?
11. How is conformity assessment applied to Q 9000?
12. How is the Qualified Product List tested by the Qualified Manufacturers List?
13. What are the custom requirements a supplier might face in dealing with individual government agencies?

Introduction

As with industry, in general, the military employs different types of standards and specifications. In general military parlance these are called "mil specs," although there exist both standards and military specifications within the military system. Standards generally relate to a process, while specifications generally relate to a product.

What makes the military system different from the commercial system is its focus on procurement. Many military specs exist as part of the defense contract system. That means they are "mandatory" for the defense contractors or suppliers that want to earn military contracts.

The U.S. military is actively replacing both quality and product-related military standards and specifications, or "specs," with commercial standards. In the last few years the Department of Defense (DOD) cancelled all military standards relating to quality in favor of commercial standards.

Note: Not all military specs will be eliminated. This is especially true in the product area.

Changes are taking place on a number of fronts simultaneously and within the DOD. Of particular concern to many contractors and suppliers is the introduction of ISO 9000 as the quality system of choice, or Q 9000. Q 9000 is the American version of ISO 9000, which has been adopted by the American National Standards Institute (ANSI) and is almost identical to the original standard.

The DOD has eliminated Mil Q9858A—the defense quality standards system—which was deactivated in August 1995. Although ISO 9000 is considered the quality system of choice by the DOD, the military in no way intends to mandate its use. There is general awareness that other quality programs exist, such as the Big Three Automakers' common quality standard QS-9000. The DOD's main concern is allowing its contractors choice and flexibility while ensuring that they create internal quality structures.

For all of these reasons, ISO 9000 is considered a baseline. Nowadays, when contractors submit a Request for Proposal (RFP), they are asked to respond with whatever quality system they have in place—"ISO 9001, 2, 3, or an equivalent." If they choose a system equivalent to ISO 9000, they must be able to prove that it provides the same level of quality assurance as the international standards series. And, in fact, the DOD will use the twenty basic ISO 9000 elements to validate that equivalency.

Various military branches and services have approached the Q 9000 process individually, causing confusion for military suppliers and defense contractors. The Navy, for example, has examined creating its own set of specific criteria that suppliers must adopt while implementing Q 9000. None of these criteria has been adopted.

At this writing, DOD has yet to require ISO 9000 registration as a condition for doing business with DOD. Moreover, the DOD still chooses to conduct a great deal of second-party auditing of suppliers. Depending on the service and agency concerned, defense contractors and suppliers must be in compliance with the ISO 9000 standard series, but do not have to be registered.

In a related area, federal acquisition requirements (D-FAR 246) have been revised to reflect this change, stating that for quality purposes, defense suppliers and contractors should use "any military, commercial, national or international standard." Once again, this means provided they meet the DOD's current acquisition requirements as they relate to a quality system.

Defense Standards System

The DOD standards system is not really a system at all, but a huge accumulation of mil specs emanating from government agencies that serve the military, as well as from the individual military branches. Many of these specs have grown out of decades of defense requirements to pass congressional authorization and subsequent budget appropriations.

Unlike private-sector standards bodies, the military is a government agency whose procurement system must withstand intense media scrutiny. The DOD is expected to maintain standards that determine product performance and quality. The department is also expected to produce conformity assessment results that assure constituents that its professional judgments are sound and will stand up to review.

History of Standards at the DOD

While many DOD standards efforts began during World War II, it was not until 1952 that the DOD acknowledged the need to establish, develop, and maintain a system of technical documentation in support of design, development, engineering, acquisition, manufacturing, maintenance, and supply management that would (1) increase efficiency and effectiveness of logistical support and operational readiness of the military services and (2) conserve resources and money. That year the Cataloguing and Standardization Act became federal law, requiring formal documentation of all material (hardware) products and support services that military departments and defense agencies were purchasing. Products and services purchased had to be described in sufficient detail to allow for multiple supply sources and competitive bids from established, capable defense industries and commercial producers.

Note: It was the DOD documentation system that served as one of the basic tools of ISO 9000—documentation as a means of creating an internal auditing system.

Since 1952, the defense establishment has created what insiders describe as "a large, complex, closed cocoon of 41,000 specifications and standards on which it bases its acquisition decisions." The bulk of these standards—approximately 34,000—have been developed by 120 separate military units or taken from the Federal Supply Service. In addition they are categorized by document type as follows:

- Military specifications (mil specs)
- Military standards
- Federal specifications and standards
- Nongovernment standards
- International standards and commercial item descriptions

The primary source of information on DOD specifications and standards is the Defense Department Index of Specifications and Standards. The DOD maintains standards management facilities to develop and validate mil specs and military standards. Military departments and defense agencies function as lead standardization creators and custodians, depending upon their authority. What is described by insiders as a "thorough yet cumbersome series of checks, balances, and review" is actively maintained.

The DOD also uses nongovernment standards. By the early 1990s, there were 5,100 nongovernment standards in use and 1,620 international ones. In addition, there were 4,300 DOD-prepared commercial item descriptions, which served as procurement specifications for off-the-shelf products.

DOD personnel participate in more than 200 voluntary standards organizations. The DOD is also well represented in international standards advisory groups and lists 1,620 international standards that have been adapted for use in defense procurement. As discussed more fully later in this chapter, a major movement is afoot to encourage government adoption of commercial standards and gradual elimination of government standards programs that duplicate the work of private-sector groups.

Military Standards: A System in Transition

When William Perry was named secretary of defense in the winter of 1994, he vowed he would remove military specs. Over the years, many mil specs had become redundant and suppliers and contractors were exerting more energy in "covering all bases" for the military, which was sapping their competitive edge and making it difficult for them to function in dual markets—commercial and military.

As noted in the introduction, there was a secondary effort to upgrade military quality efforts to better match quality efforts taking place worldwide. On February 14, 1994, the defense secretary issued a letter that allowed the services and their suppliers to substitute ISO 9000 standards for corresponding military quality specs. The two main reasons were:

1. There was pressure on defense contractors and suppliers to adopt ISO 9000 by their commercial customer base.
2. Military officials found ISO 9000 to be a satisfactory quality tool.

Note: The defense secretary's letter of February 14, 1994, produced a great deal of hype and claims from ISO 9000 consultants, seminar providers, and others involved in selling ISO 9000 services. Contrary to these claims, the DOD did not, and has not, mandated ISO 9000 as a standard of choice. The DOD has *recommended* use of this standard and suggested that ISO 9000 is probably the only standard that meets its guidelines for quality as they are evolving. However, each branch of the military has been given the right to enforce whatever quality system it believes will serve it best.

In June 1994, Defense Secretary Perry made good on his promise to remove all military specs. The DOD issued a letter to all services advising them to switch from mil specs to commercial or industry standards. In this letter, the secretary of defense said this would be "a new way of doing business." Under this altered system, still being defined, military specs are to be used only as a last resort.

At the same time that Perry announced he would eliminate mil specs, there was talk in the DOD of altering the Federal Acquisition Law to reflect these changes. In the fall of 1994, a new version of the Federal Acquisition Law was passed to reflect changes in military/spec policy. Additional amendments to the Federal Acquisition Regulations (FAR) were made in 1995 when DOD specified use of ISO 9000—or an equivalent quality system—as a requirement of the military acquisition process.

The Defense Standards Improvement Council (DSIC), an ongoing board in existence over 20 years, has the authority to make the final disposition on DOD specifications and standards. Major consideration is given to:

- Product performance
- Interface
- Design guide

Note: In an agency that's as much a behemoth as the DOD, with tentacles that reach throughout the U.S. economy, the sort of far-reaching change Perry advocated is enormous. Several years later, the DOD is still cranking in the direction of eliminating mil specs. However, there are many, many issues to resolve, especially around the area of auditing or inspection (discussed later in this chapter).

Military Specification Waiver Process

Not all military specs will be eliminated. The DOD recognizes that many product specs should be retained. For example, specifications defining wiring and adhesives are straightforward and require no altering. Information technology standards also will remain as is.

Individual agencies and services have the right to petition the head contracting office for a waiver when it makes sense to use an existing military spec. Waivers are generally part of the acquisition process and take place when an agency is preparing a request of proposal to send out to industry contractors.

Note: Where waivers are concerned, suppliers and defense contractors are expected to take their lead from the agencies that are their customer base.

Any agency that wants to use mil specs must go to its program officer and formally state the reason for using a mil spec rather than a commercial spec. The program officer then petitions the head contracting office for the waiver. See Figure 5-1.

By January 1995, the DOD had adopted more than 1,200 commercial standards. Over 160 military specs had been eliminated by mid-1996. A hot line was established to assist the public with questions on standards, implementation issues, the military specification waiver process, and general policy directions. The number is 800-327-7732. The appendix to this chapter presents a finalized list of "heartburn" standards that are slated for cancellation.

Introducing ISO 9000 (or Q 9000)

In an era of defense cutbacks, the military is facing the challenge of maintaining an industrial base large enough to supply its needs during a period of declining purchases. Many industries that have long served the military—metal tooling, for example—are undergoing massive conversion from defense-related products to civilian use. These industries need to be able to work in both the military and commercial sectors to survive.

In the face of such massive change, harmonizing DOD quality system assessment requirements with international systems of quality assessment has become extremely attractive to many DOD contractors. Defense suppliers argue that harmonizing quality system requirements can provide entry to foreign markets and can reduce the cost of producing products that currently must meet multiple sets of requirements and undergo an assortment of assessment processes.

Other challenges on the standards and conformity assessment fronts are coming from the European Union (EU) and emerging economic blocs worldwide, especially on the product standards front. DOD officials are becoming increasingly concerned about the need to simplify the massive defense standards system while working on harmonization and mutual recognition of product qualification and certification processes between the United States, the EU, and other national blocs.

Figure 5-1. Military IT standards not requiring a waiver.

Mil. Std. # and Title	Date of Publication	Prep./ Resp. Org.	Type	% Com. Std.	Based on Commercial Std. # and Title	Reason Needed
MIL-STD-188-198A Joint Photographic Experts Group (JPEG) Image Compression for the National Imagery Transmission Format Standard	15 Dec. 1993	DISA/ JIEO DC	Inter- face	75	Multiple including JPEG	Selects options and features to provide tactical digital intelli- gence imagery inter- operability.
MIL-STD-188-199 Vector Quantization Decompres- sion for the National Imagery Transmission Format Standard	27 June 1994	DISA/ JIEO DC	Inter- face		None	No commercial equiv- alent. Required by DMA for sending mapping data.
MIL-STD-188-220 Interoperability Standard for Digital Message Transfer Device Sub- systems	7 March 1993	DISA/ JIEO DC	Inter- face	40	Multiple	No commercial equiv- alent. Needed for tac- tical interoperability.
MIL-STD-974 Contractor Integrated Technical In- formation Service (CITIS)	20 Aug. 1993	DISA/ JIEO DC	Inter- face		None	No commercial equiv- alent. Contractor inte- gration standard.
MIL-STD-1582C EHF Low Data Rate (LDR) Satellite Data Link Standards (SDLS) Up- links and Downlinks (SECRET)	10 Dec. 1992	DISA/ JIEO DC	Inter- face		None	No commercial equiv- alent.

February 28, 1995

When DOD officials began work on streamlining the military standards system and making it more responsive to domestic and international economic trends, various military services were exploring use of the ISO 9000 standards series in lieu of mil specs. This was before the DOD began to tackle this issue in earnest. For example, as early as November 1993, air force brass issued a letter to their command saying they should "employ" the ISO 9000 series. In January 1994, the Joint Logistics Commanders/Joint Aeronautical Commanders Group (air force and navy air force, or NAVAIR) issued a letter to their command telling them they had the "option of choosing" ISO 9000. In fact, the standards series was already being employed.

A Strategic Quality Plan

Q 9000 grew out of the DOD's earlier 1991 efforts to redefine quality for military application. In a report released on February 23, 1991, DOD officials stated that quality should be emphasized and "integrated throughout all elements and activities of a program." This policy statement eventually led to the formation of the Joint Government/Industry Quality Liaison Panel, which was formed to work on a strategic quality plan for the military and its suppliers and contractors. Joint Government/Industry Quality Liaison Panel members include the following:

Government
  Department of Defense
  Department of Transportation (DOT)
    Federal Aviation Agency (FAA)
    Maritime Administration
  National Aeronautics and Space Administration (NASA)
  National Oceanic & Atmospheric Administration (NOAA)
  National Institute of Standards and Technology (NIST)
  General Services Administration (GSA)

Industry
  Aerospace Industries Agency (AIA)
  Electronic Industries Association (EIA)
  National Security Industrial Association (NSIA)

The panel set out to create a twofold quality plan that would improve government acquisition procedures and help defense contractors serve both military and commercial customers. It prepared a draft to promote a single quality management system for the DOD and its contractors and suppliers. Although nothing official has been issued yet, the panel has been grappling with a definition of quality and has come up with the following three goals:

1. Creation of a single quality system that contractors can easily adapt to meet all customer requirements
2. Recognition and use by government and industry of advanced quality concepts in the requirements definition, design, manufacture, and acceptance of products
3. Effective implementation of a baseline quality system and appropriate oversight methods

In the effort to create a single system, the DOD does not want to create "a rigid and uniform quality management system across government and in every contractor's facility." Rather, the panel envisions a multitier quality management framework built on the foundation of a basic quality system. It defines a basic quality system as one that meets certain criteria, such as the ISO 9000 elements (see Chapter 9), and that is recognized and agreed to governmentwide and across industry.

The ISO 9000 standards series will serve as the basis for this "flexible" quality system, just as the ISO 9000 elements are the basis for the Big Three automakers' QS-9000. Beyond that, the military envisions industry adding advanced quality concepts and industry-specific concepts as it sees fit. To create this basic quality system, the DOD—as early as 1991 in reference to acquisition policies—determined that military quality efforts must focus on three interconnected areas:

1. *Quality of Design.* Relates to the "effectiveness of the design process in capturing the operational requirements and translating them into detailed design requirements that can be manufactured (or coded) in a consistent manner."

2. *Quality of Conformance.* Relates to the "effectiveness of the design and manufacturing functions in executing the product manufacturing requirements and process specifications while meeting tolerance, process control limits, and target yields for a given product group."

3. *Fitness for Use.* Relates to the "effectiveness of the design, manufacturing and support processes in delivering a system that meets the operational requirements under all anticipated operational conditions."

Note: ISO 9000 (or Q 9000) is the only quality assurance standard that meets the foregoing requirements.

Single Process Initiative

Because industry was not moving off of military specs and standards, the DOD has introduced Single Process Initiatives (SPI), or the meshing of quality and product-performance processes in their facilities.

A main thrust of SPI is to create more flexible contract language so that contractors and suppliers can pursue the most effective process—the best practice—to move toward a quality system that produces quality products. Under the SPI approach, contractors/suppliers are encouraged:

- First, to negotiate with their customer base to implant the best standards and requirements so that they are eventually operating under a single process
- Then to negotiate with the DOD so that their contracts reflect the changes they have implemented

Example

A major Boston-based defense contractor in the electronics field recommended 80 process changes for a given product line. Under SPI, they were able to change all of their defense contracts to reflect the new process.

Note: Most, if not all, major defense contractors are participating in SPI.

The Q 9000 System as It Relates to Mil Standards

- *Q 9001.* A replacement for MIL-Q-9858 and includes MIL-STD-1520 (material review) and MIL-STD-1535 (supplier quality requirements). It applies to systems in design, production, installation, and servicing.
- *Q 9002.* A replacement for MIL-I-45208. It is an inspection system that also includes MIL-STD-1520 and MIL-STD-1535 requirements. It applies to systems in production, installation, and servicing.
- *Q 9003.* Equivalent to the MIL-I "inspection system." It is designed to be applied for a final test only.
- *Q 9004.* Equivalent in the ISO 9000 standards series to ISO 9004. It provides guidelines for implementing Q 9000.

Note: Unlike ISO 9000, the Q series has a major emphasis on distribution and service, as well as manufacturing. Also, the DOD is encouraging contractors involved with electronics, computers, and telecommunications products to buy preexisting systems rather than get involved in designing their own. These are called nondevelopmental items or commercial off-the-shelf items. If using either item, then contractors should remember that choice will be reflected in the Q series they select.

Implementing Q 9000

Q 9000 requires the following:

- A quality system in place, whether documented or not
- A quality policy
- A policy that company procedures define management's role, especially top management, and that there be regular management reviews
- A proof-of-quality plan
- A quality manual outlining (1) mission statement, (2) quality assurance policy, (3) company background/introduction, and (4) main body of information including company organization, quality records, work procedures, and change mechanisms
- A policy encouraging employee involvement
- A policy mandating frequent internal audits and self-audits

Q 9000 Certification

The question of how to audit Q 9000 is still very much up in the air. The Joint Government/Industry Quality Liaison Panel has recommended this basic quality system be certified or verified once annually by a government-approved auditor to be recognized and accepted by all government agencies. As it now stands, the military works on a second-party auditing system, conducting its own audits of suppliers and defense contractors. There are two major differences between the DOD and the ISO 9000 certification systems:

1. In the commercial sector, companies earn ISO 9000 certification when they prove conformance to the ISO 9000 standard through ISO 9000 registrars. Registrars are accredited entities that companies hire to perform certification. In the military system, at this time there is no third-party auditing because DOD has not approved third-party auditing. DOD does not require certification; it requires compliance with an ISO 9000 quality system or commensurate quality system.

2. Manufacturers and service companies pay for ISO 9000 certification and pass the cost on to customers. In the military system, the DOD bears most of the cost associated with the QML (qualified manufacturers list) process, a testing system for electronics products. QML is discussed in more depth later in this chapter.

There has been tremendous internal DOD debate over whether to train DOD auditors to conduct ISO 9000 registration. European Union officials voiced concern that this system—which would effectively mix second- and third-party auditing—might ruin the third-party registration system that ISO 9000 advocates. But with the Big Three automakers training registrars under their QS-9000 system and major electronics giants forcibly angling to create their own "mixed" auditing system, the EU seems at present to be coming around to the DOD approach.

In the meantime, there are efforts to meld the DOD and the ISO 9000 third-party registration systems. In July 1993, the Defense Electronic Supply Center in Dayton, Ohio, started a prototype certification program for implementation in 1994. The program is still in the test phase.

Interestingly, the third-party registration aspect of the ISO 9000 international quality assurance process actually had its roots in DOD procedures. The British adopted many of the DOD's unique procedures when they developed their national BS 5750 Quality Management Systems, which would ultimately serve as the model for ISO 9000 registration.

How Individual Services Are Handling Q 9000

As noted, individual branches of the military have the authority to handle quality issues as they see fit. While the air force and navy air force (NAVAIR) are adopting ISO 9000, other services have examined, but not mandated, other approaches.

Navy. In general, the navy is following DOD guidelines regarding ISO 9000. It is important for contractors/suppliers to know that there was an initiative called N 9001 that the navy issued to its suppliers and contractors in 1995. N 9001 was never adopted and is not being used in any existing or new navy contracts. There was discussion among members of the Special Project Office to rename N 9001 as D 9001, but this effort never got off the ground.

Army. The army has stated nothing in writing about use of ISO 9000/ Q 9000. Each command has the prerogative to do what it deems appropriate. With so much direct connection to the U.S. automobile industry, there's talk that some commands will be urging their contractors and suppliers to implement the Big Three's QS-9000.

Note: See "Custom Requirements a Supplier Might Face in Dealing With Individual Government Agencies" later in this chapter for advice on how your company can cope with Q 9000 requirements during this transitional period.

Mil Handbook 9000

With so many changes taking place at once, the DOD attempted to create some order by issuing *Mil Handbook 9000* to provide guidance for the application of the ISO 9000 standard. This was supposed to be a definitive "how-to" guide from the military standpoint. Although there is criticism of the handbook, military experts say is it serving as a source of guidance for quality system requirements and is being updated.

Conformity Assessment

As the world's largest buyer (second-party) of products and services, the DOD is highly conscious of the need to assure the public that standards and quality levels are being met. In this effort, the DOD employs just about every known conformity assessment procedure, including those described in international documentation, in its procurement functions. The DOD certification process is carried out under the quality assurance functions of DOD's Defense Logistics Agency (DLA).

The DLA maintains a workforce of eight thousand quality assurance personnel covering seventeen thousand facilities that have contracts requiring DLA certification. In addition, DLA certification staff conduct audits for their own department, NASA, other federal agencies, and foreign governments.

Given this sort of enormous effort, DLA staff have developed their own conformity assessment methods, many of which eliminate redundant sampling, testing, and inspection. DLA methodology, in turn, has found its way into international quality assurance standards and guidelines such as ISO 9000.

Qualified Product List and Qualified Manufacturers List

For many years the military subsidized the testing of semiconductors and integrated circuits that fell under its Qualified Product List (QPL). Suppliers, in turn, were bound to a self-declaration of conformity once their product passed an initial testing process.

With the vast growth of the electronics industry, the QPL system was found lacking. There was no standardization of testing. Moreover, with budget constraints mounting, the military could not afford to subsidize testing of supplier products. In response to these concerns, the semiconductor industry—with military support—developed a new testing system called the Qualified Manufacturers List (QML).

While responding to military budget constraints, QML's aim is to allow for introduction of new technologies and designs; to offer flexible response to problems, better utilization of customer feedback, stronger management support, and common processing of defense contracts; and to support acquisition reform. Qualification is based on the following five criteria:

1. Validation of the manufacturer's design
2. Wafer fabrication
3. Assembly
4. Test
5. Quality control processes

Manufacturers that earn QML status are allowed to use the standard military fabrication, assembly, and test methods.

Note: Defense suppliers and manufacturers that are designated on the QML after passing quality assurance procedures have not required further certification.

Custom Requirements a Supplier Might Face in Dealing With Individual Government Agencies

Longtime defense suppliers and contractors may find their main challenge to be implementing ISO 9000. Chapter 8 outlines ISO 9000 basics and Chapter 9 tackles the cost-effective route to certification, if this is something a supplier or contractor chooses to pursue. Remember, the DOD requires compliance to an ISO 9000 type of quality system, not certification.

For those defense suppliers and contractors already working on ISO 9000 certification, a main concern is keeping track of evolving requirements surrounding mil specs and quality systems. This can be accomplished by doing the following:

- Keeping tabs on DOD regulations
- Monitoring individual services and their recommendations
- Knowing the "customer," in this case one of hundreds of government agencies
- Knowing the special requirements of that customer

Specialized Criteria

Individual services may ask suppliers and contractors to meet criteria above and beyond ISO 9000. Some criteria have been required for a long time and are not directly related to changes in military specs. For example, an agency like the air force may ask for first-time test deals, meaning forcing a supplier or contractor to keep track of every product test and the pass rate.

Remember that the government is not an ISO 9000 registrar. Government inspectors still exist and will want access to a vendor's facility and to inspect the products that are being built for the government.

Note: NIST is putting together a home page on the World Wide Web that will offer help for companies working to meet DOD quality and other standards-related requirements.

Resources

Joint Government/Industry Quality Liaison Panel, "World Class Quality," 3rd draft, November 1994.
Standards and Trade in the 1990's, U.S. government publication.

Appendix

Military Standards Proposed for Cancellation

As a result of reviews, the cognizant preparing activities (PAs) have recommended the following list of "heartburn" military standards be cancelled:

Document Number	Truncated Title
MIL-STD-12D	Abbreviations for Use on Drawings, Specifications Standards & in Technical Documents
MIL-STD-14A	Architectural Symbols
MIL-STD-15/2 NOT 1	Electrical Wiring Equipment Symbols for Ships' Plans Part 2
MIL-STD-17A(1)	Mechanical Symbols
MIL-STD-17/1B(1)	Mechanical Symbols
MIL-STD-29A	Spring, Mechanical, Drawing Requirements
MIL-STD-102B	Anti-Friction Bearing Identification Code
MIL-STD-168B NOT 1	Visual Inspection Guide for All-Rubber Gloves Except Surgical
MIL-STD-172C NOT 1	Color Code for Containers of Liquid Propellants
MIL-STD-178A NOT 1	Definition Applicable to Speed-Governing of Electric Generator Set
MIL-STD-187/310	Standards for Long Haul Communications Switching Planning Standards for the Defense Communication
MIL-STD-187/320	Standards for Long Haul Communications Transmission Planning Standards for the Defense Communication

Document Number	*Truncated Title*
MIL-STD-188/100(3)	Common Long Haul and Tactical Communication System Technical Standards
MIL-STD-188/194	Integrated Services Digital Network Profile
MIL-STD-188/318	System & Subsystem Design & Engineering & Equipment Technical Standards for Closed Circuit TE
MIL-STD-188/331	Interoperability and Performance Standard for Video Teleconferencing
MIL-STD-188/340(1)	Equipment Technical Design Standards for Voice Orderwire Multiplex
MIL-STD-188/342	Standards for Long Haul Communications Equipment Technical Design Stands for Voice Frequency
MIL-STD-190C	Identifications Marking of Rubber Products
MIL-STD-195(1) NOT 2	Marking of Connections for Electric Assemblies
MIL-STD-200K(1)	Electron Tube, Selection of
MIL-STD-205 NOT 1	Frequencies for Electric Power
MIL-STD-242/1H	Electronic Equipment Parts, Selected Standards Synchros, Blowers, and Acoustical (Part 1)
MIL-STD-242/2H NOT 1	Electronic Equipment Parts, Selected Standards Crystals, Delay Lines, Coils, and Transformers
MIL-STD-242/3H NOT 2	Electronic Equipment Parts, Selected Standards Resistors (Part 3)
MIL-STD-242/4G NOT 1	Electronic Equipment Parts, Selected Standards for Capacitors (Part 4)
MIL-STD-242/7G NOT 1	Electronic Equipment Parts, Selected Standards-Switches
MIL-STD-242/9J	Electronic Equipment Parts, Selected Standards Circuit Breakers, Fuses, Lamps, & Meters (Part 9)
MIL-STD-255B	Electric Voltages Alternating and Direct Current
MIL-STD-277(1)	Static Acceptance Test for Light Output of Flash Munitions
MIL-STD-284A	Visual Inspection Guide for Rubber Footwear
MIL-STD-295	Bill of Material, Preparation of

Document Number	*Truncated Title*
MIL-STD-372 NOT 1	Welding, Gas Metal-Arc and Gas Tung-sten-Arc, Aluminum Alloys, Readily Weldable for Structures
DOD-STD-396	Weapon Caliber and Ammunition, Metric System for Identification of
MIL-STD-417A NOT 3	Classification System and Tests for Solid Elastomeric Materials
MIL-STD-606A	Helmet Welders'; Shield, Welding, Hand Held and Lenses, Helmet
MIL-STD-627A	Sprocket Wheels for Power Transmission and Conveying Chains
MIL-STD-645B NOT 1	Dip Brazing of Aluminum Alloys
MIL-STD-670B NOT 1	Classification System and Tests for Cellular Elastomeric Materials
MIL-STD-708	Formula for Binder Solution
MIL-STD-717 NOT 1	Formula for Binder Solution II
MIL-STD-725A(1) NOT 4	Method of Marking Scales for Sights and Fire Control Instruments
MIL-STD-731A(1)	Quality of Wood Members for Containers and Pallets
MIL-STD-739A(1)	Trailer and Semitrailers, Commercial
MIL-STD-771C NOT 1	Damage Control Books for Auxiliary and Miscellaneous Ships, Preparation for
MIL-STD-772C(1)	Damage Control Books for Warships and Miscellaneous Large Ships, Preparation of
MIL-STD-782D NOT 1	Reconnaissance/Mapping Data Marking
MIL-STD-783D	Legends for Use in Aircrew Stations and on Airborne Equipment
MIL-STD-787	Joint Optical Range Instrumentation Type Designation System
MIL-STD-850B NOT 1	Aircrew Station Vision Requirements for Military Aircraft
MIL-STD-858	Testing Standard for Personnel Parachutes
MIL-STD-872(1)	Test Requirements and Procedures for Aircraft Emergency Ground and Ditching Escape Provisions
MIL-STD-877(1)	Antenna Subsystem, Airborne, Criteria for Design and Location of
MIL-STD-908	Provisions for Evaluating the Quality of Spare Parts for Mechanical & Textile End Items

Document Number	*Truncated Title*
MIL-STD-912	Physical Ear Noise Attenuation Testing
MIL-STD-964(1)	Manufacture and Packaging of Drugs, Pharmaceuticals and Biological Products
MIL-STD-1005 NOT 1	Renovation, Cleaning and Glazing of Bake Pans
MIL-STD-1163	Lithographic Chemicals
MIL-STD-1169B NOT 1	Packaging, Packing and Marking for Shipment of Inert Ammunition Components
MIL-STD-1201C	Ethyl Alcohol (Ethanol), Technical and Denatured Grades
MIL-STD-1210B	Fog and Ice Preventive Compounds
MIL-STD-1212A	Industrial Safety Belts, Straps, and Related Equipment
MIL-STD-1215B	Water Purification Compounds
MIL-STD-1216A	Preventive Compounds (Corrosion) and Inhibitors
MIL-STD-1221B	Protective Compounds (For Personnel)
MIL-STD-1226A NOT 1	Engine, Gas, Air Cooled, Ind Type, 1½ BHP MILSTD, Model 1A08 Install Procedures
MIL-STD-1227B(1) NOT 2	Engine, Gasoline, Air Cooled, 3 BHP, 4-Cycle, Military Design, Model 2A016, Installation Procedures
MIL-STD-1252	Inertia Friction Welding Process, Procedure and Performance Qualification
MIL-STD-1256A(1)	Rubber Coated Parts for Machine Gun, 7.62MM, M60
MIL-STD-1258 NOT 1	Chromium Plated 5.56MM, 7.62MM, and Caliber .30 Small Arms Barrel Bores
MIL-STD-1261C(1)	Arc Welding Procedures for Construction Steels
MIL-STD-1267 NOT 1	Dimensioning of Barrel Chambers of Small Arms Weapons
MIL-STD-1270A(1)	Patching of Wood Stocks for the 7.62MM, M14 and M14E2 Rifles
MIL-STD-1272A	Door Hardware, Vehicular
MIL-STD-1278 NOT 2	Filters, Light, Photographic
MIL-STD-1281	Internal Transient Control for Solid State Power Supplies
MIL-STD-1285B	Marking of Electrical and Electronic Parts
MIL-STD-1306A	Fluerics Terminology and Symbols

Document Number	*Truncated Title*
MIL-STD-1343	Glossary of Terms for Electronic and Weapons Control Interface Functions (Naval Ship Combat Systems)
MIL-STD-1348	Knob, Control Selection of
MIL-STD-1353B(4) NOT 4	Electrical Connectors, Plug-In Sockets and Associated Hardware, Selection and Use of
MIL-STD-1361A	Fluidics Test Methods and Instrumentation
DOD-STD-1371B	Inspection Procedure for Use of Anaerobic Thread Locking Compounds with Studs
MIL-STD-1372A(1)	Process for Smoldering Accident Dosimeter to Film Badge Holder for Radiac Detecting Element
MIL-STD-1373(4)	Screw-Thread, Modified, 60 Deg. Stub, Double
MIL-STD-1399/102A	Interface Standard for Shipboard Systems Section 102 Low Pressure Dry Air Service for Surface
MIL-STD-1399/ 105 NOT 1	Interface Standard for Shipboard Systems Section 105 Sea Water Service for Surface Ships
MIL-STD-1399/1068	Interface Standard for Shipboard Systems Section 106 Compressed Air Service for Surface Ships
DOD-STD-1399/204A	Interface Standard for Shipboard Systems Section 204A Ambient Air Conditions in Surface Ship
DOD-STD-1399/ 533(1) NOT 1	Interface Standard for Shipboard Systems Section 533 Potable Water Service (Metric)
MIL-STD-1399/ 534(1) NOT 2	Interface Standard for Shipboard Systems Section 534 Auxiliary Steam Service, Surface Ships
MIL-STD-1401(1)	Engine, Gasoline, Air Cooled, 20 BHP, 4 Cycle, Military Design, Model 4A084 Installation Procedures
MIL-STD-1402(1) NOT 2	Engine, Gasoline, Air Cooled, 20 BHP, 4 Cycle, Military Design, Model 4A084 Installation Procedures
MIL-STD-1410A	Methods for Selection of Industrial Engines for End Item Application
MIL-STD-1422A	Mask, Chemical Biological

Document Number	*Truncated Title*
MIL-STD-1424	Hydrogen Ion Meters
MIL-STD-1427A	Activated Desiccants (Metric)
MIL-STD-1433B	Climber Sets, Tree and Pole
MIL-STD-1434A	Goggles (Metric)
MIL-STD-1439 NOT 1	Thickened Hydrocarbon Flame Fuels, Consistency of, Mobilometer Test
MIL-STD-1440A	Test Facility for Determining Percent Agent Recovery
MIL-STD-1442A	Inorganic Peroxides, Technical Grade
MIL-STD-1453	Ballistic Standards and Test Method for Evaluating and Selecting 5.56MM Ammunition for M16/M1
MIL-STD-1478	Task Performance Analysis
MIL-STD-1493	Contractual Service Requirements for Automatic Dishwashing Machine Accessory Equipment and Supplies
MIL-STD-1529(1)	Vendor Substantiation for Aerospace Propulsion System Items
MIL-STD-1549A	Common Termination System for Electrical and Electronic Parts
MIL-STD-1555 NOT 1	Aircrew Station Displays and Associated Equipment, Definitions of
MIL-STD-1592 NOT 1	Mockups, Air Vehicle Engines, Construction & Inspection of
MIL-STD-1598	Studs Preferred for Design, Listing of
MIL-STD-1606A	Technical Information Requirements for Air Launched Guided Missile Proposals
MIL-STD-1621A NOT 1	Acoustical and Vibrational Standard Reference Quantities
MIL-STD-16348 NOT 3	Module Descriptions for the Standard Electronic Modules Program
MIL-STD-1646B	Servicing Tools for Electric Contracts and Connections, Selection and Use of
MIL-STD-1648A NOT 1	Criteria & Test Procedure for Ordnance Exposed to an Aircraft Fuel Fire
MIL-STD-1653A NOT 1	Power Cable Assemblies
MIL-STD-1659	Sealing Condition of Ammunition Primer Tube Flash Holes
MIL-STD-1671 NOT 1	Schematic Wiring Diagram (External DC Power Connector, Aircraft)
MIL-STD-1681	Fabrication, Welding, and Inspection of HY-130 Submarine Hull

Document Number	*Truncated Title*
MIL-STD-1695	Environments, Working, Minimum Standards for
MIL-STD-1761 NOT 1	Fastener Recess Test, Method for Damage Tolerance Evaluation
MIL-STD-1774 NOT 1	Process for Cleaning Hydrazine Systems and Components
MIL-STD-1775 NOT 1	Propellant, Hydrazine-Uns-Dimethyl-hydrazine 50/50 Blend
MIL-STD-1777	Internet Protocol
MIL-STD-1778 NOT 1	Transmission Control Protocol
MIL-STD-1780	File Transfer Protocol
MIL-STD-1781	Simple Mail Transfer Protocol
MIL-STD-1782	Telnet Protocol
MIL-STD-1788A	Avionics Interface Design Standard
MIL-STD-1801	User/Computer Interface (Controlled Distribution)
MIL-STD-1816	Preservation, Packaging, and Packing of Rubber and Nylon Fuel, Oil, and Water-Alcohol Cells
MIL-STD-1819	Performance Evaluation for Plasma Spray Masking Tape
MIL-STD-1875	Ultrasonic Inspection, Requirements for
MIL-STD-1907(1)	Inspection, Liquid Penetrant and Magnetic Particle, Soundness, Requirements for Materials, Parts, and Weldments
MIL-STD-1946A(2)	Welding of Aluminum Alloy Armor
DOD-STD-2003(1) NOT	Electric Plant Installation Methods for Surface Ship and Submarine (Controlled Dist.)
MIL-STD-2065	Test Methods for Still Photographic Equipment (Less Optics)
MIL-STD-2072	Survivability, Aircraft, Establishment and Conduct of Programs for
MIL-STD-2076 NOT 1	Unit Under Test Compatibility With Automatic Test Equipment General Requirements for
MIL-STD-2078	Requirement for Preparation of Support Equipment Depot Level Rework Standards
MIL-STD-2081 NOT 1	Assembly Procedures, Gimbal
MIL-STD-2082A(1) NOT 1	Assembly Procedures, Gyro

Document Number	*Truncated Title*
MIL-STD-2094 NOT 1	Missile Guidance Set, Aim/Rim-7M, First Article Tests
MIL-STD-2095 NOT 1	Missile Guidance Set, Aim/Rim-7M, Production Verification Test
MIL-STD-2114	Electro Acoustical, Mechanical and Environmental Test Methods for Audio or Acoustical Component Parts
MIL-STD-2120 NOT 1	Connectors, Electromagnetic Interference (EMI) Filter Contact
MIL-STD-2126A	Reduced Smoke Rocket Motor Processing & Test Procedures (Sidewinder)
DOD-STD-2144 NOT 1	Induction Clutches, Low Magnetic Field Design of (Metric)
MIL-STD-2149A(1)	Standard Procedures for Explosion Testing Ferrous and Non-Ferrous Metallic Materials and Weldments
MIL-STD-2172 NOT 1	Aeronautical Equipment Service Record
MIL-STD-2189-302-1	Design Methods for Naval ShipBoard Systems Section 302-1 AC Motor and Controller Application
MIL-STD-2189-305-1	Design Methods for Naval ShipBoard Systems Section 305-1 Designation and Marking of Electric System
MIL-STD-2189-310-1	Design Methods for Naval ShipBoard Systems Section 310–1 Electric System Load and Power Analysis for Surface Ships
MIL-STD-2189-314-4	Design Methods for Naval ShipBoard Systems Section 314-4 400 Hertz Power System Test Procedures
MIL-STD-2196	Glossary, Fiber Optics
MIL-STD-2200	Requirements for Employing Standard Enclosure Systems

Part II
Europe

6

The European Standards System

Questions the Reader Will Find Addressed in This Chapter

1. What is the European Union and who are its members?
2. How does the European Union operate?
3. How does the European Union legislate standards?
4. What are the legislative tools of the European Union?
5. How is legislation adopted?
6. What is the European standards system?
7. What is the European Commission's impact on standards?
8. How do the national standards systems function in Europe?
9. Who are the European standards players?
10. How does the consensus approach affect European standards?
11. What is ISO and how does it relate to European standards?
12. What is taking place with European certification programs?
13. How can foreign companies interact with European standards organizations?
14. What is the underground route to the European Union system?
15. What is taking place with standards harmonization?
16. What are European quality-related standards bodies?
17. Who are the European ISO 9000 players?
18. Who truly determines accreditation in Europe?
19. What are the quality assurance certification issues?
20. What should U.S. companies do about rapidly changing European standards?

Introduction

As Europe forms a unified market system, standards have come to the fore as a principal unification tool. To facilitate trade, the European Union (EU) is creating harmonized, European-wide standards in key product sectors to replace the many thousands of differing national standards.

From quality assurance to the environment and product standardization, Europeans are setting the tone on many fronts, as well as setting new standards and testing criteria for entry into the European market. In 1996, the *Product Certification European Directory* listed approximately three hundred certification systems and seven hundred certification bodies operating in one or more of the nineteen countries of the European Community/ European Free Trade Association (EC/EFTA). EFTA includes Iceland, Liechtenstein, Switzerland, and Norway.

Because Europe is the United States' largest trading partner, its standards activities have a direct bearing on American trade with that region. European Community directives, the harmonization of standards, and the strengthening of European regional standards bodies and other trade policy considerations all affect U.S. exporters and their market access. European Commission (EC) testing and certification programs also directly affect U.S. business.

Commerce Department officials are discovering that U.S. exporters are concerned with having access to current information on European product standards, testing, and certification requirements. These are important financial issues for companies. Consequently, the government is allocating a significant portion of business counseling to passing on the latest information on CE Mark requirements—including the New Approach directives and related standards, and product certification under the "old approach"—as well as other EU legislation and regulation.

Example

In Europe, the International Organization for Standardization (ISO) 9000 series is tacitly mandated for electronic switch manufacturers and producers of pacemakers. CE Marking is an entry requirement for the European market for a variety of product groups. Meeting the requirements of both certification programs can be costly for many companies.

For economic reasons alone, it will serve companies to learn as much as possible about the European standards system and the new EU government that backs standards. Only with a working knowledge of the system and the players can companies register their concerns about European standards developments through the government and private-sector liaisons available to them within the National Institute of Standards and Technology (NIST) and the American National Standards Institute (ANSI). As noted in Chapter 3, ANSI and other bodies are working on increasing U.S. access to and participation in European standards activities.

Formation of the European Union

Standards harmonization is a main element of the internal market system now forming under the European Union. What has come to be known as the EU came into being in 1993, but it has been developing in one form or another since the end of World War II, when European countries awoke to the need to create a common market. In 1951, Belgium, France, Germany, Italy, Luxembourg, and the Netherlands signed the Treaty of Paris, creating the European Coal and Steel Community (ECSC). Other efforts to unite European economic interests followed. The European Economic Community (EEC) and the European Atomic Energy Community (EAEC) came into being in 1957 with the signing of the Treaty of Rome. The European Free Trade Association was also an early model for the EU. EFTA was formed in 1960 to promote trade between the United Kingdom, Norway, Sweden, Denmark, Austria, Portugal, and Switzerland. Finland became an associate member of EFTA in 1961, and Iceland became a full member in 1970. Today only Iceland, Switzerland, and Norway remain of the original EFTA members. Liechtenstein is currently a member of EFTA.

The European Community was formed in 1967 with the merger of several European economic communities. Over the years, membership swelled to the current fifteen countries: Austria, Belgium, Denmark, Finland, France, Germany, Greece, Ireland, Italy, Luxembourg, the Netherlands, Portugal, Spain, Sweden, and the United Kingdom. Bulgaria, the Czech Republic, Hungary, Poland, Romania, Slovakia, and Israel are considered eastern associates of the EC. Enlargement of the EC is projected for 1997, when Cyprus and Malta are also expected to join.

Maastricht Agreement

In December 1991, the then European Community leaders drew up a series of amendments and additions to the 1957 Treaty of Rome, which had established the original European Economic Community (EEC). These amendments related to political and monetary union and were presented and voted on at an intergovernmental conference at Maastricht, in the Netherlands. Under the Maastricht Treaty, existing responsibilities of the European Community were expanded, and policy areas not previously covered by its treaties—particularly economic and monetary union and defense—were placed under the new European economic, legislative bloc. All participating national governments ratified the treaty and protocols in 1993.

On November 8, 1993, the twelve foreign ministers making up the Council of Ministers of the European Community decided that the European Community should be reconstituted as the Council of the European

Union. The Commission of the European Communities was renamed the European Commission.

Note: The European Community was renamed the European Union in 1993. When the initials EC appear today—and in this book—they refer to the European Commission, which is one of the main European governing bodies (see next section). Often, Europeans refer to the European Union as "the Community," which is a throwback to the days when the region was called the European Community. Some European bureaucrats jokingly refer to the EC as "European Confusion."

New European Government

The European standards system is increasingly a legislative function of the evolving European Union (EU). To comprehend the standards system it is necessary to know something about how this relatively new legislative system operates. Following is a discussion of the five major institutions responsible for implementing and managing EU policy.

1. *European Commission.* The European Commission (EC) is Europe's premier legislative body, whose main task is economic integration of member states. The EC is responsible for implementation of "Community" treaties. It initiates all EC legislation, is the executive arm of the Community, and has executive and legislative powers in certain areas.

Based in Brussels with an administrative staff of fourteen thousand, the commission is made up of twenty members, with the larger member states—France, Germany, Italy, Spain, and the United Kingdom—nominating two members and the other ten member states nominating one each. The EC can conduct investigations and inquiries and enact its own legislation in certain areas. These include competition law, common politics, coal and steel industry treaties, and treaties relating to nuclear power and radiation.

All member states contribute to advisory, management, and supervisory committees that act as checks and balances against commission power. There are approximately twenty-three directorate-generals, or agencies, which function in the same fashion as U.S. government agencies, each having its own area of concentration. Each of the twenty commissioners has a support team of personal policy advisers known as a cabinet. The cabinet chief acts as the commissioner's deputy and plays a crucial role as liaison between the directorate-generals that fall under the commissioner's purview, as well as between the commissioner and other interest groups. Individual commissioners are assigned an area of concentration, such as agriculture, the environment, and so on.

2. *Council of Ministers.* Made up of representatives from the 15 member states—usually government ministers—the Council of Ministers creates the legislation that emanates from EC proposals. The council presidency is rotated among member states every six months.

3. *European Council.* Since 1974, the European Council has served as a meeting ground for heads of European governments and their foreign ministers and senior commission officials. These European summit meetings usually took place biannually in whatever country was then holding the council presidency.

Under the EU system, the European Council provides strategic guidelines in key areas such as economic and monetary union, institutional reform, and involvement of new members. In recent years, it has also served as an unofficial appeals court where contentious issues can be aired and resolved.

4. *European Parliament.* The European Parliament is a representative assembly of 626 directly elected members (MEPs), who supervise the operation and management of Community policies that are initiated through the European Commission and the European Council. The parliament participates in the legislative process by giving its opinion on commission proposals and proposing amendments.

One of the parliament's main roles is approving members of the European Commission and approving its president. Both bodies preside over a wide array of issues, ranging from monetary policy to defense. The parliament can overrule the European Council only when the council is divided. However, it has the right to reject European Council legislation.

5. *European Court of Justice.* The European Court of Justice (ECJ) is the final arbiter in disputes over interpretation of the treaties binding the European Union, or when there is failure to implement EU law. It has the power to abolish any measures member states or EU institutions introduce that are incompatible with the treaties.

The Legislative Process

Standards and standards policy can be a matter of legislation in the EU. Because the legislative option exists, it is helpful to have some understanding of the European legislative system. In general, the EU is imitating the U.S. system with its layers of local, state, and federal governments. In practice, however, the way that legislation is drafted and then adopted is quite different.

Example

The new European quality policy—now in draft form—may either be implemented through the European legislative process or may be adopted voluntarily by standards groups, standards bodies, and industry. At this writing, members of Directorate-General III plan to bring their policy proposal before the EC for a vote in November 1996. If, as expected, it passes, the quality proposal will become official EC policy with tremendous political force behind it.

Legislative Tools. The following are the EU's legislative tools:

- *Rules and regulations* are offered from member states as binding guidelines for conducting programs. Those accepted are binding to all member states.
- *Directives* are a form of legislation that state results to be achieved. Member states must translate them into national legislation.
- *Decisions* are binding on the member states, companies, or individuals to whom they are addressed.
- *Recommendations, opinions, resolutions,* and *declarations* are nonbinding policy reviews that serve as declarations of intent.
- *Essential requirements* are the portions of legislation that outline regulations.

Example

The European Council of Ministers has adopted a number of directives to cover product health and safety under the CE Marking program. Each directive is quite explicit in its description of what manufacturers must do to comply with CE Marking regulations in a given product sector. (See Chapter 7 for more examples.)

How Legislation Is Adopted. The European Council of Ministers adopts legislation in two main ways through the workings of the European Commission and other bodies.

An Abbreviated Version of the Consultation Procedure

- The European Commission initiates legislation through the urging of the parliament or outside interest groups.
- Directorate-generals within the commission (our equivalent to government agencies and offices) are asked to draft a working document.
- The working document is sent to the twenty commissioners for review. (Commissioners' offices are called cabinets.)
- A simple majority vote by commissioners is required for a proposal to be adopted. Each commissioner has the right to veto the proposal.
- Once the draft proposal is formally adopted, it is published as a commission document and a working party is established. Working

parties consist of experts from the fifteen governments. If the proposal passes muster with the working party it is passed on to the Committee of Permanent Representatives (COREPER) for formal approval.

- In the interim, the proposal is then sent to the appropriate European Parliament committees for review.
- The parliament's opinion on the proposal, along with any amendments, are forwarded to the monthly European Commission plenary session through an appointed messenger called a *rapporteur*. The EC will vote on the proposal if all members are in accord.
- In the event of a dispute between the commission and the parliament, the parliament can refer the proposal back to committee. The committee has two months to report to the commission, or can choose to table amendments in an effort to reach a compromise.
- The EC has the final vote on a proposal before it becomes law. Whether the deciding vote is by a simple majority, qualified majority, or unanimity depends on the legal aspects of the proposal.

Figure 6-1 charts the normal path that legislation takes in the European Union before it is adopted as law in member states.

The cooperation procedure has been adopted to speed up the decision-making process. This procedure applies for issues relating to discrimination, free movement of workers, business rights within member states, completion of the internal market, health and safety, and regional development, as well as research and technological development.

An Abbreviated Version of the Cooperation Procedure

- After extensive consultation with all interested parties, the EC submits a proposal to the European Parliament and to the Economic and Social Committee for their opinions.
- The Council of Ministers adopts a common position on individual proposals and the decision is communicated to the European Parliament. Votes are by qualified majority.
- The parliament has three months to accept, reject, or propose amendments to the EC's common position.
- If the European Parliament accepts the common position or fails to act, the Council of Ministers can adopt the proposal according to their common position.
- If the European Parliament rejects the common position, the Council of Ministers can accept the proposal only by a unanimous vote.
- If the European Parliament adds amendments, the commission must either accept or reject them within one month. The proposal is

Figure 6-1. Consultation procedure for legislation up for adoption as law in EU member states.

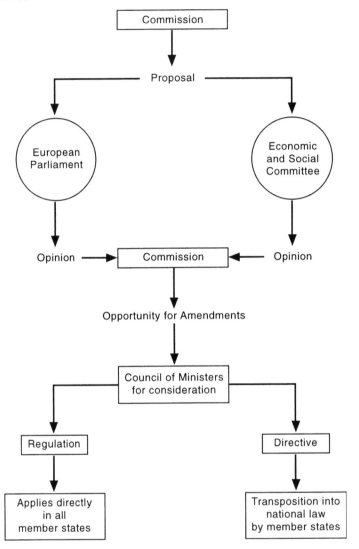

then forwarded with an explanatory statement to the Council of Ministers.

- If the commission accepts the European Parliament's amendments, a unanimous vote of the council is then required. If the council wishes to add further amendments, they too are subject to a unanimous vote.

The cooperation procedure is outlined in Figure 6-2.

Figure 6-2. Cooperation procedure.

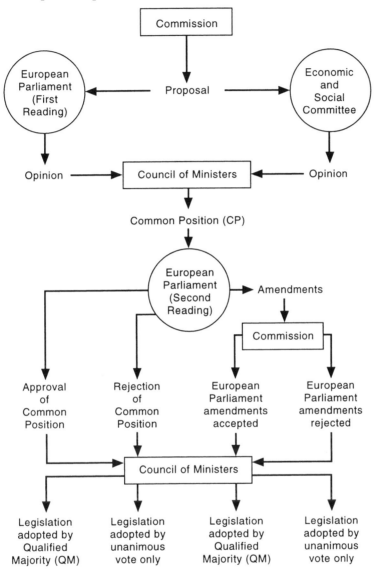

Case Study

The Toy Directive was one of the first health and safety directives passed under the CE Marking product conformance program (see Chapter 7). Concerns about harmonizing toy standards in Europe to prevent health or safety mishaps was a high priority of member states. The legislation took the following path:

1. The European Commission prepared draft legislation.
2. The legislation went to the European Parliament for a vote.
3. The parliament approved the directive and each member state then had a year to adopt it nationally.

Note: National courts or individual member states enforce EU law. The European Court of Justice plays final arbiter when there is a dispute over interpretation of EU law, or when a member state fails to comply with EU law.

European Standards System

To get a better grasp of today's European standards scene it helps to look at its antecedents. Starting in the 1970s there was growing recognition that standards could help accelerate unification of an internal European market. During this period, European standards players decided to unite the fifteen to twenty independent national standards bodies to work toward creation of European standards, as well as to provide strong input to international standards bodies.

In 1985, the Commission of the European Community (CEC) directly tackled the issue of removing technical barriers to trade within Europe through the "New Approach" (see Chapter 7). This policy stated that technical specifications (standards) should be the responsibility of major nonprofit standards bodies working in concert with the EC.

As discussed later in this chapter, the private-sector European Committee for Standardization (CEN), and an electrotechnical counterpart—the European Committee for Electrotechnical Standardization (CENELEC)—have assumed major roles in European standards development, as did the European Telecommunications Standards Institute (ETSI).

Much of this work on standardization is successfully underway. Technical barriers to trade on the standards front have been eliminated throughout the EU through harmonizing the bulk of technical requirements and preempting member state regulations where EU rules exist.

Example

Harmonized regulations and standards now exist for many regulated products, including gas appliances, electrical applications, and telecommunications attachment equipment.

European Commission Impact on Standards

The EC is uniting European standards activities in a number of ways. Here are the highlights:

- EU and its member states have joined forces to set standards priorities under the EU umbrella. This means that for the first time a single government body will set standardization priorities and require that all EU member states adopt standards that conform to the essential features outlined in EC directives.
- Agreement on standards is predicated on a majority vote of EC member states. When member states adopt an EC standard it has legal weight in all member states.
- Existing European national standardization bodies have been united into a coherent group and given a clear framework for mutual decision making.
- Work is underway to create a body of technical European standards to be applied to high-tech products and equipment sold throughout the member states.
- Any standard that earns the designation European Standard must comply with strict rules set out by EU standards bodies. The standard must meet conformity testing as well as measurement and inspection requirements.
- Private standards organizations are being tapped to generate European standards in coordination with national standardization organizations.

National Standards Systems

All European governments financially back their national standards bodies to some degree, and European standards bodies perform what would be considered public functions in the United States. This give and take is considered natural, and Europeans are not as concerned about government interference as Americans are.

In general, many European countries operate privately run standards bodies under government charter. Government backing can be partial or substantial depending on the location. There are also regional standards bodies that operate privately but may enjoy European Union support and financial backing. The EU often contracts with regional bodies to develop standards that provide technical backup and information for EU directives, or laws.

Most major European countries have centralized standards structures, with the electrotechnical sector operating separate standards entities. The standards development process is fairly uniform throughout the region and is similar to the international system that will be outlined in Chapter 8. In general, technical committees made up of volunteer experts draft standards. Documents are circulated for public comment to ensure a consensus is reached. A system is adopted for the commercial publishing and distribution of the standards. Standards sales and memberships finance standards institutions.

As discussed later in this chapter, there is a movement toward Europeanization of standards under the auspices of the European Committee for Standardization (CEN), the European Committee for Electrotechnical Standardization (CENELEC), and the European Telecommunications Standards Institute (ETSI). However, national standards and standards bodies still exist.

Note: Debate continues over the supremacy of EU standards. Germany and France, for example, are known for insisting on compliance with their national product health and safety standards. This dual system is being actively challenged.

Variations in Structure of Standards

Standards structures are not entirely uniform in Europe and may vary in size, with Britain operating the largest standards institution. In fact, American multinationals report that the British standards system is run like a business rather than like a nonprofit or governmental entity, even though the government plays a large role in standards development. In some European countries, such as France, drafting of standards is primarily the task of trade associations.

Financial support and authority, or "public service," also varies somewhat by country. Traditionally, the Swiss government (which is a member of EFTA but not the EU) has not backed its standards bodies, whereas in Portugal the main standards institution is actually part of the Ministry of Industry. In Germany and Britain, for example, the government has traditionally contracted standards services that benefit the public, while in France, Italy, and Spain these services are offered because of government mandate.

European Standards Players

As noted, there are several major European nonprofit standards organizations the EU has charged with development of European-wide standards. Most prominent are the European Committee for Standardization (CEN), the European Committee for Electrotechnical Standardization (CENELEC), and the European Telecommunications Standards Institute (ETSI), which is an outgrowth of the European Conference of Postal and Telecommunications Administrations (CEPT).

The CEN, CENELEC, and ETSI central secretariats are the guardians of the authoritative versions of the European standards, and as such are responsible for keeping master texts for distribution to all relevant government and private-sector bodies as well as EFTA countries. CEN, CENELEC, and ETSI work cooperatively through a system called "the 5 mode approach," which allows for joint work ranging from acting as observer to creation of joint committees or working groups.

All three organizations are charged with ensuring that standards work stays in tune with the demands of the internal market and that a coherent body of European standards is created.

CEN, CENELEC, and ETSI not only draft standards for the EU, they also develop standards to serve their European national member organizations. In addition, the European Organization for Technical Approvals (EOTA) provides technical assessments of the fitness of construction products.

Appendix A of this chapter provides a thorough listing of CEN National Members and Affiliate Members and CENELEC Member National Committees.

The relationships among the European standards players are charted in Figure 6-3.

The European Committee for Standardization (CEN)

Based in Brussels, the European Committee for Standardization (CEN) has actually been operating as a standards body since the 1950s, covering products, quality systems (along with CENELEC), and laboratories, to name a few of its many functions. CEN promotes European regional standardization in the nonelectrotechnical field and is the world's largest regional standards group. It is composed of national standards bodies within European member states and EFTA, countries which include Iceland, Norway, Switzerland, and Liechtenstein.

Now that the European Community exists as an official entity based in Brussels, CEN is leading the ongoing effort to create European-wide product standards. Within the Community, CEN product standards are proposed by individual national ministries and become mandatory once adopted by the European Community at large (see Chapter 8).

Membership. The membership of CEN is made up of the national standards bodies of the EU member states and the EFTA countries. The member countries are Austria, Belgium, Denmark, Finland, France, Germany, Greece, Iceland, Ireland, Italy, Luxembourg, the Netherlands, Norway, Portugal, Spain, Sweden, Switzerland, and the United Kingdom.

CEN affiliate members are the national standards organizations of Bulgaria, Cyprus, Czech Republic, Estonia, Hungary, Lithuania, Poland, Romania, Slovenia, and Turkey. The associate members are the European

Figure 6-3. Relationship among the committees and agencies of the European standards players.

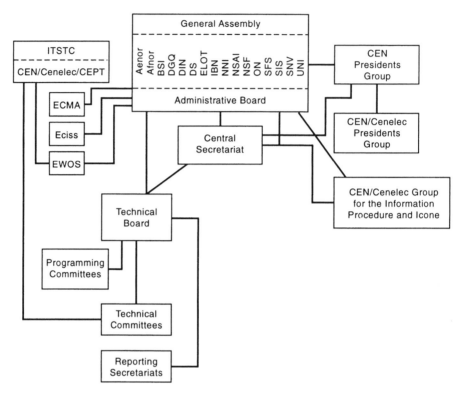

Notes:
Any official CEN body can set up *ad hoc* groups (whether for technical work or horizontal work, internal regulations, computerization, etc.)
There are continuous contacts with Cenelec on the one hand and the Commission of the European Communities and EFTA on the other through the Central Secretariat and practically all the CEN bodies.

Trade Union Technical Bureau for Health and Safety (TUTB) and the European Construction Industry Federation (FIEC). The eighteen full members of CEN are obliged to issue the adopted European standards as national standards without modification and withdraw any conflicting national standards. Affiliate members are encouraged to adopt "ENs" (EN is the prefix for a European Standard) as national standards but are not obliged to withdraw their conflicting national standards. However, affiliates are not allowed to modify an EN.

Standardization Activities. CEN develops voluntary European Standards (ENs) for mechanical engineering, building and civil engineering, health technology, information technology, biology and biotechnology, quality, certification and testing, environment, health and safety at the work place, gas and other energies, transport and packaging, consumer goods, sports, leisure, food, materials (iron and steel), and chemistry.

U.S. Access. CEN committees are not in general open to bodies outside of Europe. U.S. parties may formally request meetings with the chairs of CEN technical committees through ANSI. ISO and IEC may also nominate representatives to sit on CEN technical committees when there are working proceedings at both the European and ISO level.

Other Information. CEN normally issues its work as European Standards (ENs), and it also issues Harmonization Documents (HDs), European Prestandards (ENVs), and CEN reports. CEN European Standards are prepared in English, French, and German. They are also translated into the national languages of CEN members as they are issued as national standards by member organizations.

Technical Publications. CEN's technical publications may be purchased from its member organizations and from some ISO members outside of Europe, such as ANSI in the United States. Draft European standards (prENs) are normally available in English, French, and German at different stages of their preparation and are available from CEN member organizations as well as from a number of ISO members outside Europe, such as ANSI.

Note: Copies of CEN Central Secretariat publications—such as catalogs and the English language *CEN/CENELEC/ETSI Bulletin*, which lists adopted standards and drafts, main decisions of principal policy-making bodies, mandates received, and official citations—can be ordered from the Distribution and Sales Unit, CEN Central Secretariat, rue de Stassart 36, B-1050 Brussels, Belgium; Tel: (32 2) 519 6811.

European Committee for Electrotechnical Standardization (CENELEC)

CENELEC, also based in Brussels, promotes European standardization in the electrotechnical field, working often in concert with CEN. CENELEC has also experienced growth—especially in the electromagnetic compatibility area—since the advent of the EU.

Membership. The member countries of CENELEC are Austria, Belgium, Denmark, Finland, France, Germany, Greece, Iceland, Ireland, Italy, Luxembourg, the Netherlands, Norway, Portugal, Spain, Sweden, Switzerland, and the United Kingdom. CENELEC has affiliate members from Poland, Romania, Slovakia, and Slovenia.

U.S. Access. CENELEC committees are not open in general to bodies outside of Europe. U.S. parties may formally request meetings with the chairs of CENELEC technical committees through ANSI. ISO and IEC may also nominate representatives to sit on CENELEC committees when there are working proceedings at both the European and ISO levels.

Other Information. CENELEC standards may be purchased from CENELEC members within their countries. The official versions of the standards are available in English, French, and German, and in the national languages of the member states. CENELEC standards also are available through IEC members outside of Europe such as ANSI in the United States.

Note: Information on CENELEC's activities, as well as its catalogs and annual report, is available from the CENELEC Central Secretariat, rue de Stassart 35, B-1050 Brussels, Belgium; Tel: (32 2) 519 6871.

CEN and CENELEC: The Joint European Standards Institution

When operating jointly, CEN and CENELEC are called the Joint European Standards Institution. As part of its effort to establish standards for the EU market, the Joint European Standards Institution is translating ISO and IEC standards to the European level, as well as promoting European standards interests abroad.

European Conference of Postal and Telecommunications Administrations and European Telecommunications Standards Institute

The European Conference of Postal and Telecommunications Administrations (CEPT) publishes recommendations to harmonize and improve administration and operational services in these areas.

The European Telecommunications Standards Institute (ETSI) was an outgrowth of CEPT. ETSI's main function is to create European standards for a unified telecommunications system. It is headquartered in Valbonne, France.

Each organization is responsible for establishing a central secretariat or office structure to accomplish the following:

- See that standards mandates from the Commission of the European Community (CEC) and the European Free Trade Association (EFTA) are carried out.
- Prepare draft standards, through technical committees, according to international standards, or at the request of interested European organizations.
- Maintain a liaison with European bodies representing industry and other economic interests.
- Maintain its own financial base through membership fees, standards contracts and programs, and publication sales.

Standardization Activities. ETSI has 11 technical committees, approximately 60 technical subcommittees, and more than 140 working groups and *rapporteur* (liaison) groups. These committees deal with standards for public and private telecommunications systems and equipment, local area networks, and other electronics equipment for government and consumers. ETSI is also helping to work toward establishing telecommunications standards worldwide. To this end, ETSI has produced more than four thousand voluntary standards since it was established. Many of these have been adopted by the Commission of the European Union as the technical basis for directives and regulations.

Membership. ETSI is an open forum that brings together 373 full members, 14 associate members, and 71 observers from thirty European countries. ETSI members are from EU member national telecommunications administrations; manufacturers; public network operators, users, and counselors; and firms established within ETSI member states, albeit of foreign origin.

ETSI members are currently from Austria, Belgium, Bulgaria, Croatia, Cyprus, Czech Republic, Denmark, Finland, France, Germany, Greece, Hungary, Iceland, Ireland, Italy, Luxembourg, Malta, the Netherlands, Norway, Poland, Portugal, Romania, Russia, the Slovak Republic, Slovenia, Spain, Sweden, Switzerland, Turkey, and the United Kingdom. Australia and Israel are associate members.

U.S. Access. ETSI has granted the United States and U.S. companies observer status.

Miscellaneous Information. ETSI standards are available in English, and global dissemination of its standards has been one of ETSI's top priorities. At the European level, ETSI has reached agreement with the national standards organizations of CEN and CENELEC for the sale and distribution of documents.

Note: For information on ETSI standards, contact the ETSI Secretariat, 650 rue des Lucioles, F-06921 Sophia Antipolis CEDEX, France, Tel: (33) 92 94 42 00.

European Organisation for Testing and Certification

The European Organisation for Testing and Certification (EOTC) is an EU- and EFTA-backed organization that is working for cooperation and coordination between European suppliers, purchasers, and users of goods and services. Founded in 1990 through a memorandum of understanding between the EC, EFTA, and CEN/CENELEC, EOTC forms the focal point in Europe for all nonregulatory questions relating to conformity assessment.

Among its main purposes are

- Harmonizing conformity assessment practices to allow EC/EFTA countries one-step entry into the European market
- Coordinating general standards forums on matters of concern to the EC
- Conducting mutual recognition forums for countries concerned about EU conformity assessment issues

The EOTC includes a council, committees that focus on either industry-related or functional issues such as testing and certification, and agreement groups. Agreement groups, which are attached to committees called sectoral committees, conduct the actual work of establishing technical equivalences between various parties. EOTC agreement groups are open to non-Europeans. Sectoral committees, although not directly open to non-Europeans, are designed to establish dialogues between similar organizations in the United States and elsewhere. Some American companies are represented in EOTC agreement groups through their European subsidiaries, and some U.S. companies hold associate memberships in EOTC. Some eastern European countries also participate, as does Israel.

Members. EOTC has thirty-two members, including sixteen representatives of national conformity assessment communities and sixteen European organizations. Each national member has documented rules of operation that demonstrate it is open to representation from all parties concerned with conformity assessment at the national level, notably manufacturers, suppliers, users and consumers, conformity assessment practitioners, and public authorities. The national members are Austria, Belgium, Denmark, Finland, France, Germany, Greece, Ireland, Italy, the Netherlands, Norway, Portugal, Spain, Sweden, Switzerland, and the United Kingdom.

Role in Conformity Assessment. The role of EOTC as the focal point for conformity assessment in Europe is being achieved by actively encouraging the formation of sectoral committees through which it gives recognition to agreement groups composed of calibration or testing laboratories or certification bodies that operate in accordance with the internal regulations and relevant guidelines established by EOTC over the past four years.

Other Information. The EOTC disseminates information on European testing and certification activities. It also coordinates prestandardization work to complement or service European Commission programs. The EOTC secretariat recently took over the management of the Testing, Inspection, Certification, and Quality Assurance database (TICQA Project), launched by the Industrial Affairs division of the European Commission in 1991. The database is an inventory of more than ten thousand entities, including three thousand proven test labs. These facilities are both public and private, and work in the areas of testing, inspection, calibration, certification, and quality assurance in each member state of the European Union. EOTC staff are also helping the marketplace locate the services they want.

Joint Standards Bodies

Apart from the daily interaction of the CEN, CENELEC, and ETSI secretariats—which share common tools such as databases and telecommunications infrastructures—the three standards bodies have established a number of committees and groups to assist them organizationally, including the following:

- *Joint President Group.* The Joint President Group (JPG) acts as a forum where strategic issues affecting European standardization can be discussed and appropriate agreements can be prepared.
- *Joint Coordination Group.* The Joint Coordination Group (JCG) is responsible for monitoring and coordinating activities of CEN, CENELEC, and ETSI technical bodies where there is a common interest. It also acts as a court of last resort with the power to arbitrate disputes.
- *Information Technology Steering Committee.* The Information Technology Steering Committee (ITSTC) coordinates standards programs affecting the information technology field both within the EU and internationally.

Note: What distinguishes the evolving European standards system from the international system is the mandatory nature of European standards. Unlike international standards—which are adopted on a voluntary basis even if users later "mandate" their use—European standards become part of the EU canon. Once they are voted and accepted by all relevant legislative bodies, they become law throughout the EU and supersede national standards.

European Standards Procedures

The EU has charged CEN/CENELEC and ETSI with creating a European standards system. A main aim of standards development in Europe is to ensure that standards are not biased toward one industry, one party, or one government. Therefore, the consensus approach has been adopted and implemented as much as possible.

Here is how the European standards system operates:

- The technical board of any official CEN body can set up ad hoc technical committees to work on standards-related issues as long as continuous contact is maintained with the commission, EFTA, and other interested groups.

- In general, the secretariat of these technical committees is one and the same as the secretariat for the corresponding international standards committee of ISO or IEC.

- CEN/CENELEC may also set up programming committees to ensure consistent planning, programming, and coordination of European standardization activities within a particular sector. These committees are responsible for drawing up a European standardization program to make sure that European-wide concerns are taken into account.

- Except in rare cases, CEN/CENELEC have agreed not to publish national standards on areas where European standards work is in progress. The aim is to ensure that European standards are taken seriously, as well as to save on human and financial resources.

- Although CEN/CENELEC create European standards based on a qualified majority vote, there is a general understanding that every effort should be made to obtain unanimous support for standards.

- An appeals procedure exists to make sure that dissenting voices are heard and considered.

Note: A qualified majority in this system is not simply a two-thirds vote; it means that the largest number of countries must be in accord with the vote and that the opinion of the dissenting side is taken into account when the standard is drafted in final form.

Summary

The EC gives mandates to private-sector standards organizations to develop technical standards that are consistent with the essential safety and performance requirements of EC directives.

Products that meet the essential technical standards outlined by CEN, CENELEC, and ETSI are presumed to conform to the requirements of EC directives and allowed to circulate freely within the European Union.

For many products, a manufacturer can choose not to comply with the CEN/CENELEC/ETSI standards, but then must demonstrate that the product meets the essential safety and performance requirements of the directives.

Example

As part of the process of harmonizing health and safety requirements for toys under the CE Marking program there was a need to create standards for European companies to follow. CEN was drafted to develop detailed essential requirements for the toy directive. The essential requirements covered such concerns as the toxicity of paints and the size of allowable parts for children aged three and younger. Member states adopted this directive and enforce it within their borders.

European Standards Listings

The various categories of European standards are listed in Appendix B of this chapter.

CEN Standards

CEN, through its EN 29000 series, is the official governing body of the European version of ISO 9000 and as such regulates national accreditation bodies. CEN officials have accepted ISO 9000 documentation as a substitute for CEN documentation of quality systems for those national accreditation bodies under its jurisdiction.

Although CEN accepts ISO 9000 standards, it is also developing separate quality standards. For example, CEN has real laboratory standards and ISO doesn't. ISO only has guidelines for some categories.

Relationship With ISO

The relationship between European standards bodies and the International Organization for Standardization (ISO) is covered in Chapter 8. In general, European standards organizations aim at avoiding duplication with international standards efforts.

European Certification Systems

Like the United States, individual European countries have long maintained sophisticated testing laboratory and certification systems, some of which are based on private entities, a public-private mix, or government-run institutions.

Example

The British developed the third-party certification system (registration in the United States) that is the basis for ISO 9000 certification. In fact, the British Standards Institution (BSI) issued the first third-party certificate for ISO 9000.

At present, the Europeanization of certification systems is lagging behind standards creation. Given the amount of money and power that testing and certification represent—not to mention product and market protection—this is not surprising. Highly developed countries whose testing and certification programs are well regarded both internally and in the world market are not pleased with the prospect of adapting what they consider to be a potentially inferior, homogenized system.

Individual EU countries have been reluctant to abandon their own testing and certification schemes. Some of these well-known and well-respected schemes include the United Kingdom Kitemark, the Benor Mark in Belgium, the NF Mark in France, and the DIN Mark in Germany.

Although CEN has developed many European product standards for which companies earn a CE Mark, consumers in countries like France and Germany will not buy a product unless the manufacturer has earned the corresponding national mark. There is a belief that the national marks are more stringent than the CE Mark and offer more protection. Although this may be the case, it is also true that old habits and attitudes die hard.

Example

Rather than force the issue at this time, CEN/CENELEC promotes both European standards and national certification systems through national reciprocal recognition agreements. In one scenario a German certification body grants its certificate on the basis of tests conducted in the Netherlands, with the European standard being the guidepost.

How American Companies Can Interact With European Standards Organizations

It is true that non-European companies cannot directly affect legislative change in Europe. Avenues do exist, however, for companies to register their concerns. They can take some of the following routes to influence European standards activities and developments:

• *American National Standards Institute (ANSI).* As noted in Chapter 3, ANSI is actively working with European standards bodies to open channels for American input to standards development. American companies can join ANSI for direct input into the process or join an affiliate member.

• *Commerce Department Agencies.* As noted in Chapter 2, the National Institute of Standards and Technology (NIST), the United States Trade Representative (USTR), and the International Trade Administration (ITA) are all involved in increasing American presence in standards activities worldwide. All have public affairs offices.

NIST provides information about foreign standards and certification requirements and maintains a General Agreement on Tariffs and Trade (GATT) hot line with a recording that reports on the latest technical developments that could affect trade. The agency also helps exporters identify European standards and directives so they can correctly market products to the EU. An EU hot line provides information on directives and draft standards of the European Committee for Standardization (CEN) and the European Committee for Electrotechnical Standardization (CENELEC).

The following are NIST numbers to contact for standards information:

National Center for Standards
   and Certification Information   301-975-4040
GATT hot line   301-975-4041
EU hot line   301-921-4164
The Interagency Committee
   on Standards Policy (ICSP)   301-975-2396

See Chapter 2 for listings of other Commerce Department offices that handle standards issues.

• *National Center for Standards and Certification Information (NCSCI).* The NCSCI maintains extensive reference material on EU standards institutions. Address: Bldg. 411, Room A163, Gaithersburg, MD 20899; (301) 975-4040; fax: (301) 926-1559; e-mail: overman@micf.nist.gov.

Note: American companies based in Europe can contact the U.S. Mission to the EU at 40 Boulevard du Regent, 1000 Brussels, at this phone number: 32-2-508-2674. The mission operates like an embassy and is under the auspices of the state department.

• *European Union Offices.* The EU maintains two offices in Washington that provide access to American companies. They are:

1. The Office of European Union and Regional Affairs (OEURA), U.S. Department of Commerce, Fourteenth and Constitution Avenue, NW, Room 3036, Washington, DC 20230. Tel: (202) 482-5276; fax: (202) 482-2155.
2. The Office of European Union and Regional Affairs, part of the U.S. Department of Commerce's International Trade Administration,

works to ensure that U.S. exporters maintain access to Europe. Address: U.S. Department of Commerce, Fourteenth and Constitution Avenue, NW, Room 3036, Washington, DC 20230. Tel: (202) 482-5276; fax: (202) 482-2155.

The Underground Route

Creating contacts with European and international standards officials may be beyond reach for small and midsize companies, but there are some routes into the European system that simply require know-how. Here are two examples from U.S. government officials who regularly work within the EU system:

1. Do not approach the secretary-generals of major EU standards bodies to provide input or gain direction. Inquire with the information office of the appropriate agency for the technical directors of desired industry sectors. Technical directors are usually willing to communicate with foreign companies.

2. To obtain copies of CEN/CENELEC standards it is necessary to visit one of the agency's member state offices, where the standards are actually sold. National standards bodies in Europe derive income from standards sales and do not want to transfer these sales to private-sector agencies.

Trade Associations, Unions, and Consumer Organizations

European trade associations, unions, and consumer organizations have geared up to respond to the EU's call for European standardization. Of main concern to many of these private-sector bodies is maintaining communication with CEC institutions, being consulted on their standards work, and contributing directly to that work.

Three of the main private-sector organizations representing industry, workers, and consumers are:

1. Union of Industries of the European Community (UNICE), a major umbrella organization
2. European Trade Union Confederation (ETUC)
3. The European Bureau of Consumers' Unions (BEUC)

Associated Standardizing Bodies

Some of these organizations have earned the designation Associated Standardizing Bodies (ASB), a special status conferred on organizations that

CEN, CENELEC, and ETSI have tapped to draw up draft standards. Under these circumstances, all major standards bodies have access to the technical work in process, and drafts are then fed into the system for adoption as European standards. This process is described in full in Chapter 8.

Example

The European Association of Aerospace Equipment Manufacturers (AECMA) was the first to earn ASB designation through an agreement signed in 1986.

Other Forms of Cooperation

Not all organizations that want to participate in standards creation can meet ASB conditions. CEN, CENELEC, and ETSI have developed less formal relationships with bodies such as the European Committee for Iron and Steel Standardization (ECISS), CEPT, and the European Workshop for Open Spaces (EWOS).

There are provisions in EU law that allow cooperation between non-ASB bodies and CEN/CENELEC/ETSI through general agreement. In most cases—especially with unions and consumer groups—these organizations may participate in standards technical work only through representation in national delegations. Representation is only allowed for general contracts and planning purposes.

The EFTA Connection

The European Free Trade Association (EFTA) was set up after the signing of the Rome Treaty in March 1957, which formally established the European Economic Community (EEC). EFTA was created to form a free trade area between its member countries. Although one of EFTA's major purposes is free movement of products, its ties are looser than CEC's and it does not have the legislative mechanisms in place to mandate standards activities such as harmonization.

Even so, EFTA countries are very much committed to harmonization of standards and have long been pursuing harmonization through the European Community. Moreover, EFTA countries have been members of CEN/CENELEC from the time those institutions were created. Since 1983–84 the EFTA secretariat has been working with CEN/CENELEC to increase cooperation between all parties.

Example

Of notable importance is the united effort of all the EFTA countries regarding the standards aspect of the "New Approach" since its inception in 1985. The battle to eliminate technical barriers to trade and improve cooperation with the rest of the continent on standards issues was a prime factor in EFTA's reaching out.

Since the mid-1980s, EFTA countries have authorized their secretary-general to sign general cooperation guidelines with European standards institutions. In 1986, EFTA member states signed a framework contract with CEN/CENELEC that allows EFTA to funnel standardization mandates to this body in the same way that CEN/CENELEC accept mandates from the EC.

Quality-Related Standards Bodies

In 1987, ISO released the ISO 9000 standards series and gave birth to an international quality assurance movement. New and existing organizations developed programs to issue ISO 9000 certificates using third-party registration schemes.

It was necessary to accredit the certifiers (registrars in the United States) who would issue ISO 9000 certificates. To meet this demand, some European countries developed national accreditation bodies to handle accreditation of ISO 9000 certifiers or added departments to pre-existing conformity assessment institutions. In recent years, there has been a movement to loosely unify those bodies under the umbrella organization called the European Accreditation Council (EAC).

Foundations and institutes also came into being, or increased programming to meet educational demands on the ISO 9000 front. During this same period the European Quality Award came into being. Based on the Malcolm Baldrige Award in the United States, this national award also calls for an administrative structure as one of the criteria for winning. The European Foundation for Quality Management (EFQM) has operated the award program. Both EFQM and the European Organization for Quality (EOQ) could act as the organizational infrastructure for a new European Quality Program if such a program is implemented.

Continuing its long tradition of involvement in international standards, the EC required a forum to coordinate and facilitate standards activities between Europe and the rest of the world. As mentioned, the European Organization for Testing and Certification (EOTC) was founded by the EC in 1986 to provide a "European consensus" on certification and testing issues while providing world access to EU standards bodies. The EOTC Testing, Inspection, Certification, and Quality Assurance (TICQA) database is now in place and contains three thousand proven test labs. About seven thousand additional facilities are being researched for inclusion. EOTC staff are also helping the marketplace locate the services they want.

Some of the major standards institutions devoted to quality-related concerns are the following:

• The European Accreditation Council (EAC) serves as an umbrella organization for European national accreditation boards. EAC is moving in the direction of becoming a European-wide governing body for these boards. The following eight European countries have now signed multilateral agreements (MLAs) recognizing EAC as the sovereign European accreditation forum: Finland, Germany, the Netherlands, Italy, Norway, United Kingdom, Sweden, and Switzerland. France, Spain, and Austria are expected to sign on in 1996, which would mean that almost all major EU members will be united behind EAC by 1997. All European accreditation bodies are allowed observer status. At this time MLAs are also being discussed in the areas of product certification, quality system registration, and personnel certification. It's expected that EAC will merge with the European cooperation for Accreditation Laboratories (EAL) within the next two years.

Major European standards players believe that unification is necessary to provide the international market clout the Europeans are seeking. However, there is no indication that there will be one European accreditation office handling all certification and conformity assessment issues in the near future.

Powerhouse accreditation bodies in the U.K. and Netherlands give lip service to ceding over individual power bases, and market bases, for the larger clout a unified system would allow. Under such a system, national accreditation bodies will cease competing and will operate under the EAC leadership. It's unclear at this time how national entities will function under this system. However, insiders believe that the Dutch, British, and Swedes will dominate a European accreditation system, and maintain their influence in that fashion. One of these insiders, a major European standards official, believes it will be in the "far future, though, before there is one European accreditation office. However, most accreditation bodies have close links to individual governments and that will provide a barrier to creation of one European accreditation office." He does see individual national bodies carrying out "one European accreditation scheme."

• Other European organizations support and supplement EOTC conformity assessment activities. For example, EAC has a memorandum of understanding with EOTC to foster a European-wide system of assessment and accreditation and to promote harmonization of standards among its participating bodies. The European Organization for Quality (EOQ) and the European Committee for Quality System Assessment and Certification (EQS) have observer status in EOTC.

• European Organization for Quality (EOQ) offers a continentwide forum for quality management and quality science, as well as disseminating information worldwide.

• European Foundation for Quality Management (EFQM) administers the European Quality Award.

• The International Accreditation Forum (IAF) is a functioning worldwide body that will attempt to bring order and harmony to international ISO 9000 management systems (see Chapter 3).

European ISO 9000 Players

Because both ISO and the International Electrotechnical Commission (IEC) are both located in Geneva, Switzerland, it is sometimes difficult for outsiders to separate their international functions from their European base. Both organizations enjoy close relations with European quality assurance and standards bodies because of proximity and because Europeans, as noted, have long been boosters of international standards. However, it would be false to say ISO or IEC are European organizations. As explored in more detail in Chapter 8, it is clear that these are truly international bodies.

Accreditation in Europe

As things now stand in Europe, the national accreditation bodies still have much say over the operation of their management system standards programs within their own realms. They must conform to EN 45011 and EN 45012 guidelines—the Europeanized versions of guidelines outlined by the ISO's Committee on Conformity Assessment (CASCO). Already, however, some of these accreditation bodies are taking industry concerns into more account than they have in the past.

CEN has been investigating alternatives to the national accreditation bodies' acting as sole arbiters of ISO 9000 programs within their national boundaries. They have been investigating a more "vertical" or industry-oriented system whereby "interested parties" will define what should transpire within the ISO 9000 process. Interested parties include industry leaders, trade associations, consumer groups, ISO 9000 registrars, and others.

EU standards officials are also envisioning a larger role for EOQ and EFQM in European-wide standards and quality-related activities. Although it is too soon to say whether proposals under the new European quality program will be adopted, EU officials are already actively promoting the European Quality Award. (See Chapter 9, ISO 9000: A Program in Transition.)

Quality Assurance Certification Issues

In Europe, as in the rest of the world, companies hire third-party certifiers (called registrars in the United States) to issue ISO 9000 certificates. At present, the EU does not regulate certifiers. Instead, certifiers must earn accreditation through national accreditation bodies.

As discussed in more detail in Chapter 9, some prominent European standards officials are concerned with the resulting commercialization of the ISO 9000 standards series. As noted, the senior standards policy group of Directorate-General III for Industry is intent on altering the ISO 9000 certification process to place more emphasis on the quality process and less emphasis on passing a test. There is no plan to abolish ISO 9000 certificates.

Advice to Companies

Much of what is taking place in the European standards scene is evolutionary. Work on harmonization of product performance standards, electrical standards, and other areas of standardization is ongoing. There is much discussion about altering certification schemes in the quality assurance and other standards areas.

To cope with this transition period companies can do the following:

• Keep close tabs on European standards trends affecting their business through trade associations, the government, or ANSI.

• Attend local or regional seminars that offer education on European standards programs to keep abreast of developments.

• Do not sit in the dark wondering if they will be affected by EU standard requirements, but contact U.S. government or EU officials to make sure of where they stand.

• Be prepared to institute European standards programs such as CE Marking if there is even a 50-50 chance that a customer will require compliance.

• Follow European requirements. European standards officials are generally accessible and receptive to input from American companies. However, when it comes to meeting essential requirements for directives, U.S. government officials recommend small and midsize companies follow European regulations. Trying to convince European certification officials that a foreign product is already in compliance with European standards may prove trying and costly.

• Work as much as possible to build contacts within EU standards bodies. Standards officials have been known to help out their "friends."

Note: There is as much confusion in Europe as elsewhere about what is and is not required. A senior standards policy official has been known to joke that he does not understand what is taking place. Keep a sense of humor about the process and look at meeting European standards as a challenge that will help your company get ahead of the competition.

Finally, to aid the reader through the myriad of acronyms that accompany any degree of immersion into European standards, Appendix C to this chapter contains an alphabetized list of the standards themselves and Appendix D provides a comprehensive grouping of the numerous groups and committees of the European Union and the European Commission.

Resources

A Summary of the New European Approach to Standards Development.
Breitenberg, Maureen, ed., *Directory of European Regional Standards-Related Organizations.*
CEN/CENELEC, "European Standardization" (a booklet).
Common Standards for Enterprises.
European Standardization Statesman's Yearbook, 1995–1996.
Global Standards: Building Blocks for the Future.
Rensberger, Roger A., and van de Zande, Rene, *Standards Setting in the European Union: Standards Organizations and Officials in EU Standards Activities,* NIST Special Publication 891.
Standards and Trade in the 1990's.
The European Companion 1995.
Zuckerman, Amy, *ISO 9000 Made Easy: A Cost-Saving Guide to Documentation and Registration,* AMACOM, 1995.

Appendix A
CEN and CENELEC Membership

Note: European telecommunications companies are standardizing phone numbers in countries such as the Netherlands and Germany. Many, if not all, phone numbers are in the process of being changed. The numbers listed below will still be useful in accessing new ones.

CEN National Members

Austria
Osterreichisches Normungsinstitut / Austrian Standards Institute (ON)
Postfach 130
Heinestrasse 38
A-1021 VIENNA
Tel: (43 1) 222 213 00
Fax: (43 1) 222 213 00 818
President: Dr. Karl Korinek
Managing Director: Dr. Ing. Gerhard Hartmann
Deputy Managing Director: Mr. Hans G. Stoklasek
Head of PR and Communications: Dr. Johannes Stern
Tel: (43 1) 213 00 317
Fax: (43 1) 213 00 327

Belgium
Institut Belge de Normalisation / Belgisch Instituut voor Normalisatie
  (IBN / BIN)
Avenue de la Brabanconne 29/ Brabanconnelaan 29
B-1040 BRUXELLES / BRUSSELS
Tel: (32 2) 734 9205
Fax: (32 2) 733 4264
Head: Mr. P. M. Croon

Denmark
Dansk Standard (DS)
Baunegaardsvej 73
DK-2900 HELLERUP
Tel: (45) 39 77 0101
Fax: (45) 39 77 0202
Managing Director: Mr. Jacob Erik Holmblad
Standardization and Head of Sales and Information Department:
    Mr. Mogens Winther
Section Manager, Electrical Engineering: Mr. Jan Roed
Section Manager, Healthcare: Mr. Lars Brogaard
Section Manager, Information, Technology and Logistics:
    Mr. Hans Jorn Reuss
Section Manager, Building and Civil Engineering: Mr. Jorgen Riis-Jensen
Certification Manager: Mr. Egon Hansen

Finland
Suomen Standardisoimisliitto/Finnish Standards Association (SFS)
PO Box 116 (Maistraatinportti 2)
FIN-00241 HELSINKI
Tel: (358 0) 149 9331
Fax: (358 0) 146 4925
Internet: given name.surname@sfs.fi
Managing Director: Kari Kaartama
Director of Standardization: Raija Relander
Director of Certification: Eeva Parviainen
Chief Marketing: Satu Simula
Head of System Certification: Stefan Fagerstrom
Public Relations Officer: Jyrki Alanko
Library: Seija Koskimaa
Environmental Labeling Expert: Matti Jarv

France
Association Francaise de Normalisation (AFNOR)
Tour Europe
F-92049 PARIS-LA DEFENSE Cedex 7
Tel: (33 1) 42 91 5555
Fax: (33 1) 42 91 5656
President: Mr. Henri Marte
General Manager: Mr. Bernard Vaucelle
Deputy: Mr. Alain Durand
Public Relations/Communications: Mrs. Ghyslaine Pertusot
Manager, International and European Affairs: Mrs. Florence Nicolas

Manager, Personnel and Human Resources: Mr. Gabriel Bacq
Manager, Finance and Logistics: Mr. Daniel Geronimi
Manager, Quality and Strategic Marketing: Mrs. Claude Merle
Manager, Standards/Normative Strategy: Mr. Etienne Dupont
Manager, Certification: Mr. Jacques Beslin
Manager, Products/Services/Consulting: Mr. Bruno Dusollier

Germany
Deutsches Institut fur Normung (DIN)
Burggrafenstrasse 6
D-10787 BERLIN
Tel: (49 30) 26 010
Fax: (49 30) 26 01 1231
President: Mr. Eberhard Mollmann
Vice President: Gottfried Kremer
Director: Dr. Ing. Sc.D Helmut Reihlen
Deputy Director: Mr. Klaus Gunther Krieg
Technical Director for International Cooperation: Mr. Ernst-Peter Ziethen
Technical Director for Technical Coordination and Planning:
    Mr. Peter Kiehl

DIN's German Information Center for Technical Rules (DITR)
Information Inquiries: Tel: (49 30) 2601 2600
Euro-Info-Center: Tel: (49 30) 2601 2505

Greece
Hellenic Organization for Standardization (ELOT)
Acharnon Street 313
GR-111 45 ATHENS
Tel: (30 1) 2015 025
Tel: (30 1) 2020 776
President: Prof. G. Varoufakis
Tel: (30 1) 2234 966
Managing Director: N. Malagardi
Tel: (30 1) 2234 966
Promotion and Information: V.A. Filopoulos, Manager
Tel: (30 1) 2013 778
Standardization: D. Agapalidis, Manager
Tel: (30 1) 2019 891
Electrotechnical Standardization: Dr. P. Theofanopoulos, Manager
Tel: (30 1) 2029 367
Testing Laboratories: K. Ionas, Manager
Tel: (30 1) 5247 117
Directive: 83/189/EEC and GATT: E. Melagrakis, Manager
Tel: (30 1) 2019 890

Iceland
The Icelandic Council for Standardization (STRI)
Technological Institute of Iceland
Keldnaholt
IS-112 REYKJAVIK
Tel: (354) 587 7000
Fax: (354) 587 7409
Internet: stri@iti.is
Chairman: Mr. T. Karlsson
Secretary: Mr. J. Thorsteinsson

Ireland
National Standards Authority of Ireland (NSAI)
Glasnevin
Ireland DUBLIN 9
Tel: (353 1) 837 0101
Fax: (353 1) 836 9821
Head: Mr. E. Paterson

Italy
Ente Nazionale Italiano di Unificazione (UNI)
Via Battistotti Sassi, 11b
I-20133 MILANO
Tel: (39 2) 70 02 41
Fax: (39 2) 70 10 6106
Head: Dr. E. Martinotti

Luxembourg
Inspection du Travail et des Mines (ITM)
Boite postale 27
26, rue Ste Zithe
L-2010 LUXEMBOURG
Tel: (35 2) 478 6154
Fax: (35 2) 49 1447
Head: Mr. P. Weber

(ITM's main role is to ensure the implementation of all legislative aspects related to the working conditions and contracts, health and safety at the workplace, and so forth. Because of the size of the country and for some industrial reasons, Luxembourg does not develop national standards. The procedure for implementation of European standards is executed by ITM.)

The Netherlands
Nederlands Normalisatie-Instituut (NNI)
Postbus 5059
Kalfjeslaan 2

NL 2600 GB DELFT
Tel: (31 15) 690 255
Fax: (31 15) 690 130
Head: Mr. C. De Visser

Norway
Norges Standardiseringsforbund (NSF)
Postboks 7020
Homansbyen
N-0306 OSLO
Tel: (47 22) 46 6094
Fax: (47 22) 46 4457
Managing Director: Ivar Jachwitz
Technical Director: Liv Solhjell
Support/Services: Odd Bjornstad, Assistant Director
Assistant Director of Information: Sidsel Aarnaes Arbo
Assistant Director of Standards: Anne Kristoffersen
Assistant Director of Marketing: Frederik Hilsen
Assistant Director of Certification: Kirsten Svindahl

Portugal
Instituto Portugues da Qualidade (IPQ)
Rua Jose Estevao, no. 83-A
P-1199 LISBON Codex
Tel: (351 1) 52 3978
Fax: (351 1) 353 0033
Head: Mr. C. dos Santos

Spain
Asociacion Espanola de Normalizacion y Certificacion (AENOR)
Calle Fernandez de la Hoz, 52
E-28010 MADRID
Tel: (34 1) 310 4851
Fax: (34 1) 310 4976
Head: Mr. R. Naz Pajares

Sweden
Standardiseringskommissionen I Sverige (SIS)
PO Box 3295
Tegnergatan 11
S-103 66 STOCKHOLM
Tel: (46 8) 613 5200
Fax: (46 8) 411 7035
Director: Dr. L. Wallin
Head of Technical Department: Mr. Anders Skold

Head of Certification Department: Mr. Ivar Paljak
Head of PR and Communications: Ms. Jannecke Schulman
Tel: (46 8) 613 5227
Fax: (46 8) 10 8464

Switzerland
Schweizerische Normen-Vereinigung (SNV)
Muhlebachstrasse 54
CH-8008 ZURICH
Tel: (41 1) 254 5454
Fax: (41 1) 254 5474
Director: Dr. H. C. Zurrer

United Kingdom
British Standards Institution (BSI)
2, Park Street
UK LONDON W1A 2BS
Tel: (44 71) 629 9000
Fax: (44 71) 629 0506
Head: Sir Neville Purvis
Mr. Heinz Kull

Affiliate Members

Bulgaria
Committee for Standardization and Metrology
21, rue de 6 Septembre
BG-1000 SOFIA
Head: Mr. Y. Yordanov
Tel: (359) 2 85 91
Fax: (359) 2 80 1402

Cyprus
Cyprus Organization for Standards and Control of Quality (CYS)
Ministry of Commerce and Industry
CY-NICOSIA
Tel: (357 2) 30 3441/(357 2) 36 6185
Fax: (357 2) 36 6120
Chairman: Dr. G. Christodoulides
Director: Dr. I. G. Karis
Secretary: Mrs. Katherina Photiadou

Czech Republic
Czech Office for Standards, Measurement, and Testing
Vaclavske Namesti 19
113 47 PRAGUE 1

Tel: (42 2) 242 247 34
Fax: (42 2) 242 247 26
President: Mr. Michal Tosovsky
Tel: (42 2) 242 166 88
Fax: (42 2) 242 282 90
Department of International Relations
Vice President: Mrs. Vaclava Horakova
Tel: (42 2) 236 57 06
Fax: (42 2) 242 297 54
Department of State Testing
Director: Mr Vojtech Petrik
Tel: (42 2) 248 109 39
Fax: (42 2) 248 109 64
Department of Metrology
Director: Mr. Jiri Kraus
Tel: (42 2) 248 109 39
Fax: (42 2) 248 109 64

Hungary
Hungarian Office for Standardization (MSZH)
25 Ulloi Ut
H-1450 BUDAPEST 9PF 24
Tel: (36 1) 118 3011
Fax: (36 1) 118 5125
Head: Mr. G. Ponyai

Lithuania
Lietuvos Standartizacijos/Lithuanian Standardization Office (LST)
A. Jaksto g. 1/25
2600 VILNIUS
Tel: (370 2) 226 962
Fax: (370 2) 226 252
Director: Mr. Brunonas Sickus
Tel: (370 2) 226 962
Deputy Director: Mr. Stasys Brencius
Tel: (370 2) 224 944

Poland
Polski Komitet Normalizacji/Polish Committee for
    Standardization (PKNMIJ)
PO Box 10
PL-00-950 WARSAW
Tel: (48 2) 620 5434
Fax: (48 2) 620 5434
President: Mr. Marian Lukaszewicz

Tel: (48 2) 620 29 16
Fax: (48 2) 620 07 41
Vice-President: Mr. Andrzje Kocznorowski
Tel: (48 2) 620 6621
Fax: (48 2) 620 0741
Secretary: Mr. Krzysztof Trzcinski
Tel: (48 2) 620 2914
Fax: (48 2) 620 0741
Foreign Relations: Mr. Zygmunt Niechoda, Director
Tel/Fax: (48 2) 620 5434

Romania
Institutul Roman de Standardizare
13, rue Jean-Louis Calderon
RO-70201 BUCAREST 2
Director General: Mihail Ciocodeica
Tel: (401) 611 40 43
Fax: (401) 312 08 23
Division of Standardization
Director: Mircea Petcu
Tel: (401) 615 58 70
Fax: (401) 210 08 33
Division of Certification, Accreditation, Notification of Bodies
Quality Director: Claudiu Stefanescu
Tel: (401) 222 38 50
Fax: (401) 210 08 33
Division of Services, Consulting, Communication, International Relations
    (ISO, CEN, CENELEC, ETSI, IEC, TERMNET)
Director: Daniela Moga
Tel: (401) 615 58 70
Fax: (401) 312 47 44
Division of Human Resources, Finances, Accounting, Logistics, Marketing
Director: Clementina Enciu
Tel: (401) 615 58 70
Fax: (401) 312 47 44
Division of the Secretariat of the National Center for Training,
    Consultancy and Management in Quality Assurance
Director: Gabriela Anghelescu
Tel: (401) 222 38 60
Fax: (401) 210 08 33

Slovakia
Slovak Office of Standards, Metrology and Testing (UNMS)
Stefanovicova 3
81439 BRATISLAVA

Tel: (42 7) 491 085
Fax: (42 7) 491 050
President: Mr. Lubomir Sutek
Tel: (42 7) 491 085
Standards: Mrs. Kvetoslava Steinlova, Director
Tel: (42 7) 493 521
International Relations: Mr. Andrej Svatik, Director
Tel: (42 7) 494 728

Slovenia
Standards and Metrology Institute (SMIS)
Ministry of Science and Technology
Kotnikova 6
SI-61000 LJUBLJANA
Tel: (386 61) 131 23 22
Fax: (386 61) 314 882
Internet: ic@usm.mzt.si
Director: Mr. Bogdan Topic
Administration and Legal Advice: Mr. Vitomir Fister, Assistant Director
Standardization: Mr. Tone Pogacnik, Assistant Director
Metrology: Mr. Vasja Hrovat, Director
Accreditation: Mr. Bogdan Topic, Director
Type Approval Road Vehicles: Mr. Miha Luckmann, Assistant Director
Information Center: Mr. Dusan Zuzic, Advisor to the Director

Turkey
Turkish Standards Institution (TSE)
Necatibey Cad 112
TR-06100 ANKARA BAKANLIKAR
Tel: (90 4) 417 83 30
Fax: (90 4) 425 43 99
Head: Mr. M. Y. Ariyoruk

Associate Members

European Construction Industry Federation (FIEC)
Avenue Louise 66
B-1050 BRUSSELS
BELGIUM
Tel: (32 2) 514 5535
Fax: (32 2) 511 0276
President: Dr. Ing Thomas Rogge
Director General: Mr. Ulrich Paetzold
Technical Affairs: Mr. John Goodall

European Trade Union Technical Bureau for Health and Safety (TUTB)
Blvd. Emile Jacqmain 155
B-1210 BRUSSELS
BELGIUM
Tel: (32 2) 224 0560
Fax: (32 2) 224 0561
President: Mr. Fritz Verzetnitsch
Vice President: Mr. Emilio Gabaglio
Director: Mr. Marc Sapir
Standards Research Officer: Mr. Jean-Jacques Gueant
Standards Research Officer: Mr. Vicente Verde Peleato
Information Officer: Ms. Janine Delahaut
Tel: (32 2) 224 0552

CENELEC Member National Committees

Austria
Osterreichisches Elektrotechnisches Komitee (OEK)
    beim Osterreichischen Verband fur Electro
Eschenbachgasse 9
A-1010 VIENNA
Tel: (43 1) 587 6373
Fax: (43 1) 56 7403
President: Dipl.-Ing. Helmut Hainitz
General Secretary: Dipl.-Ing. Dr. H. Starker
Executive Secretary: Mr. P. Rausch

Belgium
Comite Electrotechnique Belge (CEB)
Belgisch Elektrotechnisch Comite (BEC)
Avenue Fr. Van Kalken 9
B-1070 BRUSSELS
Tel: (32 2) 556 0110
Fax: (32 2) 556 0120

President: M. R. Laurent
Administrateur delegue
NOVA Electro International
Overhamlaan 44
B-3700 TONGEREN
Tel: (32 12) 23 2986
Fax: (32 12) 26 2056
Secretary-General: M. J. Papier

Denmark
Dansk Standard (DS)/(Danish Standards Association)
Electrotechnical Sector
Baunegaardsvej 73
DK-2900 HELLERUP
Tel: (45) 39 77 0101
Fax: (45) 39 77 0202
President: Mr. Niels W. Holm
Managing Director: Mr. Jacob Erik-Holmblad
Standardization and Head of Sales and Information Department:
   Mr. Mogens Winther
Section Manager, Electrical Engineering: Mr. Jan Roed
Section Manager, Healthcare: Mr. Lars Brogaard
Section Manager, Information, Technology and Logistics:
   Mr. Hans Jorn Reuss
Section Manager, Building and Civil Engineering: Mr. Jorgen Riis-Jensen
Certification Manager: Mr. Egon Hansen

Finland
Finnish Electrotechnical Standards Association (SESKO)
Sarkiniementie 3
PO Box 134
FIN-00211 HELSINKI
Tel: (358 0) 696 391
Fax: (358 0) 677 059
President: Mr. Kalervo Rudanko
Vice President: Mr. Otso Kuusisto
Director: Mr. Tuomo Ilomaki
Information and Documentation Officer: Mrs. Pirkko Taavitsaien

France
Union Technique de l'Electricite (UTE)
Immeuble Lavoisier
4, place des Vosges
La Defense 5-COURBEVOIE
Mailing Address:
UTE-Cedex 64
F-92052 PARIS-LA DEFENSE
Tel: (33 1) 46 91 1111
President: M. P. R. Sallebert
Director-General: M. J. Benoist
UTE, Approval Department, Tel: (33 1) 47 89 4587
UTE, All Services, Tel: (33 1) 47 89 4775
UTE, Standardization Department, Tel: (33 1) 46 91 1265

Germany
Deutsche Elektrotechnische Kommission im DIN und VDE (DKE)
Stresemannallee 15
D-60596 FRANKFURT/MAIN
Tel: (49) 69 630 80
Fax: (49) 69 631 2925
President: Mr. Gunter G. Seip
Direktor, Siemens AG
ASI 3 GWR
Siemenstrasse 10
D-93055 REGENSBURG
Tel: (49) 941 790 2252
Fax: (49) 941 790 2700
Teletex: 2627-9418128-Sie IBJR
Secretary: Dipl.-Ing. K. Orth

Greece
Hellenic Organization for Standardization (ELOT)
Acharnon Street 313
GR-111 45 ATHENS
Tel: (30 1) 2015 025
Fax: (30 1) 2020 776
President: Prof. G. Varoufakis
Tel: (30 1) 2234 966
Managing Director: N. Malagardis
Tel: (30 1) 2234 966
Promotion and Information: V. A. Filopoulos, Manager
Tel: (30 1) 2013 778
Standardization: D. Agapalidis, Manager
Tel: (30 1) 2019 891
Electrotechnical Standardization: Dr. P. Theofanopoulos, Manager
Tel: (30 1) 2029 367
Testing Laboratories: K. Ionas, Manager
Tel: (30 1) 5247 117
Dir: 83/189/EEC and GATT: E. Melagrakis, Manager
Tel: (30 1) 2019 890

Iceland
Icelandic Council for Standardization (STRI)
Technological Institute of Iceland
Keldnaholt
IS-112 REYKJAVIK
Tel: (354) 587 7000
Fax: (354) 587 7409

Internet: stri@iti.is
Chairman: Mr. T. Karlsson
Secretary: Mr. J. Thorsteinsson

Ireland
Electro-Technical Council of Ireland (ETCI)
ESB Office
Parnell Avenue
Harold's Cross
Ireland DUBLIN 12
Tel: (353 1) 454 5819/454 5820
Fax: (353 1) 454 5821
Chairman: Mr. S. Elmore
Personal Assistant: Ms. Lucie Quesnel-Brady
Administrator: Mr. J. P. Sheehan
Ballymun Road
Tel: (353 1) 837 6773
Fax: (353 1) 836 9821
Head Secretary: Mr. D. O'Regan

Luxembourg
Service de l'energie de l'Etat
34, avenue de la Porte-Neuve
L-2227 LUXEMBOURG
Tel: (352) 46 9746-1
Fax: (352) 22 2507
Postal Address:
c/o Service de l'Energie de l'Etat
BP 10
L-2010 LUXEMBOURG
Director: M. Jean-Paul Hoffmann

The Netherlands
Nederlands Elektrotechnisch Comite (NEC)
Kalfjeslaan 2
Postbus 5059
NL-2600 GB DELFT
Tel: (31 15) 690 255
Fax: (31 15) 690 130
President: Mr. E. Ribberink
Vice President, Euro Affairs:

Holec Systems and Components BV
PO Box 23
NL-7550 AA HENGELO
Tel: (31 74) 46 4880

Fax: (31 74) 46 42208
Vice Presidents:
Prof. Ir. J. L. de Kroes
Mr. C. Ch. Smit
Director: Mr. T. D. Roodbergen
Tel: (31 15) 690 208
Fax: (31 15) 690 242

Norway
Norsk Elektroteknisk Komite (NEK)
Harbitzalleen 2A, Sky yen
Postboks 280
N-0212 OSLO 2
Tel: (47 22) 52 6950
Fax: (47 22) 52 6961
Telegrams: NORWELCOM
President: Mr. Knut Herstad
Tel: (47 7) 59 7200
Fax: (47 7) 59 7250
Director: Mr. B. I. Odegard

Portugal
Instituto Portugues da Qualidade (IPQ)
Rua Jose Estevao, no. 83-A
P-1199 LISBON Codex
Tel: (351 1) 52 3978
Telex: (404) 13042 QUALIT P
Fax: (351 1) 353 0033
President: Mr. Candido dos Santos

Spain
Asociacion Espanola de Normalizacion y Certificacion (AENOR)
Comite Electrotecnico Espanol
Calle Fernandez de la Hoz 52
E-28010 MADRID
Tel: (34 1) 310 4851
Fax: (34 1) 310 4976
Chairman: Mr. I Tornos
IBERDROLA
Calle Claudio Coello 53
E-28010 MADRID
Tel: (34 1) 577 6565
Fax: (34 1) 577 0848
General Director: Mr. R. Naz
Secretary: Mr. V. Ruiz de Valbuena

Sweden
Svenska Elektriska Kommissionen (SEK)
Kistagangen 19
Box 1284
S-16428 KISTA STOCKHOLM
Tel: (46 8) 750 7820
Fax: (46 8) 751 8470
Chairman: Mr. M. Setterwall
Sveriges Elektroindustriforening
Box 5501
S-11485 STOCKHOLM
Tel: (46 8) 783 8164
Fax: (46 8) 663 6323
Vice Presidents:
Mr. G. Sandqvist
Mr. J. Nou
Managing Director and Secretary of the Swedish Committee of
    IEC and CENELEC Committees: Mr. Hans Erik Rundqvist

Switzerland
Swiss Electrotechnical Committee (CES)
Luppmenstrasse 1
CH-8320 FEHRALTORF
Tel: (41 1) 956 1170
Fax: (41 1) 956 1190
President: Dr. Ing. Paul W. Kleiner
AWK Engineering AG
Leutschenbachstrasse 45
CH-8050 ZURICH
Tel: (41 1) 305 9511
Fax: (41 1) 305 9519
Secretary-General: Mr. R. E. Spaar

United Kingdom
British Electrotechnical Committee (BEC)
British Standards Institution (BSI)
2, Park Street
UK LONDON W1A 2BS
Tel: (44 71) 629 9000
Fax: (44 71) 629 0506
Chairman: Mr. Norman J. A. Holland
Consultant: Standards and Directives
Pinehaven, 94 Hilting Lury Road
Chandler's Ford, Hampshire S05 1NZ

Tel: (44 0703) 27 0605
Fax: (44 0703) 27 0605
Secretary: Mr. I. Campbell

Affiliate Members

Poland
Polski Komitet Normalizacji/Polish Committee for
  Standardization (PKNMIJ)
PO Box 10
PL-00-950 WARSAW
Tel: (482) 620 5434
Fax: (482) 620 5434
President: Mr. Marian Lukaszewicz
Tel: (48 2) 620 29 16
Fax: (48 2) 620 07 41
Vice-President: Mr. Andrzje Kocznorowski
Tel: (48 2) 620 6621
Fax: (48 2) 620 0741
Secretary: Mr. Krzyszbof Trzcinski
Tel: (48 2) 620 2914
Fax: (48 2) 620 0741
Foreign Relations: Mr. Zygmunt Niechoda, Director
Tel/Fax: (48 2) 620 5434

Romania
Institutul Roman de Standardizare
13, rue Jean-Louis Calderon
RO-70201 BUCAREST 2
Director General: Mihail Ciocodeica
Tel: (401) 611 40 43
Fax: (401) 312 08 23
Division of Standardization
Director: Mircea Petcu
Tel: (401) 615 58 70
Fax: (401) 210 08 33

Division of Certification, Accreditation, Notification of Bodies,
Quality Director: Claudiu Stefanescu
Tel: (401) 222 38 50
Fax: (401) 210 08 33

Division of Services, Consulting, Communication, International Relations
  (ISO, CEN, CENELEC, ETSI, IEC, TERMNET)
Director: Daniela Moga

Tel: (401) 615 58 70
Fax: (401) 312 47 44

Division of Human Resources, Finances, Accounting, Logistics: Marketing

Director, Clementina Enciu
Tel: (   ) 615 58 70
Fax: (   ) 312 47 44
Division of the Secretariat of the National Center for
  Training, Consultancy and Management in Quality Assurance
Director: Gabriela Anghelescu
Tel: (401) 222 38 60
Fax: (401) 210 08 33

Slovakia
Slovak Electrotechnical Committee (SEV)/Slovak Office of
  Standards, Metrology and Testing (UNMS)
Stefanovicova 3
81439 BRATISLAVA
Tel: (42 7) 491 085
Fax: (42 7) 491 050
President: Mr. Vladimir Adamec
Tel: (42 7) 496 847

Slovenia
Standards and Metrology Institute (SMIS)
Ministry of Science and Technology
Kotnikova 6
SI-61000 LJUBLJANA
SMIS is an affiliate of CEN, CENELEC, and a member of ETSI
Director: Mr. Bogdan Topic
Administration and Legal Advice: Mr. Vitomir Fister, Assistant Director
Standardization: Mr. Tone Pogacnik, Assistant Director
Metrology: Mr. Vasja Hrovat, Director
Accreditation: Mr. Bogdan Topic, Director
Type Approval Road Vehicles: Mr. Miha Luckmann,
  Assistant Director
Information Center: Mr. Dusan Zuzic, Adviser to the Director
Tel: (386 61) 131 23 22
Fax: (386 61) 314 882

Appendix B

European Standards Listings

European standards bear different prefixes depending on what general categories they represent, as follows:

- *EN.* This prefix is placed before newly created European standards or standards that are adopted from international standards. For example, the ISO 9000 Standards Series as adopted in the EU is called EN 29000. EU member states are mandated to implement EN standards. Corresponding national standards must be withdrawn.

- *HD.* This prefix represents harmonization documents, which are also mandated at the national level. Conflicting national standards must be withdrawn if they are within the technical scope of the HD standard. Some exceptions are allowed, though usually on a temporary basis.

- *ENV.* This prefix represents standards under creation that can be applied on a provisional basis when there is an urgent need to be met. Because a standard may be released under the ENV prefix without consensus, it assumes less obligation on the national level than the EN or HD prefix. Existing national standards may be maintained until a decision is made to convert the ENV standard into either an EN or HD standard. A standard can only bear this prefix for a five-year period, at which point it must be converted to an EN or HD standard or withdrawn.

- National standards that correspond with European standards will bear the prefix of the national standards body. For example, a corresponding German standard may be labeled DIN-EN.

Note: For the sake of regional unity, CEN/CENELEC members prefer to issue an EN rather than an HD standard. Both are mandatory, even for dissenting member states, and are published in the three official EU languages: English, French, and German. ENV text is often made available in one of the three languages only.

Eventually, European standards are expected to substitute for all national standards. European standards developers recognize that national standards often better reflect the habits and cultures of domestic markets. On the other hand, the European standard is valid throughout the EU and allows for easier market penetration.

Appendix C

EU Acronyms by Country (as of 1995)

BC	Bon de Commande, mandate
BCR	Community Bureau of Reference
CAD	Computer Aided Design
CAM	Computer Aided Manufacturing
CASE	Computer Aided Software Engineering
CTR	Common Technical Regulation
CTS	Conformance Testing Service
DIS	Draft International Standard
ECU	European Currency Unit
EG	Expert Group
EMC	Electromagnetic Compatibility
EMS	Environmental Management Systems
EQA	External Quality Assessment
EQA-Protocol	External Quality Assessment–Protocol
EQAS	External Quality Assurance Scheme (organizers in medical laboratories)
GALP	Good Analytical Laboratory Practice
GATT	General Agreement on Tariffs and Trade
GLP	Good Laboratory Practice
GOSIP	Government Open Systems Interconnection Profile
GSM	Global Mobile Communications
IS	International Standard
ISDN	Integrated Services Digital Network
IT	Information Technology
MOU	Memorandum of Understanding
MRA	Mutual Recognition Agreement
OSI	Open Systems Interconnection
PICS	Protocol Implementation Conformance Statement
POSIX	Unix-based operating system standardized by IEEE & ISO/IEC

PPL	Preferred Product List (USA)
QA	Quality Assurance
QC	Quality Control
QMS	Quality Management System
QPL	Qualified Products List (USA)
R&D	Research & Development
SAST	Strategic Analysis of Science & Technology
SME	Small & Medium Sized Enterprise
SPC	Statistical Process Control
SQC	Statistical Quality Control
TBR	Technical Basis for Regulation
TICQA	Testing, Inspection, Certification, and Quality Assurance
TQM	Total Quality Management
VANS	Valid Analytical Measurement (UK/DTI/LGC)

Appendix D

European Union Standards and Conformity Assessment Bodies

ACTE	Approvals Committee for Terminal Equipment (in the EC Commission)
AECMA	Association Europeenne des Constructeurs de Materiel Aerospatial
BRITE/EURAM	Basic Research in Industrial Technology for Europe/European Research in Advanced Materials
CAA	CENELEC Certification Agreement
CAPIEL	Coordinating Committee of the European Associations of Industrial Switchgear and Control Gear
CCC	CEN Certification Committees
CEA	European Insurance Committee
CEC	Commission of the European Communities (replaced by EC)
CECAPI	European Committee of Electrical Installation Equipment Manufacturers
CECC	European Harmonised System of Quality Assessment for Electronic Components (CENELEC)
CECED	European Committee of Manufacturers of Electrical Domestic Equipment
CECOD	European Committee for Manufacturers of Petroleum & Measuring and Distribution Equipment
CEEP	European Center of Public Enterprises (Centre Europeen de l'Entreprise Publique)
CEFACD	Association of European Domestic Gas Appliance Manufacturers
CEFIC	Council Europeen des Federations de L'Industrie Chimique (European Chemical Industry Council)

CEICIP	European Committee for Constructors of Weighing Instruments
CEIR	European Committee for Valves & Fitting Industry Manufacturers
CEL	Committee of EC Lighting Manufacturers Association
CEN	European Committee for Standardization/Comite Europeen de Normalisation
CENELEC	European Committee for Electrotechnical Standardization/Comite Europeen de Normalisation Electrotechnique
CEOC	Confederation Europeene d'Organismes de Controle—(Certification of Inspection Personnel)
CEPT	Conference Europeen des Administrations des Postes et des Telecommunications
CFPA Europe	Confederation of Fire Protection Associations
CIS	Customs Information System [EC Member State and Commission computerized network for information exchange; external security of the internal market.]
COCOR	Iron & Steel Nomenclature Coordination Committee / Coordinating Commission of ECISS
CONSCERT	European Group for the Certification of Construction Steels
EAA	European Elevator Association
EAC	European Accreditation Council
EASEM	European Association of Security Equipment Manufacturers
ECSC	European Organisation for Testing and Certification
ECUI	European Committee of User Inspectorates (see EEMUA)
ECEQAO	European Conference of External Quality Assessment Organisers
ECTIC	European Committee for IT&T Testing & Certification [EOTC Sectoral Committee]
ECISS	European Committee for Iron & Steel Standardization
ECMA	European Computer Manufacturers Association
ECNDT	European Council for Non-Destructive Testing
ECOSA	European Consumer Safety Association
ECTRA	European Committee for Telecommunications Regulatory Affairs
ECUI	European Committee of User Inspectorates [EEMUA refers]
EEA	European Economic Area

EEC	European Economic Community
EEMUA	Engineering Equipment & Materials Users Association (UK) European Community
EFOCA	European Federation of Quality Circle & Quality Management Association
EFQM	European Foundation for Quality Management
EFSAC	European Fire & Security Advisory Council
EESCE	European Fire and Security Group [EOTC Agreement Group]
EFTA	European Free Trade Area
EGOLF	European Group of Official Laboratories for Fire
EIA	European Industries Association
IBIPA	European Institute of Public Administration
ELC	European Lighting Council
ELSECOM	European Electrotechnical Sectoral Committee for Testing & Certification (EOTC Sectoral Committee)
EMAS	Eco-Management and Audit Scheme (EC's)
EMEDCA	European Active Medical Devices Certification Agreement
EMCIT	Recognition Arrangement for European Testing of EMC of Information Technology Products [EOTC Agreement Group]
EN	European Norm/Standard
ENV	European Pre-Standard
EOQ	European Organisation for Quality
EOTA	European Organisation for Technical Approvals (see CPD)
EPHOS	European Procurement Handbook for Open Systems (ITT)
EPTA	Association of European Portable Electric Tool Manufacturers
E-Q-NET	European Network for Quality System Assessment & Certification
EQS	European Committee for Quality System Assessment and Certification
ERMCO	European Ready Mixed Concrete Organisation
ESA	EFTA Surveillance Authority
ESCIF	European Sectoral Committee for Intrusion & Fire Protection
ESED	European Society for Environment and Development
ESRA	European Safety & Reliability Association
ESPRIT	European Strategic Programme for Research & Development in Information Technology

ETCRAF	Recognition Arrangement for European Testing for Certification of Office and Manufacturing Protocols [EOTC Agreement Group]
ETSI	European Telecommunications Standards Institute
ETSI TC ATM	ETSI Technical Committee on Advanced Testing Methodology (precursor to ETSI TC MTS)
ETSI TC MTS	ETSI Technical Committee on Methods for Testing and Specification
EU	European Union
EURALARM	European Association of Manufacturers of Fire and Intruder Alarm Systems
EURIFI	European Association of Research Institutes for Furniture
EUROBAT	European Accumulator Manufacturers
EUROCER	Federation of Certification Bodies Working in the Area of the Building & Construction Industry
EUROFEU	European Committee of the Manufacturers of Fire Protection and Safety Equipment and Fire Fighting Vehicles
EUROMET	Agreement of metrological institutes within Europe to collaborate through an MOU promoting the coordination of metrological activities
EUROSAFE	European Committee of Safe Manufacturers Associations
EUWA	Association of European Wheel Manufacturers
EWOS	European Workshop for Open Systems
FEACO	Federation Europeene des Associations de Conseils en Organisation (European Federation of Management Consulting Organisations)
FIEC	European Construction Industry Federation
IEEP	Institute for European Environmental Policy
ITQS	Recognition Arrangement for Assessment and Certification of Quality Systems in the Information Technology Sector [EOTC Agreement Group 3]
LOVAG	Low Voltage Agreement Group [EOTC Agreement Group]
NET	Norme Europeanne de Telecommunications
OPMC	European Confederation of Construction Products Manufacturers
ORALIME	Organisation for the Representation of Industrial Trade Associations in Europe
OSTC	Open Systems Testing Consortium [EOTC Agreement Group]

PRISMA	Programme for the Regions Industry for the Single Market
STLA	Short-circuit Testing Liaison Agreement Group [EOTC Agreement Group]
UEAPME	Union Europeenne del'Artisanat et des Petites et Moyennes Enterprises—European Authority for Craft & Small and Medium Enterprises
UEATC	European Union of Agreement/Union Europeenne pour l'Agrement Technique dans la Construction
UNICE	Union of Industrial and Employers' Confederations of Europe
UNIFE	Union of European Railway Industries
WECC	WECC Calibration Laboratory Accreditation System [EOTC Agreement Group]
WECC	Western European Calibration Cooperation
WELAC	Western European Laboratory Accreditation Conference
WELMEC	Western European Legal Metrology Cooperation
WRC	Water Research Centre (UK)

7

CE Marking

Questions the Reader Will Find Addressed in This Chapter

1. What is the New Approach versus the Old Approach to product standards certification?
2. How does the CE Mark work?
3. What are the mandated industrial categories for CE Marks?
4. What inconsistencies have resulted from the transition period?
5. What rules apply in this transition period?
6. What is the inspection or conformity assessment process?
7. What happens when third-party certification is required?
8. What is the role of foreign certifiers?
9. What are ten tips for earning CE Marks?
10. What happens when quality systems are required?
11. What happens when quality systems are not mentioned?
12. Is the CE Mark a trade barrier that will prevent or delay a company's entry into the European market?
13. What is keymarking?

The main tool employed in harmonizing European product standards is the CE Mark. Companies that pass testing requirements for a number of product groups may then affix a label to their products—the CE Mark—that allows them to market the products throughout Europe.

European officials consider the CE Mark "a passport for industrial products" that allows them to circulate freely throughout the internal market. The CE Mark indicates that products have passed certain European Union (EU) and European Commission (EC) health, safety, and environmental standards. EU officials consider the CE Mark a sign that products are safe and that the interests of consumers are protected. The CE Mark is not a quality mark, however, and does not indicate product conformance with particular quality standards. It indicates that the manufacturer has followed all relevant conformity assessment procedures laid down in EC directives that apply to the product.

The CE Mark is an important sales factor for any company entering the European market and, in some cases, is a legal requirement in Europe. Ideally, harmonization of standards is expected to reduce technical barriers to trade as manufacturers are required to meet only one European-wide standard, rather than make costly changes to a product to meet a variety of different national standards. The harmonization of standards, of which the CE Mark is a part, is also expected to boost trade both within the EU and with major trading partners such as the United States.

Old Approach Versus New Approach

In Europe, not all products are regulated in the sense that government mandates design. Many products circulate throughout Europe without restriction because they do not fall under government requirements, and national voluntary product standards are increasingly giving way to European standards.

Old Approach

In areas such as foods, drugs, automobiles, and airplanes, the EU has relied on the "Old Approach" to product standards certification. This is a form of harmonized legislation at the EU level that preempts some aspects of local member state authority. Although outlined in legislation, Old Approach requirements are carried out without a marking system. The focus is on individual products rather than on product groupings.

The Old Approach is considered cumbersome, with such detailed requirements that ten to fifteen years are sometimes required to develop a standard under this process. Member states often supersede this process with their own standards, creating a backlog of harmonization work.

New Approach

Under the "New Approach," the harmonization of technical standards for regulated products centers on the health and safety aspects of these products, and is intended to produce minimum health and safety levels throughout the EU. New Approach directives are limited to essential safety or other performance requirements considered to be in the general public interest. The technical details of meeting these requirements are left to manufacturers who self-certify products; to the three regional European standards organizations, CEN, CENELEC, and ETSI; and to government-appointed product certification bodies.

As a result of the New Approach, a product manufactured in conformity with EU legislation in one member state will be guaranteed automatic access to the markets of all the other member states. European and foreign manufacturers who comply with health and safety requirements in the New Approach directives may affix the CE Mark. The mark signifies that a product meets essential conformity assessment requirements and guarantees its legal access to all of the markets in the member states of the European Union.

The New Approach deals with large families of products—machinery, gas appliances, pressure equipment, toys, and construction products—or "horizontal" risks such as those addressed in the EU's Electromagnetic Compatibility Directive. Some products may be governed by more than one directive because different risks may be dealt with under separate directives. The manufacturer is responsible for ensuring the product meets the requirements for all applicable New Approach directives.

Note: Not all product requirements are harmonized; there are still products and product sectors where national or member state regulations function as mandatory requirements. Gas connectors and analog-type telecommunications terminal equipment are examples of products that still require national approvals. Moreover, the Old Approach still remains in effect for a range of products, such as automobiles, tractors, chemicals, pharmaceuticals, foods, and aircraft. These products do not require the CE Mark, but must meet Old Approach directives that contain detailed requirements for standards and test methods, and specify required marks that must be applied to indicate conformance.

Summary

The CE Mark does not eliminate national quality or performance marks representing levels of quality, safety, or performance higher than those specified in EU legal requirements. Although member states cannot bar access to their markets without national marks, certain marks can be specified in commercial contracts. The CE Mark also does not supersede national marks relating to environmental control, ergonomics, or workplace safety.

CE Mark Issues

Although American manufacturers appreciate the need to eliminate often redundant and conflicting product health and safety requirements, there is also concern that the CE Mark is fast becoming yet another trade barrier to Europe (see "Is the CE Mark a Trade Barrier?" later in this chapter). Not only is the process so laborious and time consuming that a manager of a major electronics company says it defies explanation, but individual national product, safety, and environmental regulations still exist. There is fear that the CE Mark will add just another layer of work and expense to prospective exports, discouraging trade with Europe. The United States Trade Representative and Commerce Department officials share these concerns and are keeping tabs on the CE Mark and its implementation requirements (see Chapter 12).

How the CE Mark Works

EU directives are addressed to the member states, who then must transpose them into national law. The directives define a schedule for adopting and publishing national provisions to implement each directive. Directives also define when national provisions must be applied.

New Approach directives also recognize a transitional period during which existing national provisions and new legislation will coexist. In such cases, the manufacturer may choose to follow either of these series of conditions.

Products may fall under one or several EC directives. Each directive spells out

- Whether the mark is mandatory.
- Whether quality assurance certification is required to earn a mark.
- Which party—the manufacturer, third-party testing laboratory, or other—actually places the mark or label on the product. In most cases the manufacturer will actually place the mark on a product.

A list of New Approach directives by identification number and subject is found in Figure 7-1.

Note: There are two cases where the CE Mark is not mandatory. Certain types of simple pressure vessels and construction products do not require marks. However, the CE Mark is required for many simple pressure vessels. Companies should check with EU or U.S. government officials, or hire knowledgeable consultants, to ensure a product is covered under an EU directive before proceeding.

To earn a CE Mark, manufacturers must present products for testing at EU-designated laboratories (see case studies later in this chapter). When approval is earned, an actual label is affixed to the product bearing the CE Mark, just as private testing laboratories in the United States affix their seals of approval to products. When appropriate, a numerical code accompanies the actual CE Mark label, identifying the laboratory that inspected

Figure 7-1. "New Approach" directives that have so far been adopted by council.

* DIR 87/404/EEC (Simple Pressure Vessels)
* DIR 88/378/EEC (Safety of Toys)
* DIR 89/106/EEC (Construction Products)
* DIR 89/336/EEC (Electromagnetic Compatibility)
* DIR 89/392/EEC (Machinery)
* DIR 89/686/EEC (Personal Protective Equipment)
* DIR 90/384/EEC (Non-Automatic Weighing Instruments)
* DIR 90/385/EEC (Active Implantable Medical Devices)
* DIR 90/396/EEC (Appliances Burning Gaseous Fuels)
* DIR 91/263/EEC (Telecommunications Terminal Equipment)
* DIR 92/42/EEC (Hot-Water Boilers)
* DIR 93/42/EEC (Medical Devices)
* DIR 93/15/EEC (Explosives for Civil Uses)
* DIR 94/9/EC (ATEX)
* DIR 94/25/EC (Recreational Crafts)

and passed the product. Products subject to specialized product safety requirements must bear both the CE Mark and other marks required under EC legislation.

New rules regulating how CE Marks or labels are placed on products are expected to be in place by January 1, 1997. Because the process of earning a CE Mark can be technically complicated, the aim of the new rules is to provide a simplified, more coherent approach to this process.

Mandated Industrial Categories for CE Marks

Although there is a general approach to earning a CE Mark, much of the process is product specific. The first step for product manufacturers, therefore, is determining whether a product fits into one of the following categories in which CE Marks are required:

Product	Category	Directive Period When Adopted
Simple pressure vessels	87/404/EEC	1/90–7/92
Toys (safety)	88/378/EEC	1/90–
Construction products	89/106/EEC	6/91–
Electromagnetic compatibility	89/336/EEC	1/92–12/95
Machinery	89/392/EEC	1/93–12/94
Personal protective equipment	89/686/EEC	7/92–12/94

Product	Category	Directive Period When Adopted
Nonautomatic weighing instruments	90/384/EEC	1/93–1/2003
Active implant medical devices	90/385/EEC	1/95–5 years post adoption
Appliances burning gaseous fuels	90/396/EEC	1/92–12/95
Telecommunications terminal equipment	91/263/EEC	11/92–
Hot-water boilers	92/42/EEC	
Medical devices	93/42/EEC	
Explosives for civil uses	93/15/EEC	
ATEX	94/9/EC	
Recreational crafts	94/25/EC	
Low-voltage		1/95–1/97
Construction products		1/95–1/97
Load-lifting machinery		1/93–12/94
Personal lift machinery		1/95–12/96
Satellite earth station equipment		5/95–

Product areas where requirements are in development are: in-vitro diagnostics, flammability of furniture, pressure equipment, measuring instruments, cable ways, and playground equipment (includes sports equipment).

Coping With the Transition Period

There are differences from one EC product safety directive to another regarding what the CE Mark signifies, who is responsible for affixing the CE Mark, and what the mark should look like. Work is underway to make the marks more consistent. In the meantime, CE Mark enforcement periods are staggered, and manufacturers have complained of being confused about what is and is not required to meet EC approval.

The following are examples of staggered deadlines:

• As of January 1, 1995, the EC Directive on Machines became mandatory, and all products falling under this directive had to meet the essential requirements of that directive on a self-certification basis. Those not meeting requirements could be effectively banned from sale in the internal market.

• As of January 1, 1996, an electric or electronic product that is not considered a machine does not have to meet essential requirements other than those spelled out in the low-voltage directive. CE Marking is not required, although the manufacturer has the option of marking its product. The mark *is* required for machines.

Note: Electric or electronic products that are used in telecommunications are not exempt under this category.

Transition Period Rules

Recognizing that gray areas exist and that the requirements for CE Marking are somewhat flexible, European Commission officials have created the following rules for this transition period:

- National inspectors have the right during this period to decide whether a product that conforms to EC directives, but does not carry CE Marking, can be released into their individual market without the manufacturer actually earning a CE Mark.
- It is recommended that national inspectors act in proportion to the risk involved.
- National authorities have the right to place questionable products in bonded warehouses until it is determined whether the product qualifies for a CE Mark. This is a temporary move and is not considered confiscation, which implies loss of ownership.

Case Study: ETAs and Construction Products

Because of their long transition period, construction products offer a good case study for how foreigners can sell products in Europe and still meet EC directives. EC officials predict at least a ten-year transition period for this sector, during which construction products will have to meet what is called European technical approvals (ETAs) through the European Organization for Technical Approvals (EOTA).

A nonprofit organization officially established on October 10, 1990, the EOTA will essentially replace the European Union for Technical Approvals in Construction (UEATC), which formerly conducted "fitness-for-purpose" assessments. The new EOTA will act as an umbrella organization for participating member state bodies, which at present are the national members of the former UEATC.

Once granted an ETA, a product is deemed fit for its intended use. ETAs may be granted in some of the following cases:

- There are no harmonized European standards regulating the product in question.
- There is no recognized national standard.

> • There is no mandate for a harmonized standard and the EC Commission determines that a standard could not be developed.

Applications for ETAs will normally go through a member-state body. The Standing Committee on Construction—created under the Construction Products Directive—accepts ETA proposals. After securing EOTA authorization, the manufacturer can place the CE mark on its product. An ETA is valid for a five-year period with one additional five-year extension allowed. EC officials are presuming that standards will be developed after this period and an ETA will no longer be needed.

Inspection, or Conformity Assessment, Process

EC directives spell out requirements for earning CE Marks. These range from a manufacturer's self-declaration of conformity to third-party testing and certification. Quality assurance audits are required in some cases (see "Products and Quality Assurance" later in this chapter).

The Modular Approach to Conformity Assessment

New EC conformity assessment procedures are subdivided, based on risk factors, into eight modules, each requiring a different inspection process that relates to both the design and production phases of product development. Risk factors play a major role in designating in which module a product will fit. The modules, listed below, dictate the level of certification required to earn a mark:

1. Manufacturer self-declaration of conformity
2. EC-type examination, the basic certification exam for product conformance to EC standards (called a lab test when chemicals analysis is involved)
3. EC declaration of conformity to type
4. Production quality assurance (ISO 9002/EN 29002)
5. Quality assurance: final inspection and testing (ISO 9003/EN 29003)
6. Product verification by an EC third party—series production
7. Product verification by an EC third party—unit production
8. Full quality assurance (ISO 9001/EN 29001)

Note: Modules 2 and 3 are not stand-alone conformity assessment options and must be used in conjunction with one another. Module 8 can also be used in conjunction with any one of modules 4 through 6 as specified in individual directives.

Because the EC wants to allow for choice, EC directives usually set a range of possible procedures manufacturers may follow to earn a CE Mark. For example, product certification under the EC directive on gas appliances can be accomplished through module 2, an EC-type examination, accompanied by any one of modules 3 through 6.

Manufacturer self-declaration of conformity to EC requirements is permitted for machinery (except for specified high-risk equipment), toys, electromagnetic compatibility, and weighing instruments for noncommercial use, as well as for certain classes of personal protective equipment, pressure vessels and equipment, medical devices, and recreational craft (with certain provisos specified in the individual directives).

Note: Manufacturers may face requirements for the same product addressed in different directives. For example, compressor generators may be covered under both the machine safety directive and the simple pressure vessel directive.

Certification Bodies

EC member states have the job of designating competent test labs and certification bodies when third-party certification is required. Member states notify the EC of their selections, which are then called "notified bodies." The commission has the right to request information from member states on the competence of certification bodies and can require verification of qualifications.

Notified bodies must be headquartered within the EU. Subsidiaries or related entities located in a third country will not be accepted. However, notified bodies have the right to subcontract specific tasks to contractors inside and outside the EU. Subcontractors must comply with the EU equivalent of ISO 9000—the EN 29000 standards in Europe—and test to the same standards as the notified bodies that hire them.

Foreign Certifiers. Foreign testing and certification bodies can perform third-party certification, accreditations, and approvals for the EU if their governments negotiate a mutual recognition agreement with EC officials. As noted in Chapter 3, the U.S. government and the EC have been currently negotiating such an agreement to allow recognition of U.S. testing and certification processes in Europe.

Example: Inspection Requirements

The following are some examples of the CE Mark inspection requirements for different product categories:

Simple Pressure Vessels. The directive allows the manufacturer to choose between two types of compliance assessment procedures at the design level—EC-type certification and certification of adequacy— and two types of compliance assessment at the construction level— EC declaration of conformity and EC verification.

Safety of Toys. Manufacturers are offered two means of demonstrating compliance with the essential requirements. After preparation of the technical file, they may (1) use the manufacturer's declaration of compliance with the harmonized standards or (2) conduct an EC-type examination through an authorized certification body that will offer proof of compliance.

Construction Products. (See also "Products and Quality Assurance" later in this chapter.) Either the manufacturer or an approved testing facility must perform the following procedures:

1. Conduct initial type tests.
2. Set up a regular test schedule for factory samples, and conduct those tests.
3. Make random tests of factory samples.
4. Test samples from batches that are ready for delivery, or already delivered.
5. Inspect the factory and the production system (third party).
6. Continuously monitor, evaluate, and assess in-house production (third party).

Electromagnetic Compatibility. The manufacturer may use a supplier's declaration of conformity, coupled with either a technical file or type examination, plus a declaration of conformity to match type approval.

Machinery. With the exception of dangerous machinery, the directive mandates preparation of a technical file plus a manufacturer's declaration of compliance. Declaration of compliance can be made on the basis of a third-party testing laboratory or by following an EC-type examination by a third party.

Tips on Earning CE Marks

The U.S. Commerce Department International Trade Administration offers the following "Ten Steps to a CE Mark":

1. Identify all applicable EU laws relating to a given product before attempting to jump into the CE Marking process.
2. Assess the product in relationship to all applicable requirements.

3. Choose the prescribed conformity assessment module.
4. Choose applicable CEN/CENELEC product standards and test methods.
5. If third-party testing is required, choose a notified body to perform conformity assessment work.
6. If desired, establish an authorized company representative to shepherd the project.
7. If required, prepare a technical file.
8. Maintain all documentation, supplier's declaration, and other files in one of the EC's official languages—English, French, or German.
9. Assemble required test approvals and certificates and prepare a declaration of conformity.
10. Apply the CE Mark on the product in accordance with the laws.

Case Study

Motorola's Radio Products Group, a subsidiary of Land Mobile Products in Europe, has been in the vanguard of American and European companies seeking CE Marks. In some cases, Motorola personnel have actually helped set some laboratory criteria and procedures for CE Marking for the 135 products for which they have sought CE Marks.

What Motorola managers learned was that the CE Mark criteria in their product areas resembled many of the European product marks they had already earned to do business in individual European countries. Even so, the company had to convince third-party testing labs that individual or rote tests were not required on all 135 radio models, but that conformity assessment could be accomplished through comparing similarities between products. The company approached foreign testing laboratories with respect and willingness to comply with the spirit of the CE Mark directives. The aim was not to save money but to save time and effort, both at present and in the future.

At this writing, Motorola has earned CE Marks for its entire product line. It has proved to be a major effort to accomplish this while simultaneously redesigning future product lines to meet European requirements. Expense has been a major consideration, of course. The cost of retroactively fixing the current product line was estimated at the cost of paying ten engineers their annual salaries. Future design work was proving less costly and was hailed as a means of getting a leg up on the competition. Some of the biggest challenges were not scientific ones, like ensuring compliance with frequency regulations, but administrative. For example, printing correct labels under the CE Mark regulations was trickier than meeting testing requirements.

Placement of the Mark

When manufacturers have completed the eight-step process already out-lined, they qualify to earn a CE Mark that is affixed to the product in much the same way that laboratory testing labels are affixed to products—elec-trical appliances, for example—in the United States. In most cases, inde-pendent testing laboratories carry out the testing that is necessary to earn this European seal of approval.

CE Marking is the placement of a metal label, sticker, or data plate on the actual product that has earned the CE Mark. If absolutely necessary be-cause of design issues, CE Marks can be affixed to packaging and to accom-panying manufacturer documents. The primary requirement is that the mark be visible, legible, and indelible and be at least five millimeters in height, if possible.

An identification number must follow the actual CE Mark. This num-ber identifies the body that was involved in the production control phase, the independent testing laboratories or testing houses that performed the certification work for the product. Other marking may be attached to the product as long as the CE Mark is clearly visible and legible.

Products and Quality Assurance

Although the CE Mark is not used as a quality standard, some of the direc-tives defining acceptable health, safety, and environmental standards also tacitly mandate the European version of the ISO 9000 international quality assurance standards as part of the certification process. The word *tacit* is applied here because the ISO 9000 standard may not be specifically re-quired, but the directives may not offer any other standards or guidelines as a substitute.

ISO 9000 certification is not a blanket requirement for all regulated products under CE Mark mandate, but it is the recommended base quality system for a number of product categories. Registration to one of the Eu-ropean standards equivalent to the ISO 9000 series—EN 29001 through 29003—is cited as a component of the product certification process for medical devices, construction products, personal protective equipment, telecommunications terminal equipment, gas appliances, and commercial scales. Planned EC legislation for pressure equipment, recreational craft, cable ways, and lifting equipment for persons also references EN 29000 compliance.

For most of these regulated products, ISO 9000 registration is an alter-native for product certification, not an absolute requirement. In fact, as cited in most EC legislation, quality system registration is neither manda-tory (there are other paths to product certification) nor is it a stand-alone procedure. Manufacturer compliance to either EN 29002 or 29003 is usually combined with product-type testing at the design stage for full certification to EC legal requirements.

Companies must make a careful reading of EC directives before choosing to ignore ISO 9000, however. In some sectors, such as computer switches, ISO 9000 compliance is not mandated, but no guidance documents exist for other certification procedures. That means that ISO 9000 certification may be a tacit requirement for earning a CE Mark in that category.

Example: Quality Systems Are Required

Terminal Equipment. The directive regarding terminal equipment relating to telecommunications was issued on April 29, 1991, and mandates EN 29001 and EN 29002 (ISO 9000 equivalents) as part of the requirement for passing an EC-type examination. Without the appropriate certificates, or without proof of conformity to these standards, the directive allows EU member states to "take all appropriate measures to withdraw such products from the market, or to prohibit or restrict their being placed on the market."

The EC directives call for companies doing business in Europe to have in place a quality system that meets or exceeds the ISO 9000 requirements. Outside Germany, there reportedly is no guidance document outlining how a manufacturer's declaration would substitute for ISO 9000 certification. American-based electronics companies want the EU to remove sections of directives that tacitly make the ISO 9000 quality assurance standard part of the CE Mark requirement in Europe. European standards officials at this writing were considering the situation, but had not offered any alternative to ISO 9000.

Medical Devices. For active implantable medical devices (such as pacemakers) the directive states that a quality system is required but does not identify any specific applicable standard. However, the directive describes use of ISO 9001 for a full quality assurance system and ISO 9002 as applied to the production aspect. EN 46001—specific requirements for medical devices—is also mentioned. No other quality system is described, and no other guidelines are provided. Manufacturers meeting ISO 9000 criteria are considered to meet the minimum criteria as laid out in the directive.

Example: Categories in Which
Quality Systems Are Not Mentioned

There are a number of product categories in which it is assumed that manufacturers either have quality systems in place, or for which no quality system is required. The following are some examples:

Electromagnetic Compatibility. No mention is made of setting up a quality system. This is considered the manufacturer's responsibility.

Construction Products. The directive presupposes that the manufacturer already has a quality system in place that proves that production is meeting relevant technical specifications. Some products under this category are required to pass quality certification requirements, but no specific quality system is required. However, the interpretative documents refer explicitly to the EN 29000 (ISO 9000) standards as a model.

Machinery. No mention is made of a quality system (see "Additional CE Marking Case Studies" later in this chapter).

Personal Protective Equipment. No quality system standard is mandated or even identified. The quality system criteria mentioned in the directive resembles ISO 9002.

Nonautomatic Weighing Instruments. No quality system is mandated or even identified. The quality system criteria mentioned in the directive resembles ISO 9002.

Appliances Burning Gaseous Fuel. The directive does not identify any quality system standard. However, the quality systems that are presumed to be in place resemble ISO 9002 for the production quality system and ISO 9003 for the final product quality system.

Additional CE Marking Case Studies

American manufacturers are just starting to enter the CE Marking process, which places them in a pioneering position. The following are some additional case studies based on the experiences of Weinstein Associates, Brunswick, Maine, CE Marking consultants with expertise in engineering and law. Most of the information presented here is based on machinery.

Case Study: Compact Disc Machine Manufacturer

Needs. An American manufacturer of compact disc machines exports products to a number of European countries, and one of their main concerns was identifying the EU directives that pertained to their products. It turned out their products fell under both the Machinery Safety Directive and the new Electromagnetic Capability Directive, which went into effect on January 1, 1996, and relates to moving equipment, electronics, robotics, and conveyor systems.

Focus. Weinstein Associates focused mainly on the risk assessment portion of the CE Marking process. They examined the product design and conducted a failure analysis for every moving part to ensure that there was nothing unsafe about the product. The detail work involved in this process was described as "excruciating."

Outcome. Product redesign was required.

Case Study: Vacuum Pump Manufacturer

Needs. A small American manufacturer of specialized vacuum pumps for woodworkers became aware of CE Marking while exporting to Europe. The owner did not become aware of the magnitude of meeting CE Marking requirements until he ordered some CE Marking labels and found that he could not simply affix them to his product.

Focus. Weinstein Associates determined that the vacuum pumps had to be CE Marked because they contained moving mechanical parts and were electrically driven. Compliance was required with both the Machinery Safety Directive and the Electromagnetic Capability Directive.

Outcome. The company was required to compile a technical construction file and maintain safety records for ten years. The owner also had to alert the vendor of the motor used in the product of EU documentation requirements because the motor fell under the Electromagnetic Capability Directive.

Note: If a product falls under one or more EC directives requiring CE Marking—but no lab testing is required—manufacturers still must perform risk assessment. They must also create a technical construction file that contains product drawings and documentation and a parts list to demonstrate that the product complies with European standards.

Commonly Asked Questions About CE Marking

Weinstein Associates commonly fields questions about CE Marking. The following are the concerns that arise most frequently:

What directives apply to my company? Companies must reach consultants or EU resource guides (see "CE Mark Resource Information" later in this chapter) and conduct a thorough study of the EC directives for CE Marking that may apply to their product. Labs that advertise CE Mark testing may also advise. Remember, a product may fall under one or more directives.

Are some European countries more strict about CE Marking compliance than others? The experience of American companies is that Germany and Sweden are very strict in terms of compliance; in England supplier's declaration suffices, and the French conduct spot checks at the border. Companies should be prepared to comply even though inspection varies from country to country.

How is a machine defined in European terms? The EC directives clearly define what is and what is not a machine. Companies should take care to ensure their product fits the European definition.

What if my product is assembled from components? Systems are examined as totalities. Each component may have earned a CE Mark, but they cannot be assembled and pass inspection unless the final product meets CE Marking requirements.

Is it necessary to earn a CE Mark if I am only shipping components? No, it is the integrator's responsibility to earn the mark. However, safety components must be CE certified and shipped with a declaration of incorporation.

When does a European notified body have to be involved in the process? In the machinery safety category is a list of high-risk equipment that requires notified-body involvement. Equipment that is not on this list can be self-certified.

How does my company perform risk assessment? CE Marking directives do not prescribe any one approach to risk assessment. Companies should ask consultants trained in engineering and risk assessment for advice.

If we are ISO 9000 registered, do we qualify for a CE Mark? No. In some cases (see "Products and Quality Assurance" earlier in this chapter) ISO 9000 is the recommended quality base that is tacitly required to begin the CE Mark process. CE Marking tests product performance and safety, not quality assurance.

If I manufacture in volume—a serial manufacturer—do I have to earn a CE Mark for every piece of equipment I sell, or can certification be based on a prototype? The first unit is certified. Then the company has to demonstrate that they have a quality program in place that will ensure continued product performance. ISO 9000 certification should be sufficient.

Note: Experience in the field indicates that earning CE Marks puts American companies ahead of the game, especially when meeting product liability law requirements in this country. Companies may find CE Mark requirements exacting, but they should bear in mind that a safe machine is a good machine.

Is the CE Mark a Trade Barrier?

As always, barriers to trade are in the eyes of the beholder. What one country or economic bloc considers necessary for internal market functions, another country or national bloc will find cumbersome and costly enough to label the requirement a trade barrier.

U.S. government officials are keeping tabs on the CE Mark to ensure that it does not create unnecessary costs through redundant product testing against U.S. standards, by shipping product designs overseas for testing, and by transporting foreign engineers to the United States for factory inspections. Current mutual recognition talks between the United States and Europe aim at eliminating this sort of wasted effort that stifles trade. However, the United States Trade Representative's office retains the CE Mark on its list of possible trade barriers worldwide.

Cases of American companies facing increased product regulation under the New Approach are starting to crop up in newspapers like *The Wall Street Journal.* Dormont, a Pennsylvania manufacturer of rubber hosing, has found countries like France and Britain maintaining their national standards—even creating new ones—and insisting that companies meet these standards along with earning the CE Mark that is supposed to obviate national requirements. General Electric is expected to take its battle with the German government over product entry to the Court of Justice based in Luxembourg.

European standards officials claim ignorance of all these cases. They maintain the EC party line that a "CE Mark on a product allows entry into all EU countries. If a product has received a CE Mark and it has been duly affixed, a member state cannot refuse this product in their market."

If CE Marks are refused, the issue is supposed to become a state affair. In this case, businesses should make sure the mark is "duly affixed" before filing an official complaint with a member state. States, in turn, are supposed to notify the EC if they feel they cannot accept a preapproved CE Mark. It will then be up to the commission, not an individual member state, to decide whether a product should be withdrawn from the market.

If the product is safe according to EU legislation, it is recommended that the company in question sign a grievance statement to the European Commission and win legal jurisdiction (to enter the European market). Companies should write to The Commission of the European Community, General Secretary, Directorate General 15, Brussels. (Members of the U.S. Mission to the EU based in Brussels can help with this process.)

In general, American companies working through the CE Mark system believe the requirements fit into the gray area of *potential* trade barriers. The process certainly is laborious and time-consuming. But, as Motorola is learning, jumping into the game early means possibly beating the competition—European as well as foreign—within the EU market.

Managers from U.S. companies now based in Europe also see the need for harmonization of EU product standards. What seems unreasonable, possibly even a trade barrier, from a distance appears more sensible when an American company is trying to function in the foreign market. A number of managers say they have changed their opinion of the CE Marking process since working with European certifiers. Europeans have confided that until the formation of the European Union in 1993 they had to contend with fragmented, dense, and highly diversified national markets and Europeans envied the United States its large, homogeneous market.

In the case of radio frequencies, for example, European harmonization efforts are more advanced than those in the United States simply because the airwaves are more crowded there. To meet CE Marking requirements companies sometimes have to go back to the design phase. Europeans contend that they are not trying to create market barriers through CE Marking and other harmonization efforts in the area of radio frequencies, even when product redesign is required. They argue that American companies in particular will be facing these same design issues down the road as frequencies in this country become overutilized.

CE Mark Resource Information

Information on European Commission directives, third-party certification bodies, and certification entities that have earned EC authorization are published regularly in the *European Community's Official Journal.* Contact:

Directorate-General III, Industry, The European Commission
200 Rue de la Loi
B-1049 BRUSSELS
BELGIUM
Tel: 32-2-299-1111
Fax: 32-2-295-3877

Commission of the European Communities
Washington, D.C. Office
2100 M Street, NW (7th floor)
Washington, DC 20037
Tel: 202-862-9500
Fax: 202-429-1766

For information on EC product safety legislation, policies, or practices, telephone Mary Saunders, Single Internal Market Information Service (SIMIS), Office of EC Affairs, U.S. Department of Commerce, 202-482-5276; fax: 202-482-2155.

Copies of standards, either European or international, may be ordered from

American National Standards Institute
11 West 42nd Street
New York, NY 10018
Tel: (212) 642-4900
Fax: (212) 302-1286

Global Engineering Documents
2805 McGaw Avenue
P.O. Box 19539
Irvine, CA 92714
Tel: (800) 854-7179, (714) 261-1455, (202) 429-2860
Fax: (714) 261-7892

Information Handling Services (IHS)
P.O. Box 1154
8 Inverness Way East
Englewood, CO 80150
Tel: (800) 241-7824, (303) 790-0600
Fax: (303) 799-4097

Additional information on EC testing and certification procedures and the role of ISO 9000 can be found in the SIMIS guide on the topic. Call SIMIS at 202-377-5276.

Keymarking

The European Committee for Standardization (CEN) and the European Committee for Electrotechnical Standardization (CENELEC)—CEN/CENELEC—are promoting a scheme called Keymarking that provides a more stringent set of requirements than the CE Mark in the product liability area. A fully voluntary program, the Keymark is largely considered a marketing tool for companies that want to offer indication of a superior product to consumers.

CEN/CENELEC are the two major European nonprofit standard bodies entrusted with creating harmonized EU standards. The Keymark is their program, not the EU's, and is compatible with New Approach directives, the CE Mark, and national certification marks.

For more information contact the CEN Central Secretariat or the CENELEC Central Secretariat, both located at rue de Stassart, 36, B-1050 Brussels. The CEN Central Secretariat's phone number is 32 2 550 08 11; for the CENELEC Central Secretariat, phone 32 2 519 68 71.

Resources

International Trade Administration, "EC Testing and Certification Procedures Under the Internal Market Program," Commerce Department.

International Trade Administration, U.S. Department of Commerce, "Background: Product Approval in the European Union" [document].

Rensberger, Roger A., and van de Zande, Rene, *Standards Setting in the European Union: Standards Organizations and Officials in EU Standards Activities*, NIST Special Publication.

Wettig, Jurgen, Directorate-General III, Industry, European Commission, "Information About the CE-Marking."

Part III

The International Standards System

8

How the International Standards System Works: The Players, the Issues

Questions the Reader Will Find Addressed in This Chapter

1. What is the ISO/IEC system?
2. Who are ISO members and what do they do?
3. What types of membership does ISO offer?
4. How is ISO organized and governed?
5. What are the committees for policy development?
6. How do ISO committees develop policy?
7. How is committee work put into action?
8. Who works on general standardization issues?
9. Who does the technical work?
10. How do member bodies participate in technical concerns?
11. How does technical work originate?
12. What are the steps from draft to international standard?
13. How are standards revised?
14. How does the International Electrotechnical Commission function?
15. What is the IECQ system?
16. How do ISO and IEC work together?
17. What are the joint ISO/IEC committees?
18. What official languages are used?
19. How do ISO and IEC relate to the European Union?
20. How do the goals of ISO/IEC and ISO 9000 differ?
21. How does Quality System Assessment Recognition solve problems resulting from the worldwide acceptance of ISO 9000?
22. How will QSAR work?

To understand how much international standards are growing in world-wide importance, browse through the International Organization for

Standardization's (ISO) 1996 budget requests. Woven through a document called "ISO Central Secretariat Programmatic Assumptions for 1996" is a call for increased financial support for ISO programs. These appeals do not stem from overspending, but rather are made to meet needs caused by rampant growth.

There are other indications that international standards have moved to center stage. The 1994 Uruguay Round of the General Agreement on Tariffs and Trade (GATT) recognized that nontariff trade barriers were not only increasing in response to drops in direct protectionist activities, but that these sort of barriers can be tremendously costly. As discussed in Chapter 12, GATT established new World Trade Organization (WTO) codes on technical barriers to trade (The Standards Code) and on trade and the environment.

In the spring of 1995, a major U.S. business publication picked up on growing tensions between the U.S. software industry and Japan over alleged misuse of the ISO 9000 series. Finally, the mainline media was recognizing the increasingly important role of international standards in the era of GATT, which is now under the auspices of the World Trade Organization.

Other standards disputes are brewing throughout the world. As noted in earlier chapters, major electronics giants are fighting to streamline the ISO 9000 registration system. And the Korean government has been making noises about refusing to recognize the national ISO 9000 accreditation bodies of other nations. On a more positive note, ISO committees are actively working to create criteria for registrars and accreditation bodies worldwide. The United States and the European Union, in the meantime, are inching toward mutual recognition of testing laboratory results, which will free trade between both entities.

Chapter 1 notes the interlocking of national/regional standards systems and the international standards system with ISO and IEC sitting at the heart of international standards development worldwide. This chapter moves in for a closer look at the ISO, IEC, their committees, subcommittees, and working groups, as well as the issues they are confronting. Since this chapter considers standards from a global viewpoint, key international standards organizations are listed in Appendix A of the chapter.

The next two chapters examine two major ISO management standards—ISO 9000 and ISO 14000. Chapter 11 focuses on standards players worldwide and standards-related activities. And Chapter 12 looks at international standards trends.

Review

- ISO, IEC, and ITU are the three principal international standardization bodies.

- ISO is a worldwide federation of 118 national standards bodies, each representing the standards concerns of their country. Its purpose is to promote the development of standardization and related activities worldwide.

- In its preparation of international standards, ISO brings together the interests of producers, users (including consumers), governments, and the scientific community. This work is carried out through 2,832 technical bodies. Approximately forty thousand experts from all parts of the world participate each year in the ISO technical work, which to date has resulted in the publication of 10,060 ISO standards.

- The result of this activity is ISO international standards whose scope includes all fields except electrical and electronic engineering standards. Once again, these are the purview of the IEC.

- IEC members come from the national committees of each participating country, representing the electrotechnical interests in the country concerned. The individual national committees include manufacturers, users, governmental authorities, and teaching and professional bodies. Most national committees are industry- and government-backed.

- Over the years, numerous liaisons have been established between ISO and IEC committees. Specifically, a joint ISO/IEC technical committee has been established in the field of information technology.

- The International Telecommunication Union (ITU) prepares "recommendations" that cover the "information highway" industries, from telephones to radio, cable TV, and so on. The ITU and the ISO are both located in Geneva and work frequently together.

The ISO/IEC System

- The primary function of the ISO/IEC system is to garner international consensus in the creation of international standards. The process of negotiation and consensus between countries is carried out through the technical committees of ISO and IEC. These committees consist of delegations appointed by national standards bodies and given the job of representing the consolidated national position on a given subject.

- Every member body has the right to participate in any of the international technical committees and subcommittees established to draft standards in the different fields. The work of the technical committees and subcommittees is highly decentralized, with technical committees meeting worldwide. On average, there are fifteen meetings taking place on any given workday throughout the world. Approximately forty thousand voluntary delegates participate in the actual creation of international standards.

- Central offices for both organizations are maintained in Geneva,

Switzerland, where a small staff carries out the planning and coordination of technical committee work and international meetings. The ISO's Central Secretariat also publishes the ISO standards.

A Closer Look at the International Standards System

ISO administrative offices, known as the Central Secretariat, are housed in a modern building on the Rue de Varembe in Geneva. ISO headquarters is situated in Geneva's international sector. The United Nations' impressive headquarters and grounds are a stone's throw from ISO, and the World Trade Organization (WTO) sits in an elegant structure not far away on the shores of Lake Geneva.

For such a large, significant organization, ISO's headquarters are actually quite modest, because most of the organization's activity takes place far from Geneva in working groups scattered throughout the world. A small central staff is based in Geneva to coordinate ISO operations, administer voting and approval procedures, and publish international standards.

Following is a more in-depth look at the international standards system with primary focus on ISO, the organization serving as the fulcrum of much of the world's standardization work. As noted, IEC focuses mainly on electrotechnical issues, while ISO's work covers a wide array of technical matters, both in terms of products and quality assurance. Per agreement, ISO involves IEC in much of its standards-related work to ensure that pertinent electrotechnical issues are covered.

ISO Members

The 118 ISO members are national standards bodies that are "the most representative of standardization" in their own country. Only one standards body per country can act as an ISO member. More than 70 percent of ISO member bodies represent government institutions. Members can participate and exercise full voting rights on any ISO technical committee, are eligible for ISO Council membership, and sit in the ISO General Assembly.

See Appendix B to this chapter for the current ISO membership list.

Each member body brings to ISO its own national concerns and various degrees of responsibility within its own national standards system. For example, metrology is considered the responsibility of the standards bodies in only about a third of the member bodies. But for the rest of the member bodies, metrology issues are handled outside the standards sphere. Quality and certification matters may also fall outside the purview of some member bodies.

Types of Membership

ISO offers different types of memberships to accommodate the varying re-sources of member bodies.

- *Full Members.* Full members enjoy all the rights of voting and par-ticipation. There are currently eighty-five full members of ISO.

Example

Government records show the American National Standards Institute (ANSI) pays $2 million annually in dues to ISO and IEC. For this amount—which apparently reflects real costs of maintaining a U.S. presence in the international system—ANSI as the U.S. representative receives one vote.

- *Correspondent Members.* A correspondent member is normally an or-ganization representing a developing country that does not yet have its own national standards body. At present, ISO has twenty-four correspon-dent members, most of which are government institutions. Correspondent members do not actively participate in technical work. They are entitled to be kept fully informed about the work of interest to them and to attend the General Assembly as observers.

- *Subscriber Membership.* For very small countries, ISO recently estab-lished a third category, called a subscriber membership. Subscriber mem-bers pay reduced membership fees for the privilege of keeping abreast of ISO standardization activities. At present, ISO has nine subscriber members.

ISO Organization and Government

Like many nonprofit organizations, ISO functions with small, paid ad-ministrative staffs who work under the direction of the secretary-general. ISO's administrative staff coordinates the efforts of nearly forty thousand volunteers who carry out the technical work of developing standards worldwide.

The staff, in turn, works with a number of governing bodies and policy-making committees that do everything from determining the organization's budget and creating technical committees to providing a structure for ISO worldwide communications and promoting ISO and standards interests internationally.

In 1993, ISO initiated a major restructuring of its governance procedures in an effort to allow for more input from a wider variety of member bodies. Geographic representation was encouraged—as was industrial diversity—by the addition of appointed posts.

ISO has a governing system that aims for consensus. Critics have raised concerns that this sort of cumbersome system does not work well in crisis or when speedy decisions are necessary, an issue ISO officials considered when restructuring the organization in 1993. At that time the Executive Board was dissolved, at its own recommendation, with duties transferred to a reconstituted ISO Council and Technical Management Board.

The main ISO governing bodies and policy committees are considered next and are displayed visually in Figure 8-1.

Figure 8-1. ISO organizational structure.

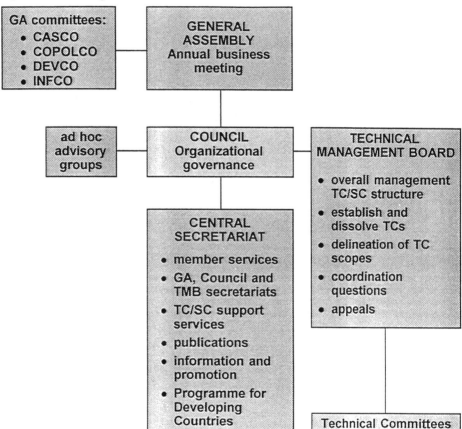

General Assembly

The General Assembly is the highest governing authority of the ISO. Only the General Assembly decides ISO policy, which is developed within the ISO Council and Technical Management Board.

Member bodies nominate delegates to the ISO General Assembly, which then elects the ISO Council president and officers. Correspondent and subscriber members may attend as observers. The Central Secretariat handles all administrative tasks for the General Assembly and subsidiary bodies.

During the 1993 restructuring, the annual General Assembly meeting was assigned the task of reviewing, discussing, and taking action relating to creation of an ISO annual report, a treasurer's report on the financial status of the Central Secretariat, and a multiyear strategic plan with financial implications. Certain parts of the annual business agenda then delegated to the council reverted to the General Assembly.

Also reporting to the General Assembly are policy development committees (see "Policy Development Committees" later in this chapter) that deal with matters of interest to the total membership.

The Council

The ISO Council is the main ISO governing body. One of its prime duties is setting the Central Secretariat's annual budget. The council is made up of thirteen elected and five appointed member bodies. This body, in turn, appoints a treasurer and twelve members of the Technical Management Board. The Technical Management Board oversees the operation of ISO technical committees.

The General Assembly elects the council president and two vice presidents. The president, who usually chairs the council, is elected for a three-year term. One term is served as president-elect. The term is not renewable.

In 1993, it was agreed to have two vice presidents: a vice president for policy, who is a member body chief executive officer or a business executive, serving a two-year term of office, eligible for two consecutive terms; and a vice president for technology, who serves as chairman of the Technical Management Board for a three-year term of office and is eligible for two consecutive terms.

In an attempt to bring more input into the process, council members' terms of office were reduced to two years during the 1993 ISO governance restructuring. It was emphasized at this time that elections of council members should take broad geographic representation and industrial diversity into consideration.

Currently council members include AFNOR of France, ANSI of the

United States, CSBTS (China), DIN (Germany), GOST R (Russian Federation), INN (Chile), INNORPI (Tunisia), IPQ (Portugal), JISC (Japan), KIAA (Republic of Korea), SABS (South Africa), SII (Israel), SIRIM (Malaysia), SMIS (Slovenia), TTBS (Trinidad and Tobago), UNI (Italy), BSI (Britain), and ABNT of Brazil.

The council appoints regional liaison officers to help the secretary-general (ISO director) represent ISO interests and concerns in their regions. Regional liaison officers also act as the advisory committee to the Committee on Developing Country Matters (DEVCO).

Policy Development Committees

Membership for major ISO policy committees is open to all interested member bodies on either a participating or observer basis. Correspondent members can observe. The following are the four major ISO policy development committees:

1. *Committee on Conformity Assessment (CASCO).* Currently, fifty-six member bodies belong to CASCO as active participants and sixteen other countries act as observers. CASCO's main goals and activities are:

- To study means of assessing the conformity of products, processes, services, and quality systems to appropriate standards or other technical specifications
- To prepare international guides relating to the testing, inspection, and certification of products, processes, and services, and the assessment of quality systems, testing laboratories, inspection bodies, certification bodies, and their operation and acceptance
- To promote mutual recognition and acceptance of national and regional conformity assessment systems, and the appropriate use of international standards for testing, inspection, certification, assessment, and related purposes

Note: ISO/CASCO has completed the development of guidelines for accreditation of registration-certification bodies. Both ISO and IEC have accepted them, and they are soon to be published as ISO/IEC guides.

2. *Committee on Consumer Policy (COPOLCO).* Currently, there are thirty-three members actively participating in COPOLCO and thirty-four observers. COPOLCO's goals and activities are:

- To study means of assisting consumers to benefit from standardization and means of improving their participation in national and international standardization

- To promote, from a standardization perspective, the information, training, and protection of consumers
- To provide a forum for the exchange of experience on consumer participation, the implementation of standards in the consumer field, and any other question of interest to consumers in national and international standardization
- To maintain contact with various ISO offices whose work is related to consumer interests

3. *Committee on Developing Country Matters (DEVCO).* At present, fifty-six member bodies actively participate in DEVCO work and twenty-six are observers. Main DEVCO goals and activities are:

- To identify the needs and requirements of the developing countries in the fields of standardization and related areas (e.g., quality control, metrology, and certification) and to assist the developing countries as necessary in defining those needs and requirements
- To recommend ways of helping the developing countries meet standards-related goals
- To provide a forum for the discussion of all aspects of standardization and related activities in developing countries, as well as offer a means of sharing experience in coordination with the United Nations and other ISO and IEC policy development committees
- To advise the General Assembly on standardization matters that affect the developing world

4. *Committee on Information Systems and Services (INFCO).* At this time sixty-one countries are active participants in INFCO and sixteen are observers. INFCO's main goals and activities are:

- To coordinate and harmonize the activities of ISO and its members in relation to information services, databases, marketing and sales of standards, technical regulations, and related matters, including providing these services and products in electronic form
- To monitor and guide the activities of ISONET (see next section) and to promote its activities
- To advise the General Assembly on policy development relating to the above matters

Information Services

There are two computer communication systems:

1. *ISO Information Network (ISONET).* ISONET is governed by INFCO, and the ISONET Management Board runs the day-to-day operations of this worldwide communication network. ISONET works both nationally and internationally to coordinate and systematize information exchange on standards and standards-type documents through computer linkage to ISO information centers worldwide. Each of ISONET's seventy-two members is responsible for dissemination of information on standards, technical regulations, and standards-related matters within its own territory or area of technical concern.

2. *ISO Online.* As of the beginning of 1995, the ISO has operated an electronic information service to Internet users via the World Wide Web. ISO Online provides the following services in both English and French:

- The full catalog of ISO International Standards and drafts classified into technical fields, groups, and subgroups
- Complete lists of ISO members and ISO technical committees
- The meetings calendar of ISO technical committees and subcommittees
- General background on the ISO, its structure and organization, the scope of activity of each technical committee, and information on contacting their secretariats
- Facts on ISO 9000 from the ISO 9000 Forum information service
- Information on the many other publications that ISO produces in addition to *International Standards,* and on upcoming events
- The texts of ISO press releases

ISO Online is located at the ISO Central Secretariat in Geneva. Users can gain access through the following Uniform Resource Locator (URL): http://www.iso.ch/

For more information on ISO Online services, or for help in gaining access to ISO Online, contact the Webmaster at: webmaster@isocs.iso.ch

For general information: central@isocs.iso.ch

Or send press inquiries to Roger Frost, press officer: frost@isocs.iso.ch

ISO Policy Development Committees in Practice

ISO policy development committees are special advisory groups with tremendous influence on both the development of standards through technical groups and how standards practices take place worldwide. ISO Policy Development Committees cannot act by fiat. The General Assembly must approve all recommendations for them to be put into action. However, the committees are highly regarded and respected by ISO governing bodies and the membership at large.

Example

CASCO develops ISO/IEC Guides on aspects of conformity assessment. These are voluntary, but the criteria they contain represent an international consensus on what constitutes acceptable practice. Their use contributes to the consistency and coherence of conformity assessment worldwide, facilitating global trade.

How Committee Work Is Put Into Action

Responding to inquiries from ISO members and governing bodies, as well as to internal committee concerns, the policy development committees conduct studies—or public sessions such as workshops and seminars—to investigate issues for ISO to address. These issues may range from international accreditation policies to new areas of standards focus. Proposals are then written and sent to the General Assembly for a vote.

Example

At the 1994 General Assembly, COPOLCO raised the issue of whether the service sector could benefit from international standards. With permission from the assembly, COPOLCO then held a workshop in 1995 to investigate the need for standards in this sector. As a result, the committee recommended that the issue of international standardization for services be given high priority within ISO. It was further recommended that there be intensive study, review, and strategic consideration of how standardization work for services could be identified, promoted, and enhanced within future ISO programs or in collaboration with its partners.

Since then, encouraging new work on service-sector standards has been incorporated within ISO's long-range strategies. In addition, the ISO Central Secretariat is working closely with the World Trade Organization to identify service sectors that could most benefit from harmonization of business practices through standards. The aim, once again, is to facilitate world trade.

Example

At the 1995 General Assembly, the ISO members accepted a proposal from COPOLCO for a revision of *ISO/IEC Guide 50: Child Safety and Standards, General Guidelines,* which reflected recent developments in safety philosophy. The ad hoc ISO/IEC Technical Advisory Group will actually handle the revisions, which will then be circulated to other technical committees preparing standards that include safety aspects.

General Standardization Principles

As with ISO policy committees, general standardization committee membership is open to all member bodies as active participants or observers. Correspondent members can observe. *The Committee on Reference Materials (REMCO)* is the main committee that addresses general standardization principles. REMCO has nineteen participating member bodies and thirty-four observers at this writing. Established in 1975 as an international seminar on Certified Reference Material (CRM), the committee's main goals and activities include:

- Carrying out and encouraging a broad international effort for harmonization and promotion of certified reference materials and their applications
- Establishing definitions, categories, levels, and classification of reference materials, as well as proposing action on reference materials required for ISO work
- Formulating criteria for the application of sources and references in ISO documents
- Preparing guidelines for technical committees for making reference to reference materials in ISO documents

Example

The guidelines that REMCO develops are especially useful in the field of measurements, where results have to stand up to serious scrutiny. Chemical measurements of various kinds increasingly form the basis of important decisions in technical as well as social fields because they can serve as the basis for national, regional, and international environmental regulations. Certified reference materials often serve as the basis for these sorts of measurements.

   Although considered highly prestigious, REMCO has no legislation authority and the guidelines it develops are voluntary. Many of the experts serving on REMCO are considered worldwide leaders in their field. For this reason, the guidelines are widely accepted and used by industries and governments alike.

Note: The Committee on Standardization Principles (STACO) has been disbanded and its responsibilities redistributed. Its main goals and activities included the following:

- Providing an international forum for the exchange of views and sharing of experience relating to fundamental aspects of standardization

- Serving as a research arm for the ISO Technical Management Board on subjects related to the basic principles of standardization, including methodology and terminology

Technical Work

Currently, there are 185 technical committees, 636 subcommittees, 1,975 working groups, and 36 ad hoc study groups that carry on the actual work of developing international standards that ISO members then disseminate.

- *Technical Committees (TCs).* The actual work of drafting international standards takes place in technical committees. The ISO Technical Management Board makes the decision to establish a technical committee and defines the scope of its coverage. The TC defines its own work program within the parameters of the general assignment. Technical committees have the right to establish subcommittees, which are commonly called SCs, and working groups (WGs).
- *Technical Management Board.* As previously noted, the Technical Management Board, also known as the Technical Board, is made up of twelve appointed council members with the technical vice president serving as chair. Its main duty is to oversee technical committees. As part of this function, the Technical Management Board is responsible for general management of the technical committee/subcommittee structure, including the establishment and dissolution of TCs, the assignment of TC secretariats, revision of the ISO directives for technical work, and annual reports and recommendations of REMCO.

The board resolves technical coordination issues between TCs, vis-à-vis IEC and other international or regional organizations; appeals against TC/SC action or inaction; seeks to correct unsatisfactory performance of TC secretariats; and engages in general monitoring of TC/SC project management requirements.

- *Technical Advisory Groups (TAGs).* The Technical Management Board (and the IEC Committee on Action in some cases) sets up TAGs when necessary to advise the board (and IEC Committee) on matters of basic, sectoral and cross-sectoral coordination, coherent planning, and the needs for new work. The ISO TAGs are appointed from Central Secretariat staffers and the ISO/IEC TAG members come from either ISO or IEC central offices. TAGs exist in the following technical categories: TAG 4, metrology; TAG 8, building; TAG 9, distribution of goods; ISO/IEC JTAG 1, health care technology; and ISO/IEC JTAG 2, image technology.
- *Technical Committee Chairmen.* Chairmen are nominated for three-year terms through the Technical Management Board. They do not have to

represent the country holding the secretariat. The ISO Technical Management Board and IEC Council are responsible for naming chairmen to their joint technical committees.

   • *Secretariats and Conveners.* ISO national members who assume the administration of technical committees are called secretariats. They are responsible for appointing a chairman and committee secretary, coordinating committee activity, and serving as liaisons to ISO member bodies. The Technical Management Board makes these assignments for technical committees. The "parent" TC appoints a convener for each working group it establishes.

Member Body Participation

Member bodies have the right to be represented on any technical committee that concerns them. When a member body takes an active role in a technical committee or subcommittee it is called a participating member. As a participating member, it is obligated to vote and, when possible, attend technical committee meetings. One of the participating members will be designated secretariat. Member bodies are called observers when they only want to be kept informed of committee or subcommittee work.

How Technical Work Originates

Proposals to begin new standards work in a technical field usually come from within ISO, but may also originate at the recommendation of another international organization. Technical committees can be established at the request of five member bodies. When a new work item is assigned for development as an International Standard it is circulated within the TC or SC as a committee draft (CD).

From Draft to International Standard

There are many stages from the time ISO or an international body recommends creation of an International Standard to the acceptance of a standard for international dissemination. The general steps in the life of an International Standard are as follows:

   1. Technical committees, subcommittees, and working groups turn the committee draft (CD) into what is known as a draft proposal.
   2. The draft proposal is circulated for study within the technical committee or subcommittee.

3. When the subcommittee approves the draft proposal it becomes a draft International Standard (DIS). The DIS is submitted to the technical committee with overall responsibility for the subject area.
4. When the committee reaches consensus on the document it is submitted to ISO Central Secretariat for registration as a draft International Standard (DIS).
5. The Central Secretariat is allotted four weeks to circulate the DIS to all member bodies for a five months' vote.
6. Depending on the voting and eventual comments, the document may need to be modified.
7. Once modifications are complete, the final draft International Standard (FDIS) is circulated to all national bodies for a two months' vote.

Figure 8-2 provides a list of committee drafts and draft international standards being considered during a one-month period.

More Details on the Voting Process

- Seventy-five percent of the member bodies that cast a vote must approve of the standard for it to be accepted and published as an international standard. The balloting process can take anywhere from eighteen to thirty-six months. Several ballots may be taken at all levels until an acceptable level of agreement is reached.
- Member bodies are not required to vote on standards they believe to be irrelevant to their industry.
- On average, it takes up to eight months from the time a member body vote is taken until a revised text is proofed and then a standard is published.
- A positive vote by a member body may be accompanied by editorial or minor technical comments, on the understanding that the secretary, in consultation with the chairman of the technical committee or subcommittee, will decide how to deal with them.
- At any time the TC may decide not to press to create an international standard because of problems reaching a consensus, developmental dilemmas, or other reasons. In those cases, the TC may authorize publication of a technical report on the topic.
- If the overall voting is negative, the draft goes back to the technical committee or subcommittee, which may decide to submit a modified version for voting by ISO member bodies.

(For more specific information on this subject, see the *ISO/IEC Directives, Part I: Procedures for the Technical Work,* 3rd edition, 1995.)

Figure 8-2. International standards in progress.

An International Standard is the result of an agreement between the member bodies of ISO. A first important step toward an International Standard takes the form of a committee draft (CD)—this is circulated for study within an ISO technical committee. When consensus has been reached within the technical committee, the document is sent to the Central Secretariat for processing as a draft International Standard (DIS). The DIS is submitted to all ISO member bodies for voting; publication as an International Standard requires approval by at least 75% of the member bodies casting a vote.

CD registered

(Period from 14 April 1995 to 11 May 1995)

These documents are currently under consideration in the appropriate ISO technical committee. They have been registered at the Central Secretariat.

TC 22	**Road vehicles**
CD 11992-3	Electrical connections between commercial vehicles and trailers equipped with 24V systems—Interchange of digital information—Part 3: Application layer for non-braking equipment
CD 12097-1	Road vehicles—Environmental simulation and testing of air bags—Part 1: Terminology
CD 14230-1	Keyword protocol 2000—Part 1: Physical layer
CD 14230-2	Keyword protocol 2000—Part 2: Communication
CD 14230-3	Keyword protocol 2000—Part 3: Implementation
TC 28	**Petroleum products and lubricants**
CD 6297	Petroleum products—Aviation and distillate fuels containing a static dissipator additive—Determination of electrical conductivity (Revision of ISO 6297:1993)
TC 34	**Agricultural food products**
CD 14797	Animal feeding stuffs—Determination of furazolidone content—Method using high-performance liquid chromatography
TC 43	**Acoustics**
CD 3747	Acoustics—Determination of sound power levels of noise sources—Survey method using a reference sound source (Revision of ISO 3747:1987)
CD 4869-4	Acoustics—Hearing protectors—Part 4: Methods for the measurement of sound attenuation of amplitude-sensitive hearing protectors
CD 13475-2	Acoustics—Determination of sound emission quantities for stationary sirens—Part 2: Test room measurements
TC 92	**Fire tests on building materials, components and structures**
CD 10294-2	Fire-resistant tests—Fire dampers for air distribution

Source: ISO Bulletin, June 1995.

	systems—Part 2: Classification, criteria and field of application of test results documents	
CD 10294-3	Fire-resistant tests—Fire dampers for air distribution systems—Part 3: Commentary document	
TC 115	**Pumps**	
CD 12396	Centrifugal pumps—Forces and moments applied to flanges	
TC 184	**Industrial automation systems and integration**	
ISO 8373:1994/ DAM 1	Manipulation industrial robots—Vocabulary Addendum 1: Annex B—Multilingual annex	

DIS circulated

(Period from 14 April 1995 to 11 May 1995)

These documents have obtained substantial support within the appropriate ISO technical committee. They have been submitted to the ISO member bodies for voting by the date shown.

		Vote terminates
JTC 1	**Information technology**	
ISO/IEC ISO 7813:1990/ DAM 1	Identification cards—Financial transaction cards AMENDMENT 1	1995-09-11
ISO/IEC 9945-1:1990/ DAM 2	Information technology—Portable Operating System Interface (POSIX)— Part 1: System Application Program Interface (AOI) (C Language) AMENDMENT 2: Threads Extension	1995-09-04
ISO/IEC 10164-13/ DAM 1	Information technology—Open Systems Interconnection—Systems Management: Summarization Function AMENDMENT 1: ICS proforma	1995-09-18
ISO/IEC 10728:1993/ DAM 2	Information technology—Information Resource Dictionary System (IRDS) Services Interface AMENDMENT 2: ADA Language Binding	1995-09-04
ISO/IEC DISP 12059-13	Information technology—International Standardized Profiles—OSI Management—Common information for management functions—Part 13: Summarization function	1995-09-04
TC 4	**Rolling bearings**	
DIS 3030	Needle roller bearings—Radial needle roller and cage assemblies—Boundary dimensions and tolerances (Revision of ISO 3030: 1974)	1995-11-11

Note: There is some disgruntlement in U.S. standards circles that since the formation of the European Union the United States is underrepresented in the ISO/IEC system. ANSI, the U.S. representative, is allowed one vote in each system as opposed to at least fifteen votes for the EU. That is because individual European countries are still represented as ISO members but now also act under the legislative powers of the EU. No solution is being offered on an official basis at this time.

Case Study

The ISO 9000 standards series is likely the most famous standard ISO has ever developed. The concept behind ISO 9000 of documenting work procedures to track performance consistency emerged from the American military's quality efforts that were designed during World War II.

In the decades following the war, the commercial sector worldwide became familiar with defense department practices and started adapting them for commercial use. In 1975 Canada created a national quality assurance standard for commercial application called the CS A 299 standard. The United Kingdom followed with a similar standard—BS 5750.

The British and Canadian models were not identical. Europe adapted the British model, and a number of countries, including Australia and New Zealand, followed the Canadian route. German standards officials called for a uniform model.

Addressing these concerns, ISO in 1980 formed Technical Committee (TC) 176, the International Technical Committee on Quality Assurance and Quality Management, to work on developing an international quality assurance standard. Canada was asked to hold the secretariat for TC 176, and the first meeting was held in Ottawa. It took seven years to develop the ISO 9000 series, with the British three-part model eventually serving as the basis when the series was released in 1987.

Here are some pertinent dates from that developmental period:

- *1979:* A working group of experts was formed to represent their member countries' interests on quality assurance.
- *1980:* TC 176 is formed and its first meeting takes place in Ottawa.
- *1983–1984:* A committee draft of the ISO 9000 series is circulated to all member bodies, who then circulate the draft within their country's standards bodies for comment. Later that year the committee draft is accepted as a draft International Standard.
- *1987:* The ISO 9000 Standards Series is published after several years of refinement and revisions.

These are rough dates culled from members of TC 176. In general, each of the pertinent phases—committee draft, draft International Standard, and International Standard being readied for publication—took place over a period of at least a year.

Standards Revisions

Technical evolution, new methods and materials, and new quality and safety requirements are among the many factors that will make a standard dated or even obsolete. To keep standards as current as possible, ISO rules mandate standards review at least every five years.

International Electrotechnical Commission

As noted, the aim of the International Electrotechnical Commission (IEC) is to promote international cooperation on all standardization issues that relate to electricity and electrical engineering.

IEC members include forty-two national committees representing the majority of the world's population and the bulk of world energy consumption. Delegates come from national standardization bodies, many of which are government-backed. Delegates to national committees are expected to represent a wide spectrum of related interests in their own countries, from the manufacturer's perspective to users, government authorities, and educational and professional organizations.

IEC operates a "registered subscriber's scheme" for countries that have not established national committees. Subscribers may be electric power companies, manufacturers, telecommunications authorities, as well as national standards bodies. Observer status is allowed, but subscribers cannot vote.

Like ISO, IEC works through a system of technical committees and subcommittees to develop standards in the electrotechnical sector. However, its structure and working procedures are different from ISO's. While ISO secretariats do most of their organizational work, from the distribution of documents to duplication, IEC committees rely heavily on their Geneva headquarters. Since the late 1980s, ISO and IEC have been working on harmonizing their procedures and work methods.

The IECQ System

In 1982, IEC introduced what is known as the IECQ third-party certification system for manufacturers and users of electronic components worldwide. Manufacturers earn an IECQ Certificate of Conformity after demonstrating that a component conforms to prescribed quality levels.

IEC operates the IECQ certification program through a network of member countries. Each must operate a National Authorized Institution (NAI) and a National Standards Organization (NSO) that comply with IECQ rules. Each must agree to recognize all IECQ regulations for manufacturers, distributors, and test labs. Under this system, manufacturers and test laboratories must also comply with ISO 9001 or 9002 requirements (or *ISO/IEC Guide 25* for test laboratories).

Relationship With ISO

ISO and IEC have a formal agreement to complement each other's work without duplicating efforts in the field of international standardization. Questions related to electrical and electronic engineering are IEC's responsibility, with ISO handling other subject areas. When gray areas arise, the two organizations come to a decision on which will assume primary responsibility through mutual agreement.

ISO and IEC team up on many standardization issues that relate to electrical and other concerns. Some of the committees established for this purpose are the following:

• *Joint Technical Committees.* When ISO and IEC team up on standards, they form what is called a Joint Technical Committee, or JTC. Only one such committee exists to date, JTC 1, Information Technology.

• *ISO/IEC Joint Technical Programming Committee.* The ISO/IEC JTPC resolves work allocation and organizational questions in an effort to reduce overlap and redundancy between the two organizations, especially relating to technical committees and standards development.

• *Joint Presidents' Coordination Group (JPCG).* The ISO/IEC presidents, secretaries-general, president-elect, or immediate past president and ISO vice president serve on this joint committee. JPCG's main goal is to strengthen and advance the voluntary international standards system of ISO and IEC through coherent policies and cooperation. It also ensures that appropriate collaboration exists with the International Telecommunication Union (ITU) at relevant levels and in appropriate fields. The ITU secretary-general or representative may attend sessions when there are interests common to all three organizations, and sometimes specialists are brought in to address specific issues.

Official Languages. Both ISO and IEC have adopted French, English, and Russian as their official languages. Documents are developed and distributed in both English and French. Technical committee and subcommittee meetings may be conducted in both English and French while working group sessions are generally held in one language. The Russian member body provides interpreters and translators.

ISO/IEC'S Relationship With the European Union

In 1991, the European Committee for Standardization's (CEN) administrative board concluded a technical cooperation agreement with ISO/IEC aimed at avoiding duplication of standardization work. Under the so-called Vienna Agreement, CEN works with ISO to harmonize European and international standards, reduce technical barriers to trade within its sector, and use international standards to meet deadlines for EU standards development.

The Vienna Agreement allowed for the general exchange of information, cooperation on standards drafting between CEN and ISO organizations, and the adoption of existing international standards as European standards. The same year the European Committee for Electrotechnical Standardization (CENELEC) and IEC came to a similar arrangement under the so-called Lugano Agreement of 1991. In both arrangements CEN/CENELEC will develop their own standards only when international standards do not exist and are unlikely to be developed to meet specific European needs. To this end, the ISO may appoint representatives to CEN/CENELEC technical committees, and vice versa.

ISO/IEC Tackling Development Issues

ISO and IEC create standards but do not administer standards programs. Until the advent of ISO 9000, the first effort to create an international quality assurance program that affects all industries, there seemed no need for either body to play an administrative role. Standards created were highly technical and relatively straightforward, with testing laboratories and certification institutes able to handle their "interpretation" and implementation.

It is not part of ISO's mission to verify that its standards are being implemented in conformity with the requirements of the standards. Conformity assessment is considered a matter for suppliers and their customers in the private sector, and a responsibility of regulatory bodies when ISO standards are incorporated into public legislation. ISO, in partnership with IEC, develops ISO/IEC Guides covering various aspects of conformity assessment activities. The voluntary criteria contained in these guides represent an international consensus on what constitutes acceptable practice.

The ISO 9000 Standards Series is an entirely different story and has created a new set of issues for ISO, especially. The aim of the standard is to produce quality assurance through creation of an internal auditing system based on documentation. It is entirely nonprescriptive, meaning that there is no one acceptable implementation route. National accreditation bodies operate as they fit. They, in turn, accredit registrars. Registrars are the entities that issue ISO 9000 certificates, and they are allowed to set their own criteria.

Quality System Assessment Recognition (QSAR)

Problems have developed with the explosive worldwide acceptance of ISO 9000. Many unqualified people have joined the ISO 9000 bandwagon, leading to rampant commercialization—and cheapening—of the standards' implementation. Recognizing these problems, ISO/IEC have established the Quality System Assessment Recognition (QSAR) committee to offer guidelines for national accreditation bodies and registrars that want to use the ISO/IEC logo. The aim of QSAR is to create uniformity within ISO 9000 programs worldwide, and ensure that the standards are implemented in a quality fashion, free of conflicts of interest and unprofessional business practices. In turn, the hope is that QSAR will encourage the international recognition of ISO 9000 certificates.

For example, once member bodies accept QSAR recommendations, registrars will not be able to operate consultancies, which is a main concern of QSAR committee members. Registrars that continue operating consultancies may find they cannot use the ISO/IEC logo (QSAR under the new system).

QSAR Timetable. National accreditation bodies should be able to apply for QSAR membership shortly. Once a minimum of ten member bodies have joined QSAR, ISO will create a central QSAR staff and take nominations for the QSAR board. ISO/IEC will have to jointly approve all board members. When the board is created, it will prepare final operating rules and procedures, as well as licensing and pricing procedures for the QSAR logo. These will also require ISO/IEC approval.

How QSAR Operates. ISO/IEC and the International Accreditation Forum (IAF) have created a board of directors for QSAR. The board is made up of made up of industry representatives, registrars, and accreditors. Once created, the QSAR Board has the task of drafting a memorandum of understanding (MOU) with IAF and will be charged with the following responsibilities:

- Issue criteria for accreditation bodies that want to bear the ISO/IEC logo, which will be designated as a QSAR logo. To do so, accreditation bodies must become QSAR members.
- Make decisions about whether national accreditation bodies are meeting QSAR criteria through a peer assessment process based on ISO/IEC conformity assessment guides.
- Be able to either grant use of the ISO/IEC logo or disallow its use for parties found to be not meeting criteria.

Once accepted as QSAR members, accreditation bodies will be open to requests for recognition and accreditation from quality system registrars that want to be recognized under the QSAR system. Registrars that pass muster under the system will be able to bear the QSAR logo, as will their client businesses.

Note: The QSAR board members have been selected, but the names have not been released for publication as of this writing. Contact ISO News Service for more information.

QSAR is expected to be self-financed, though ISO may provide some seed money to launch the program. It is estimated that QSAR's initial membership of ten accreditation bodies will grow by ten per year for a three-year period, then hold at forty around year four. Between 200 and 350 registration bodies are expected to seek accreditation under the QSAR system.

Note: As of this writing, IEC had requested a number of changes to the QSAR program, including means of accommodating those operating under the IECQ conformity assessment scheme. Most of the proposals were minor and did not involve drastically altering the QSAR system as laid out in this chapter.

International Accreditation Forum Involvement in QSAR. Made up of eighteen of the approximately thirty national accreditation bodies, the IAF will act as the operating arm for QSAR. It will carry out the peer assessment of accreditation bodies wishing to join QSAR. Accreditation bodies do not have to belong to the IAF to be accepted for peer assessment review under QSAR.

There is general consensus between Dutch and European Union standards officials that QSAR efforts should be moved under the auspices of the IAF. QSAR, which currently operates as an ISO committee, is endeavoring to create common rules and regulations for accreditation bodies worldwide. European officials consider it a major conflict of interest that ISO operates QSAR because so many ISO members themselves are national accreditation bodies, registrars, and even consultants that could benefit from QSAR—the "fox guarding the chicken coop" syndrome.

They see the fact that ISO has named IAF administrator of QSAR as a major step forward, and would like ISO to eventually cede over the entire QSAR process to IAF.

Resources

ISO Bulletins, 1994–1996.
A Review of U.S. Participation in International Standards.
Standards and Trade in the 1990's.

Appendix A

International and Foreign Organization Acronyms

AECMA
Association Europeene des
   Constructeurs de Materiel
   Aerospatial
(European Association of Aero-
   space Manufacturers)

AFNOR
Association Francaise de
   Normalisation
(French Association for
   Standardization)

CAA
Civil Aviation Authority Air-
   worthiness Division

CCIR
Comite Consultatif International
   de Radio
(International Radio Consultative
   Committee)

CCITT
Comite Consultatif International
   Telegraphique et Telephonique
(International Telegraph and Tele-
   phone Consultative Committee)

CECC
CENELEC Electronic Compo-
   nents Committee

CEN
European Committee for
   Standardization

CENELEC
European Committee for Electrotechnical Standardization

CEPT
Conference Europeene des Ad-
   ministrations des Postes et des
   Telecommunication
(European Conference of Post and
   Telecommunications
   Committee)

CGSB
Canadian General Standards
   Board

CNS
Chinese National Standards

CPPA
Canadian Pulp and Paper
   Association

CSA
Canadian Standards Association

DIN
Deutsches Institut fur Normung,
   e.V.
(German Institute for Standardization)

ECMA
European Computers Manufac-
    turers Association
EUROCAVE
European Organization for Civil
    Aviation Electronics
ETSI
European Telecommunications
    Standards Institute
ICAO
International Civil Aviation
    Organization
IEC
International Electrotechnical
    Committee
ISO
International Organization for
    Standardization

JIS
Japanese Industrial Standards
JESI
Joint European Standards Institute
SASO
Saudi Arabian Standards
    Organization
SBAC
Society of British Aerospace
    Companies
SAA
Standards Association of Australia
MOD UK
British Defense Standards
VDE
Verban Deutscher Electrotech-
    niker, e.V.
(Association of German Electrical
    Engineers)

Appendix B

ISO Member Bodies

Although this list is current at the time of writing, ISO membership is in flux, and by publication time there will almost certainly be additional member countries.

Algeria	Guyana	Poland
Argentina	Hungary	Portugal
Australia	Iceland	Romania
Austria	India	Russian Federation
Barbados	Indonesia	Saudi Arabia
Belgium	Iran, Islamic Republic of	Singapore
Brazil	Ireland	Slovakia
Brunei Darussalam	Israel	Slovenia
Bulgaria	Italy	South Africa
Canada	Jamaica	Spain
Chile	Japan	Sri Lanka
China	Kenya	Sweden
Colombia	Korea, Republic of	Switzerland
Costa Rica	Malawi	Syrian Arab Republic
Croatia	Malaysia	Tanzania, United Rep. of
Cuba	Mauritius	Thailand
Cyprus	Mexico	Trinidad and Tobago
Czech Republic	Mongolia	Tunisia
Denmark	Nepal	Turkey
Ecuador	Netherlands	Ukraine
Egypt	New Zealand	United Kingdom
Estonia	Nigeria	Uruguay
Finland	Norway	USA
France	Pakistan	Venezuela
Germany	Papua New Guinea	Viet Nam
Greece	Peru	Yugoslavia
Grenada	Philippines	Zimbabwe

9

ISO 9000 International Standards: Coping With a Program in Transition

Questions the Reader Will Find Addressed in This Chapter

1. What are ISO 9000's growing pains?
2. What are industry-specific ISO 9000 programs (the hybrids)?
3. Why is the ISO registration system under attack?
4. What debates have developed around trade barriers?
5. Who is encouraging ISO 9000 and who is not?
6. Why do U.S. companies pursue ISO 9000 and what hot issues endanger ISO 9000's survival?
7. How is ISO 9000 a system in transition?
8. What are the highlights of the 1994 ISO 9000 revisions?
9. How is ISO 9000 fine-tuned?
10. What implementation changes have resulted from hybridization?
11. What concerns ISO officials?
12. What regulations are on the way?
13. What are the best ways to cope with ISO 9000 changes?
14. How does a company reap ISO benefits?
15. What business strategy leads to savings?

Although a standards series, ISO 9000 fits under the umbrella of quality assurance, which measures a company's quality level in terms of process rather than the end result. ISO 9000 is the first-ever attempt to create an international quality assurance standard to cover all industries as well as the service sector. The standard couples a total quality management approach with documentation methodology to create an internal auditing system.

As of January 1, 1995, slightly over six thousand ISO 9000 certificates have been awarded in the United States and between eighty thousand and one hundred thousand worldwide. Experts in the field say they expect these numbers to double each year.

Although the original ISO 9000 series, released in 1987, is designed for implementation in manufacturing, the standard has proved transferable to the service sector. Industries and sectors such as transportation, which are heavily documentation-based already, are finding ISO 9000 a good organizational tool for preexisting documentation systems.

With U.S. companies continuing to venture into the international trade arena, there is a definite demand for some sort of international standard that will offer instantaneous recognition of quality. This sort of reassurance is tremendously appealing when a company's money is sitting in that letter of credit awaiting clearance by a foreign bank.

Companies who buy into the ISO 9000 program—companies from Minneapolis to Mombasa—are supposed to be able to select among ISO 9000 certificate bearers worldwide and feel confident that they are dealing with a "quality" company. By offering this assurance of quality, ISO 9000 is ideally expected to breed credibility in the world market and thereby make overseas business arrangements far easier. In reality, ISO 9000 is experiencing severe growing pains and its efficacy as a total quality program is under dispute, especially by many major electronics companies and certain European standards officials.

ISO 9000 Growing Pains

Many companies and many industries consider ISO 9000 a solid benchmark tool to establish an internal auditing system and to test consistency. However, an increasing number of ISO 9000 critics complain that the standard does not serve well as a complete quality system. The old saw that one could create cement life preservers and still earn an ISO 9000 certificate still holds.

In reaction to these issues and to continued high costs of implementation, some of the developments affecting ISO 9000 that are discussed more fully later in this chapter are noted here.

Industry-Specific ISO 9000 (the Hybrids). Members of both European and American industry have been examining means of overlaying industry-specific quality processes onto ISO 9000 to make it more responsive to individual industry needs. In this area, the Big Three automakers are leading the way with their ISO 9000 hybrid, QS-9000.

ISO 9000 Registration Reform. The ISO 9000 registration system is under attack in Europe and within electronics industry circles worldwide. Efforts to streamline the system and curb costs are being explored.

Trade Barriers. Whether ISO 9000 is a barrier to trade in the European Union (EU), Japan, or whether the Big Three are creating a trade barrier with their joint QS-9000 has been a matter of major international debate.

EU Quality Program. The senior EU standards policy group is determined to push for a Malcolm Baldrige sort of approach to quality assurance, deemphasizing ISO 9000 certification in Europe. The European Council is expected to vote on these proposals in November 1996.

With the EU backing off from encouraging ISO 9000 certification, it appears that U.S.-based multinationals—especially the Big Three automakers—have become the most active boosters of the ISO 9000 standard worldwide. Whereas in 1991 it seemed that ISO 9000 was a prerequisite to doing business in Europe, by 1995 ISO 9000 had become a prerequisite for doing business with General Motors and Chrysler. However, General Motors is also exploring a streamlined registration approach for its first-tier suppliers.

ISO 9000 Coercion. Interviews with hundreds of companies throughout the U.S. industrial sector—from steel to transport, textiles to restaurant equipment manufacturers, to hospitals and even law firms—indicate customer pressure is still the main reason for pursuing ISO 9000 certificates. Marketing was listed as the second most popular reason.

All of these hot issues, and more, endanger ISO 9000's survival as an international standard. As ISO 9000 splinters along industry-specific lines there have been warnings that companies will experience ISO 9000 gridlock if the trend toward hybridization is not curbed. Already, some electronics companies face the possibility of seeking ISO 9000 through at least two different registration schemes: European and QS-9000. There could have been a third, JIS Z9901, if this software variant of ISO 9000 had been implemented.

In the words of a senior EU standards official, "There isn't much we can do about QS-9000 because it's market-led, and they're in a position to impose it in their sector. What can we do? Whenever we get the opportunity, we do say they've overshot and are doing more harm to ISO 9000. What will happen if industry plays around too much with ISO 9000 and ISO 9000 certification is that we'll have to forget ISO 9000 and invent something else. Industry is breaking its own toys."

At the same time, quality officials worldwide continue to voice confidence in the ISO 9000 standards series and in documentation methodology as bases for an internal auditing system. Members of basic industries and some service industries also regard documentation highly as a baseline auditing tool. However, the more complicated, intuitive industries—software, for example—consider documentation a hindrance.

ISO 9000: A System in Transition

ISO 9000 is changing on two major fronts:

1. The standards series is being fine-tuned continuously. Major revisions were issued in 1994 and continued updates and additions will be released throughout this decade.
2. Governments and industries worldwide are challenging application of the series, as well as the current registration system.

This section will examine alterations to the actual standard and will then present international developments in ISO 9000 implementation and registration schemes.

Highlights of the 1994 Revisions

Following are ten highlights of the revised ISO 9000 standards based on information provided by the ISO 9000 Forum in Geneva, Switzerland, and the National ISO 9000 Support Group:

1. The original standards focused largely on manufacturing, or things that could be made. The new standards include process materials, services, and software. There is now an emphasis on generic product categories instead of manufactured goods and hardware.

2. The new standards take into consideration how registrars really conduct ISO 9000 audits. This is with preventative as well as corrective action in mind. In the 1994 standards, both corrective and preventative action are listed as separate elements to consider.

3. For the first time since ISO issued standards in 1987, there is mention of third-party audits as an official part of the ISO 9000 program. When originally conceived, ISO 9000 was expected to be a process that corporations utilized to audit suppliers. As the program was adopted on an international basis and national entities became involved, third-party audits were introduced.

4. Quality plans are introduced in the design phase of a project. Designers assess critical inspection junctures and established these inspections as part of the manufacturing process. This is the common practice in the automobile industry. Quality plans will be required for each product produced or each service offered.

5. ISO 9000 terminology has been harmonized in the new standards. The earlier standards used different terminology, which was a major source of confusion.

6. All the series are now presented in a consistent format and organization, each addressing checkpoints that are now uniform throughout the series. Each of the series lists the same twenty elements, though requirements may vary from series to series. If an element is not required, this will be stated in the standards.

7. ISO 9002 now includes repairs or postdelivery servicing of products. This has been copied directly from ISO 9001.

8. ISO 9003 has been expanded to include contract review, control of customer-supplied products, productive action, and internal quality audits. More management involvement is encouraged.

9. ISO 9004, to be renamed ISO 9004-1, has been extensively rewritten with a focus on the product life cycle. There is an emphasis on quality improvement, market input, and feedback. Handling and storage are included throughout the process, for example, and not after the process. In addition, health, safety, and other product issues are addressed, if cursorily. More standards and guidelines are expected in these areas by the year 2000.

10. Loopholes for exemptions are being closed. For example, in the past, companies that wanted to avoid being audited for statistical methods never mentioned statistical methods in their documents. Now they must demonstrate why they do not use statistical methods, opening the door to being audited in this area.

Note: To purchase copies of the revised ISO 9000 standards, contact ANSI, 11 West 42nd St., New York, NY 10036, or U.S. RAB, 611 East Wisconsin Avenue, P.O. Box 3005, Milwaukee, WI 53201. For free information on the standards, contact the National ISO 9000 Support Group computer network at 616-891-9433.

Fine-Tuning ISO 9000

More revisions are underway as ISO/TC 176 continues to fine-tune the standards series in what is called Phase 2 of the standards revisions.

Comprehension and Interpretation. ISO/TC 176, in cooperation with ISO Central Secretariat, is setting up a structure to provide to customers interpretations and clarifications of the original intent of specific clauses and paragraphs within the ISO 9000 standards. To this end, the committee is harmonizing the vocabulary in document 8402, which establishes ISO 9000 terminology, and working on providing additional "support technology" to customers, including development of standards for auditing and for writing a manual.

ISO Hybrids. ISO/TC 176 is closely examining the trend toward industry-specific use of the standards. Committee members are asking whether the ISO 9000 series will be maintained in the future as a generic system of principles and practices, based on international consensus and applicable to all economic sectors worldwide. They also wonder whether there will be a tendency over the next few years for specific industry and business sectors to develop their own individual programs based on, or drawing from, the generic ISO 9000 standards, but not identical to them.

TC 176 members argue that the series will have lasting benefit only if the generic nature of the standards is maintained and if the ISO 9000 series is implemented in an integrated manner for maximum benefit.

Quality Management and Environmental Management. With organizations increasingly facing management challenges on the environmental front, ISO/TC 207 is developing the ISO 14000 series of generic environmental standards (see Chapter 10). ISO/TC 176 and ISO/TC 207 have committed themselves to ensuring compatibility between their respective series of standards. Current ISO policy calls for two separate but compatible systems. The challenge will be to ensure that the two systems have similar architecture, are compatible, and that third-party requirements, assessments, and audits are designed, planned, and structured so that the costs incurred in meeting them do not place an overwhelming burden on individual businesses.

Integrated Use of ISO 9000. Encouraging companies to pursue ISO 9000 in an integrated fashion is a main concern of TC 176 members. This means that users focus first on implementing the quality management aspects of the series, company setup and operation, according to the guidelines of ISO 9000-1 and ISO 9004-1.

As discussed later in this chapter, TC 176 members recognize that the main benefit of ISO 9000 is working through the quality process. This means setting up an internal auditing system that relies on employee-management cooperation and teamwork. Only then is it appropriate to turn to the quality assurance models as outlined in ISO 9001, 9002, or 9003.

The standards outline an end result, but do not dictate a process. There are guidelines included, however, in the areas of calibration, statistical tools, metrology, and for creating a quality plan.

ISO 9000 and National Quality Awards. Companies often ask ISO/TC 176 members whether there is any need to pursue ISO 9000 if they are already working on a national quality award. Major awards include:

- U.S.: Malcolm Baldrige National Quality Award
- Canada: Canadian Awards for Business Excellence

- Europe: European Quality Award
- Japan: Deming Award

TC 176 officials consider ISO 9000 a foundation system that is part of a company's ongoing quality system, while national awards are "a quest for excellence." ISO 9000 may be considered a setup for pursuit of a national award, or a satisfactory, stand-alone system.

ISO 9000 detractors worldwide argue that the standards may serve as a strong benchmark, but fall short of producing the full quality environment that awards like the Malcolm Baldrige and the European Quality Award promote. The argument is that ISO 9000 falls short on several fronts, including continuous improvement, corporate culture, and leadership fronts. Companies must pursue both ISO 9000 and a quality award to produce a full quality system, ISO 9000 opponents contend.

The Malcolm Baldrige system is divided into seven main elements and twenty-eight subelements. Quality experts report that some Malcolm Baldrige elements are compatible with ISO 9000 and others are not. The main Malcolm Baldrige elements are:

1. Leadership
2. Information and analysis
3. Strategic quality planning
4. Human resource utilization
5. Management of process quality
6. Quality and operational results
7. Customer satisfaction

TC 176 officials counter that when ISO 9000 is implemented properly—with the process, not a certificate, in mind—it does provide a basis for continuous improvement. Pursuing a national quality award is also beneficial for companies that want to move beyond a base system.

On a larger scale, ISO 9000 is an attempt to unite global markets by creating the assurance of quality. The standards, through their emphasis on sound organization, competence, and discipline, are designed to promote confidence in business and minimize government regulation. Quality awards do not particularly promote an international approach.

Quality Assurance Trends. It is anticipated that by the late 1990s the standards series will move beyond contract support to verifying broader process challenges. TC 176 is working on eliminating variation in internal management structures and processes and shifting emphasis from demonstration of meeting stated and implied needs to include verification of how these needs are met and can be subjected to continuous improvement. Future ISO 9000 certificates will reflect these goals.

ISO 9000 Trends: Hybridization, Trade Barrier Disputes, and Reform Efforts

By the mid-1990s, ISO 9000 was rapidly splintering along industry-specific lines. This move toward verticalization actually started in Europe. For example, the Dutch Council for Accreditation (RvA) had started to work on industry-specific guidelines with input from manufacturers, trade associations, and government, as early as 1992. (The RvA is the Dutch national accreditation body, which now includes conformity assessment organizations—for example, testing labs—under its umbrella.)

The movement to hybridization accelerated in the fall of 1994 when the Big Three automakers unleashed their ISO 9000 hybrid, QS-9000. As noted in Chapter 4, major truck manufacturers like Freightliner, Mack, Navistar, Paccar, and Volvo/GM have adopted QS-9000. Other industries, specifically steel and metal tooling, are reportedly spinning off their versions of QS-9000.

But the hybridization trend did not end with the Big Three, the metal tooling, or steel industries. By unveiling JIS Z9901 in the spring of 1995 (see Chapter 1), the Japanese revealed the possibility that ISO 9000 could splinter further along industry-specific or even national market lines. Had the Japanese implemented JIS Z9901, which they did not, this would have meant yet another set of specialized ISO 9000 registration criteria for the software industry to follow.

Another potential misuse of the ISO 9000 standard involved the Korean government. Communications from Korea suggested the government might not accept accreditation by foreign accreditation bodies, meaning that ISO 9000 registrars would have to operate under a Korean accreditation scheme to work in that market. There have been no new developments along those lines as of this writing.

In an ironic twist, a senior European standards official, in the spring of 1995, accused the Big Three of acting as a cartel and creating a trade barrier by mandating that suppliers worldwide earn QS-9000 certificates. Jacques McMillan, chief of the EU's Senior Policy Standards Group for Directorate-General III, Industry, had spent a good part of recent years squashing suggestions that the EU had used ISO 9000 as a trade barrier to Europe when the EU adopted the ISO 9000 standards and tacitly mandated their use for a select group of industries, including computer switches and pacemakers.

Despite the fact that the Japanese backed off of JIS Z9901, the Koreans have not yet acted, and the EU never took action against the Big Three. At present, the ISO 9000 Standards Series was being associated as much with trade barriers as with quality. This trend was leaving even the leadership of TC 176 wondering about the future of this international standard that was to replace all standards.

For while QS-9000 has the support of the ISO and the backing of EU officials, some in the ISO 9000 "community" are watching the hybridization of the international standards program with some concern. These experts include Jacques McMillan, EU standards official; Willem Deken, deputy director of the Dutch Council for Accreditation (RvA); Reg Shaughnessy, international chairman of the ISO TC 176 committee that creates the ISO 9000 Standards Series; Peter Ford, secretary of TC 176; and Larry Eicher, secretary-general of ISO.

They all concur that ISO 9000 is, and should be, a living and evolving standard that meets industry needs. On the other hand, they are worried that the trend toward a more industry-specific approach may lead to the dissolving of ISO 9000 as an international standard and will raise auditing and certification costs in the long run.

The aforementioned experts have the following concerns:

- That the industry-specific "supplements" could take over or supersede the original standard, which is designed to be nonprescriptive to cut back on internal bureaucracy
- That companies will be forced back into a situation of meeting many standards at high costs
- That third-party auditing will be replaced by less objective second-party auditing
- That the standards, through hybridization, will lose their global vocabulary

ISO 9000 should not be confused with quality awards, say the experts. The ISO 9000 system is a "journey to quality," while attempting to win a national quality award becomes "a quest for excellence."

In defense of the ISO 9000 system, McMillan, Deken, Shaughnessy, Ford, and Eicher make the following points:

- The ISO 9000 system is a foundation for managing quality and continuous improvement. It is voluntary, its criteria are based on international consensus, and it is available for use by all enterprises, everywhere. When implemented with diligence and integrity, this system will satisfy the needs for quality, dependability, predictability, and cost efficiencies.

- To be useful, the ISO 9000 series has to be capable of being implemented on a broad, international basis. It creates the "level playing field" for free trade and open competition in the developing global economy.

- One of the strong points of the ISO 9000 series is that it deliberately avoids dictating to organizations how to meet its requirements.

A more in-depth look at these developments, as well as "reform" efforts is presented here.

Electronics-Software Battles: Supplier Audit Confirmation

Efforts are being made worldwide to "reform" the registration or certification aspects of ISO 9000. In a joint effort, Motorola and Hewlett-Packard have gathered the support of thirty-seven other major electronics companies to support streamlining of the ISO 9000 registration process. Companies include AT&T, Xerox, Digital Equipment, Microsoft, Matsushita Electric, Philips Electronics, Whirlpool, Bausch & Lomb, Stala Oy (Finland), and many others.

These companies have signed a so-called supplier's declaration of conformity as part of the proposed Supplier Audit Confirmation (SAC) program. (See Figure 9-1 for a description of the program.) They are seeking approval from the EU, the ISO, and other major international standards institutes to eliminate plant-by-plant ISO 9000 registration. They want one-stop registration based on internal manufacturer certification.

At present, SAC has the approval of the American National Standards Institute's (ANSI) conformity assessment committee, and the U.S. Registrar Accreditation Board (RAB) is working with SAC participants on creating mutually acceptable registration criteria. If SAC wins worldwide support, it would create a unique form of third-party auditing.

European Quality Program

The European Union (EU), in the meantime, is moving ahead with plans to create its own European quality program that will be based more on a Malcolm Baldrige than an ISO 9000 approach. ISO 9000 methodology will be included in the EU plan, but ISO 9000 certification will be downplayed under this proposal.

In a series of reports issued between 1994 and 1996, EU standards officials announced their intent to downplay the for-profit aspect of European quality and reemphasize the quality process. What was supposed to be the final draft proposal, called "A European Quality Promotion Policy," was issued the first week of June 1995, and reemphasized the approach outlined since 1994.

At that time, EU standards officials wrote: "The use of the ISO 9000 standards by companies can be regarded as a first step towards overall quality management. The certification of the quality systems based on these standards cannot be regarded as an end in itself because it does not provide all the means necessary for an increase in the competitiveness of the company."

To this end, they intend to reinforce the fairly new European Quality Award. If all goes as planned, national accreditation bodies will operate under the jurisdiction of standards chief McMillan. They will no longer operate for profit or compete with each other. The EU also wants to

Figure 9-1. Supplier audit confirmation program.

SAC Is	SAC Is Not
Third-party certification	Supplier's declaration, self-declaration, self-certification
Evolutionary Allowed under present, existing rules and standards for certification and accreditation (no "permission" needed)	Revolutionary New certification and accreditation rules needed to start pilot programs
• Maximum leverage of internal resources for • Third-party verification and certification at • Company level	Inferior or superior third-party certification as compared to standard certifications

strengthen a "harmonized European system for qualification of quality professionals, managers, and auditors."

The intent of this report remains the same at the time of this writing, although it is being revised slightly to add information on the economic impact of ISO 9000 certification/registration. When rewritten, this proposal will go before the European Council for a vote in November 1996. EU standards officals say they have the backing of the requisite number of EC members to enable the vote to pass and to make their proposal on quality official European Union policy.

More Regulation on the Way

Over the last year or so, concern has been voiced both inside and outside the Geneva-based ISO that this organization should set up a regulation arm. One possible solution would be the creation of an international accreditation body to replace the current national system. Two main ISO committees are working on these issues, which are addressed more fully in Chapter 8:

1. CASCO (the ISO Council Committee on Conformity Assessment) is seeking some means of instituting an international accreditation system whereby there would be mutual recognition of national accreditation body standards for registrars.

2. Quality System Assessment Recognition (QSAR) is a small group of experts created by ISO and IEC to develop an international system aimed at promoting the worldwide recognition of quality system registrations.

How to Cope With ISO 9000 Changes

These are confusing times on the ISO 9000 front, but there are ways to avoid pitfalls and additional costs. Here are some suggestions for businesses.

• *Follow industry-customer recommendations in selecting an ISO 9000 program to implement.* As ISO 9000 splinters along industry-specific lines and different hybrids emerge with differing criteria for registration, the most crucial concern of any manufacturer or service company is choosing the right ISO 9000 program. Although there will be no harm in earning a basic ISO 9000 certificate, companies may find themselves performing the process all over again—at additional cost—for yet another set of customers.

Example

Suppliers to the U.S. automobile and trucking industry should be pursuing QS-9000, not ISO 9000. A QS-9000 certificate is accepted in lieu of an ISO 9000 certificate, but the Big Three automakers and truck manufacturers do not accept ISO 9000 certificates.

• *Use some of the following secondary criteria to select an ISO 9000 program.* Many companies commonly fall into a gray zone between ISO 9000 and QS-9000. They perform some work for the auto-truck industries, but this makes up only a portion of their business. Overlaying the Big Three quality programs onto their quality system—a major portion of QS-9000—seems taxing. Some criteria a company should consider when making a decision include its percentage of sales to the auto-truck industries, whether other customers are requesting an ISO 9000 certificate, and the company's resources.

If resources allow, it might be best to pursue QS-9000 despite the extra work entailed. The Big Three are committed to QS-9000 for the time being and to seeing that their entire supply chain worldwide passes through this program. Remember, a QS-9000 certificate is the equivalent of an ISO 9000 certificate. Pursuing the basic version of ISO 9000 cannot hurt a company, however. ISO 9000, as was discussed earlier, is the basis for QS-9000. All the work of organizing an internal auditing system based on documentation will be the same.

• *Select a registrar that can cover as many fronts as possible.* Because there is no worldwide administration of ISO 9000, or standard practicing procedures for ISO 9000 registrars, selecting an appropriate registrar has always posed concerns for companies, as noted in the beginning of this chapter. With emerging ISO 9000 hybrids spawning specialized registration requirements, it is extremely important that companies select registrars that can cover as many bases as possible.

Example

Most QS-9000 registrars also issue ISO 9000 certificates. For companies that face the possibility of earning both certificates—a distinct possibility in industries like steel and electronics—it is best to select a registrar that can perform in both systems.

- *Stick to the process rather than racing to pass a test.* Realistically, many companies are mandated to pursue ISO 9000 or QS-9000. Even so, there is no need to hurry the process. Most customers will stretch deadlines if they see a company earnestly pursuing these quality assurance programs.

Always keep in mind that the major benefit of ISO 9000 is not earning a certificate to please a customer, though that may be necessary. The major benefit is the process of establishing a solid quality base within a company.

Creating a long-term, low-maintenance documentation system takes some time, but it also provides benefits as an internal auditing system. Moreover, this same methodology can be transferred to other areas of company concern that are documentation-based, such as sales, purchasing, and meeting import-export regulations.

- *Keep tabs on ongoing ISO 9000 developments worldwide.* As always, awareness equals cost savings. For example, a company might be able to convince a customer to delay requiring certificates because changes are imminent or because there is controversy brewing. For example, knowing that EU standards officials want to deemphasize ISO 9000 certificates in favor of the ISO 9000 process (for example, the European Quality Program) may offer some leverage with European customers. Make a case that, with changes brewing in Europe, showing conformity to the standard should be adequate until the EU charts a definitive course.

Example

Learning of Japanese plans to unleash yet another set of industry-specific criteria with their JIS Z9901 program, electronics and software giants rallied industry support to fight this proposal. The Japanese seem prepared to compromise on requiring JIS Z9901 because industry giants voiced their opposition.

How to Reap ISO 9000 Benefits

Even ardent backers of ISO 9000 as a means of global quality assurance acknowledge that the program is costly. Companies can expect to spend at least $35,000 for basic certification and six-month checkup fees over a three-year period. Then the cycle begins again. These figures do not include hidden costs like employee time and money spent on internal improvements required to meet ISO 9000 certification.

Employee time and the cost of bringing in outside consultants contribute the most to ISO 9000 costs. For example, many so-called ISO 9000 consultants charge upward of $1,800 a day.

ISO 9000 "Danger Zones"

From interviews with hundreds of companies that have achieved ISO 9000 certification, both here and abroad, it has been possible to identify "danger zones" during the certification process that lead to increased spending. Four "danger zones" are:

1. Initial panic
2. Lack of information about ISO 9000
3. Internal disorganization
4. Reaching for outside help unnecessarily

The Right Strategy Equals Savings

In what order and fashion a company pursues ISO 9000 certification will have a direct bearing on savings. Following is a condensation of the "Ten Steps to Savings" outlined in my book *ISO 9000 Made Easy* (AMACOM, 1995). Following these steps means fewer expenditures and fewer headaches for companies concerned with ISO 9000 certification once they have chosen this path.

1. *Do not embark on ISO 9000 certification in a hurry.* Know as much about ISO 9000 as possible before embarking on a certification program. If a customer is pressuring you to become certified, negotiate a realistic timetable given your company's resources. Some customers are willing to subsidize the cost of ISO 9000 certification, so check with your customer base before proceeding.

2. *Rely on employees to run the process.* Appoint someone in-house to oversee your certification process. Make sure this individual is aware of all aspects of your operation. As much as possible, ISO 9000 should be a homegrown process involving employees throughout your company.

The more you can rely on an employee(s) to oversee certification, the less you will need to rely on outside consultants. Employees offer the advantage of knowing the most about your company, its operating procedures, and culture. They can be assisted by consultants on a piecemeal basis.

3. *Shop around for a registrar that meets your company's bureaucratic style, and do this early in the process.* Negotiate the best price possible. Registrars are free-market entities and are facing tough competition in the United States and Europe. Make sure your registrar can handle ISO 9000 hybrids.

While new standards are being designed and new guidelines for ISO 9000 implementation are being drawn up over the next five years or so, individual registrars will still serve as the "interpreters" of the ISO 9000 standards. For this reason, it is important that companies embarking on ISO 9000 registration find the right registrar to suit their own needs and the requirements of their overseas customers. Small companies report that it is best to pick a registrar that is aware of the needs of a smaller business and will not enforce needless work and bureaucracy where none is required. Your registrar should be accredited to issue ISO 9000 certificates in all countries where your company does business. Interview as many registrars as time permits. Use these interviews as a means of learning more about the ISO 9000 certification process. Do not hire a registrar until you are ready to start the ISO 9000 process.

4. *Organize your management and employees to work under an ISO 9000 team system.* Read between the lines and you can tell that ISO 9000 is employee-intensive, meaning that it encourages involvement by as many employees as possible. Although employee input may be extremely positive and beneficial to a company in the long run, involving employees in unfamiliar tasks can prove difficult, confusing, and costly in the short run.

Those who have succeeded in earning ISO 9000 certificates did so because management was firmly behind the process but did not actively lead the process. Management assisted in the creation of a team system that involved employees as ISO 9000 coordinators, data collectors, and ultimately as in-house auditors. It is recommended that the person chosen to oversee ISO 9000 certification be well respected by employees at all levels.

5. *Determine a system for collecting, processing, and formatting documentation of your operating procedures before embarking on meeting a registrar's ISO 9000 demands.* Lack of in-house preparation and coordination may cost a company thousands of extra dollars. ISO 9000 is heavily oriented toward documentation of procedures. Companies that lack quality control manuals will find that they must devise a means of culling information from employees, recording that information, and formatting it, while continuing to operate their businesses. Even those with quality control departments and manuals may find their systems require an overhaul.

Because few manufacturers or service companies tend to involve employees in documenting their functions, ISO 9000 can seem overwhelming. Organizing the work that leads to certification while running a business can seem daunting. Rather than take time to create a system, many companies hire outsiders to move the process along for them.

Up-front organization and creation of a documentation system that suits your company may save countless hours of confusion in the long run. Saving hours almost always equals saving dollars. Follow these steps for the best coordination and most efficient operation of a data collection and formatting system:

- Organize your management and employees into teams for the collection and processing of data.
- The management advisory board should establish a framework for data collection and processing based on the ISO 9000 requirements and the company's organization.
- Uniform methods of data collection should be established up front, along with formats—graphs, tables, listings, headings—under which to organize information.
- Set up all formats in your computer network first, if such a network exists. In the absence of a computer system, establish typists who will sort and codify material employees gather.
- Ensure that employees receive ample instruction in data collection before starting. Make sure those in charge of sorting data, formatting, and producing your manual receive some instruction in editing and formatting.
- Be flexible within the set formats you have established. Allow the process to dictate where additional topics may need to be added and others deleted.
- Do not concern yourself with levels of ISO 9000 documentation until all data collection-processing systems are in place and tested.

6. *Once you have your employees organized and have set up a system for collecting and processing data, hire the registrar of your choice.* A quality registrar will guide you through the ISO 9000 standards. Use outside consulting help sparingly. All companies may need outside assistance. When selecting a consultant, search for one who offers ways of saving costs and streamlining your ISO 9000 certification system, rather than adding needless hours of work. A quality consultant can help interpret the ISO 9000 standards, determine where your company ranks vis-à-vis ISO 9000 standards, conduct preassessment audits, train employees in internal auditing, and assist in creation of a quality manual that meets ISO 9000 regulations.

What is important in selecting outside help is doing so at a time in the process when that assistance is most needed. Learn as much about the ISO 9000 process, as a company, as you can, to get the most "bang from your bucks" when outside assistance appears beneficial. Never hire a consultant without checking all references thoroughly. This tip seems unnecessary, but officials at the U.S. RAB report countless cases of companies that have rushed forward with ISO 9000 certification, hired someone to assist without checking his background, then complained when the so-called consultant overcharged them or proved otherwise deficient.

A National ISO 9000 Support Group reports that a survey of roughly eight hundred ISO 9000 consultants indicates that less than a third of those surveyed had received formal ISO 9000 training. The survey agrees with the RAB that companies should be most selective when hiring outsiders. Take a little more time up front, they advise, and do proper screening.

ISO 9000's goal is quality at all levels of an operation. Checking references is the first step in seeking ISO 9000 certification properly.

Note: For more information on ISO 9000, contact

- American Society for Quality Control, (800) 248-1946
- American National Standards Institute, (212) 642-4900
- National Institute of Standards and Technology (NIST), Office of Standards Code and Information, (301) 975-4040

NIST also operates five regional manufacturing technology centers, which serve as resource facilities to help manufacturers improve their competitive position through the application of manufacturing technologies. Manufacturers can contact these centers for information and assistance in the preassessment process for ISO 9000 qualification at (301) 975-3414.

Finally, the National ISO 9000 Support Group may be helpful to you. It is located at 9964 Cherry Valley Road, Building No. 2, Caledonia, MI 49316, 616-891-9114.

Resources

Shaughnessy, R. N., "Debate on the Future of the ISO 9000 Series, *ISO 9000 News: The International Journal of the ISO 9000 Forum,* vol. 4, no. 4, July/August 1995.
Zuckerman, Amy, *ISO 9000 Made Easy.* New York: AMACOM, 1995.

10

Emerging International Management System Standards: ISO 14000 for the Environment

Questions the Reader Will Find Addressed in This Chapter

1. What can be expected from the latest in standards, ISO 14000?
2. What are the environmental concerns of ISO 14000?
3. What development issues are being addressed in the drafting of ISO 14000?
4. What advice can prepare a company for the advent of ISO 14000?
5. What are some additional tips companies can consider in preparing for ISO 14000?

Introduction

Increased globalization has brought international environmental concerns to the attention of regional economic blocs, nations, industries, and consumers. While the news media focus on issues such as depletion of the Brazilian rain forests and the possibility of nuclear disasters such as Chernobyl, businesses involved in international trade face the everyday concerns of adhering to environmental regulations both in the United States and abroad.

Any business working abroad faces a vast amount of environmental regulation, especially in Europe. American companies must meet foreign regulations, as well as the myriad local, regional, and national regulations they work with in the United States. Keeping track of the literally thousands of regulations that affect a company is a major chore.

Members of the International Organization for Standardization (ISO) Technical Committee 207 (TC 207), Environmental Management, have been listening to the concerns of businesses and governments worldwide. They understand that both businesses and governments face management as well as compliance concerns when coping with environmental regulations. Therefore, TC 207 has been working on providing international environmental guidance on the following issues:

• In the face of industry disputes, consumers and environmental interest groups want to be able to determine the environmental impact of certain products.

• Under pressure to manufacture goods in an environmentally sound fashion, manufacturers want to find ways to cut pollution in the production cycle, as well as in their products' life cycle.

• Governments and other regulatory bodies want reliable information on products so they can produce workable environmental legislation and environmental programs.

These sorts of demands have created a push for international environmental standards that will offer manufacturers help on the environmental front, allow for consumer confidence, and provide governments worldwide with the information they require to create legislation that will not stifle trade.

The ISO has a two-pronged approach for meeting these needs:

1. ISO technical committees have created a wide range of sampling, testing, and analytical methods to deal with specific environmental issues. More than 350 international standards now exist for activities ranging from monitoring air and water to providing industry and government with data on the environmental impact of economic activity. In some countries these standards serve as the basis for environmental legislation.

The following ISO technical committees prepare environmental standards:

ISO/TC 22	Road vehicles	ISO/TC 146	Air quality
ISO/TC 43	Acoustics	ISO/TC 147	Water quality
ISO/TC 61	Plastics	ISO/TC 190	Soil quality
ISO/TC 85	Nuclear energy	ISO/TC 200	Solid waste
ISO/TC 108	Mechanical vibration and shock	ISO/TC 207	Environmental management
ISO/TC 116	Space heating appliances		

2. ISO technical committees are developing generic standards for environmental management that can be applied to any industry worldwide. ISO/TC 207, environmental management, was formed in 1993 to develop generic solutions to environmental challenges that cross technologies. Areas of focus are environmental management systems, environmental auditing, environmental labeling, environmental performance evaluation, life cycle assessment, and terms and definitions, as well as creation of a guide for merging the environmental process with product standards.

ISO 14000: The New International Draft Standard

By the late 1990s, the International Organization for Standardization is expected to release its ISO 14000 environmental management standards (EMS) for application globally. Now in the draft International Standard (DIS) phase, the draft standard has been released for discussion and a final vote of ISO members is expected in 1996.

Note: ISO 14000 is very much in the developmental phase. There is talk within standards circles that a final version may not be truly applicable until the year 2000. Small to midsize companies should take note of the development of the standard but hold on implementation until the bigger companies have worked it through its initial phases. (See "Preparing for ISO 14000" later in this chapter.)

Like its predecessor, ISO 9000, the ISO 14000 series is being designed for all industries worldwide. Its aim is to help organizations manage and evaluate the environmental aspects of their operations without being prescriptive. The series is intended to:

- Provide a platform for companies to demonstrate commitment to environmental protection
- Offer a means for management to pursue continual improvement in the environmental realm
- Provide a worldwide focus on environmental management
- Promote a voluntary consensus standards approach in the environmental area
- Harmonize national environmental rules, labels, and methods
- Promote environmental predictability and consistency
- Demonstrate commitment to moving beyond regulatory environmental performance compliance
- Minimize environmental trade barriers

The ISO 14000 Series

The ISO Environmental Management Technical Committee (TC 207) is responsible for the new ISO 14000 series, which has been in creation since 1992. Nine documents relating to the environment are at the committee draft stage:

1. *CD 14000.* Environmental management systems. Provides general guidelines on principles, systems, and supporting techniques.
2. *CD 14004.* Environmental management systems. Gives specifications with guidance for use.
3. *CD 14010.* Guidelines for environmental auditing. Provides general principles.
4. *CD 14011.* Guidelines for environmental auditing. Details audit procedures.
5. *CD 14012.* Guidelines for environmental auditing. Gives qualification criteria for environmental auditors.
6. *CD 14021.* Environmental labeling. Gives terms and definitions of self-declaration environmental claims.
7. *CD 14024.* Environmental labeling. Provides practitioner programs with guiding principles, practices, and certification procedures of multiple criteria programs.
8. *CD 14040.* Life cycle assessment. Lays out principles and guidelines.
9. *CD 14060.* Guide for the inclusion of environmental aspects in product standards.

ISO 14000 Development Issues

Although ISO 14000 is moving toward reality, it is still very much in the design and fine-tuning stages. Here are some major concerns that TC 207 is addressing:

• *Taking national regulations and technology into account.* Given that environmental regulations differ from country to country, providing generic international environmental standards is quite a challenge. In developing the ISO 14000 series, members of TC 207 have attempted to allow for national regulations and environmental trends while making individual companies more attentive to environmental standards.

To avoid turning ISO 14000 into a performance-based standard, registrars will not require that companies work with a set technology. It is understood that many countries lag behind developed nations technologically. Companies will be required to use the best technology readily available.

• *Avoiding conflict with ISO 9000.* Another problem TC 207 faces is avoiding redundant work for companies with an ISO 9000 system in place. Both TC 207 and TC 176—the ISO committee that develops ISO 9000 standards—have been coordinating efforts to avoid building unnecessary duplication into the new ISO 14000 Standards Series.

• *Four major concerns.* TC 207 faces four major considerations while still in the developmental phase of ISO 14000:

1. Finding a means of documenting environmental issues, which are highly regulated and legalistic
2. Focusing efforts on management (the process), rather than on the goals
3. Promoting third-party management audits
4. Establishing principles and uniform approaches for product evaluation that consider environmental attributes

ISO 14000 Compliance

To be in compliance with ISO 14000, companies will have to perform the following:

• Create an environmental management system (EMS).
• Show evidence that their work procedures are in compliance with relevant laws, meaning the regulations of countries where they do business.
• Show commitment to continuous improvement and pollution prevention (e.g., recycling, process changes, energy efficiency, use of environmentally sound materials).

At present, no international accreditation or registration schemes exist to handle third-party auditing of the ISO 14000 standard. Most people involved in ISO 14000 development expect third-party registration to evolve around the standard. Already, the U.S. Environmental Protection Agency is talking about easing reporting requirements for companies that earn ISO 14000 certification. The Environmental Auditing Roundtable has announced plans to issue accreditation criteria, and some European standards bodies are gearing up to offer ISO 14000 certification.

Members of TC 207 are discussing conformity assessment options that range from voluntary self-declaration to third-party certification. Many small and midsize companies have voiced concern about the cost of earning certificates for yet another international program.

In addition, the American National Standards Institute (ANSI) Board Committee on Conformity Assessment (BCCA) is currently studying how to implement accreditation for EMSi5 registrars. BCCA members expect to have some registration scheme launched in the United States in 1996 or 1997.

A battle royal will ensue in the next year or so unless industry worldwide and registration bodies can agree on creation of a vastly different registration system than what now exists for ISO 9000 and QS-9000 and what could evolve for ISO 14000. European Union and Dutch standards officials are united in their intent that industry not face multiple registration schemes.

Note: For copies of ISO 14000 drafts, call 800-248-1946 or 414-272-8573 and ask for auditing drafts Nos. B5R14000 and B5R14001 or management drafts Nos. B5R14010, B5R14011, and B5R14012.

"ECO Audit" or the Eco Management and Audit Scheme (EMAS)

The EU's Directorate-General XI for Environment, Nuclear Security and Civil Protection administers the Eco Management and Audit Scheme (EMAS), less formally called the "Eco Audit." An entirely voluntary scheme, EMAS provides a harmonized environmental management system for use throughout the member states of the EU.

Countries that offer the EMAS have established accreditation systems for environmental auditors, or what the Europeans call environmental verifiers. In February 1996, the European Commission recognized the British, Irish, and Spanish management system standards for the environment. In all three cases, national environmental management schemes predated the EU's creation of EMAS. The British standard BS-7750 was the first such environmental standard created.

Companies that join the EMAS scheme pass through a series of set requirements and then hire accredited environmental verifiers to determine whether they qualify for an EMAS certificate.

To date, 189 companies have earned certificates. Of these, 150—the vast majority—are German. EU officials speculate that the EMAS appeals to Germans both because they are environmentally conscious and because their companies must pass stringent environmental regulations. The EMAS provides a system for managing and tracking those regulations.

EU officials are exploring the cost of the EMAS program and are expected to have some figures by mid-June of 1996. The main direct cost is verification fees, which reportedly vary.

EMAS's Relationship to ISO 14000. EMAS bears no direct relationship to the upcoming ISO 14000 environmental management system standard that the International Organization for Standardization is expected to publish by September 1996. European officials will not make any decision on what to do about EMAS in relation to ISO 14000 until they see the final publicized standard. At that time, they will compare ISO 14000 to the requirements under EMAS and make a decision on how, if at all, to alter their program.

The official EU position is that they favor whatever can be done to improve the environment. To that end, officials will support whatever range of instruments helps companies in that regard.

Preparing for ISO 14000

Although ISO 14000 is still in draft form, companies are already seeking advice on how to implement the new standard. For companies that are not ISO 9000 certified, note that ISO 14000 will require ISO 9000 as a quality system. (See Chapter 9 for information on implementing ISO 9000.)

Richard Clements, executive director of the National ISO 9000 Support Group, has put together tips for companies that want to get a head start on environmental management and are already familiar with the ISO 9000 process. The following are requirements of ISO 14000 not covered in ISO 9000:

- ISO 14000 requires a very thorough environmental assessment by companies that should include these three elements:

  1. Knowledge of current local, state, national, and international environmental regulations that apply to individual companies.
  2. An outline of goals and targets to achieve on the environmental management front, for example, reducing a certain chemical in wastewater to so many parts per million.
  3. An emergency preparedness and response plan (for chemical spills, hazardous waste, and so on). U.S. companies are already bound by the Community Right to Know law for hazardous chemicals. Under the new legislation, reports must be filed with local emergency response agencies, such as the police and fire departments.

- Companies are required to create a procedure for handling internal and external communications relating to the environment.

- Companies are required to do more monitoring of manufacturing systems, air discharge, and other technical aspects of maintaining environmental control. Once again, this aspect of ISO 14000 may be bound to existing regulation.

An informal survey of American companies finds them advanced on the environmental technology front but lax in knowing which regulations apply to them in the United States and world markets. American companies are also accustomed to an adversarial, litigious approach to environmental controls. ISO 14000 is preventative and encourages cooperation between government and industry. (*Note:* ISO 14000 also applies to the service sector. For example, a service company may have to record how many recycled goods it uses, the air quality in its offices, and so forth.)

Additional Tips on Prepping for ISO 14000

Here are some additional recommendations for preparing for the introduction of what may be a second management system standard for businesses:

- Learn as much about ISO 9000 documentation as possible because ISO 9000 will serve as the basis for ISO 14000. Documentation techniques can be applied to meeting environmental requirements.
- Appoint a staff person to track the progress of ISO 14000.
- Keep tabs on national and international environmental regulations and standards affecting your current or future business.
- Assess aspects of your operation where you may be out of compliance with national and international environmental regulations should you plan to do business outside the United States.
- Ease into the process. ISO 14000 has not been released, and it is strictly voluntary at this time.

Note: These tips are designed for companies already in full compliance with U.S. environmental law, whether on a local, regional, or national basis. Companies that have been lax on the environmental home front will have double the work and should get moving on compliance now.

Resources

The following are resources for companies seeking information on ISO 14000:

International Organization for Standardization press office, 1 rue de Varembe, CH-1211, Geneva, Switzerland.

National ISO 9000 Support Group, 9964 Cherry Valley Road, Building No. 2, Caledonia, MI 49316, 616-891-9114.

11

Standards and Conformity Assessment Activities Worldwide: The Players, the Issues

Questions the Reader Will Find Addressed in This Chapter

1. Who are key global standards players?
2. What are major standards activities taking place worldwide?
3. What is taking place in the former Soviet Union?
4. What is taking place in Latin America?
5. What is taking place in the Pacific Rim?
6. What are common standards and conformity assessment issues companies expect to face worldwide?
7. What is taking place with ISO 9000 worldwide?

There is no international standards system that encompasses the work of both the private and public sectors in one entity. Although the International Organization for Standardization (ISO) and International Electrotechnical Commission (IEC) are recognized world leaders in international standardization, these organizations provide only a percentage of standards work taking place worldwide. Regional economic blocs and individual nations and their private sectors all continue to create standards, some of which will emerge as international standards under the ISO/IEC system, and many of which will not.

In developed countries, much standards work relates to breaking down barriers to trade that standards and conformity assessment practices can create. As noted in Chapter 3, for example, the United States and the European Union (EU) are working on mutual recognition on the conformity assessment front. On an international level, conformity assessment harmonization is most evolved on the electrotechnical front, especially regarding safety of electrical equipment.

Many developing countries are creating standards infrastructures for the first time. Others are seeking harmonization of standards within their economic regions, as well as harmonizing national standards to meet international criteria.

To present a full picture of standards activities worldwide would be encyclopedic and far beyond the scope of this book. The aim of this chapter is to offer a glimpse of standards work taking place around the world and a sense of emerging standards players and standards issues. As noted in the introduction, countries that are actively producing standards—or gearing up to do so—may very well prove to be the movers and shakers of the new world order.

Global Standards Players

It is no surprise that the European Union and the United States lead the world in standards development and dissemination. But new standards players are emerging to add input—and create issues—for standards players worldwide. Japan and Korea are asserting their needs and requirements on the standards front. Malaysia and India are becoming active standards participants, as are Brazil, Chile, Argentina, and others.

Economic blocs are also forming to challenge the European Union and NAFTA countries. Some of these economic blocs are forming regional standards bodies. The following are some examples of regional economic blocs concerned with standards and conformity assessment:

- GCC (Gulf Cooperation Council): Saudi Arabia, Bahrain, Qatar, United Arab Emirates, and Oman
- ASEAN (Association of Southeast Asian Nations): Singapore, Malaysia, Thailand, Brunei, Indonesia, and the Philippines
- Mercosur (Common Market of the South): Argentina, Brazil, Paraguay, and Uruguay
- CACM (Central American Common Market): Guatemala, El Salvador, Honduras, Nicaragua, and Costa Rica
- CEFTA (Central European Free Trade Area): Czech Republic, Hungary, Poland, and Slovakia
- SAARC (South Asian Association for Regional Cooperation): India, Pakistan, Sri Lanka, Bangladesh, Nepal, the Maldives, and Bhutan

Although the U.S. is rallying on the international standards front, Europe is really the nerve center of the international standards movement.

Countries worldwide are working on mutual recognition and other agreements with EU standards officials. (See the Appendix at the end of this chapter for a list of these countries.) A breakout of standards organizations and bodies that have been working with the EU provides an overview of the players in the worldwide standards arena:

- Among developed countries the major standards players that have come calling on the European Union include the United States, the United Kingdom, Germany, Italy, Spain, Denmark, Sweden, France, Holland, Belgium, Ireland, Austria, Switzerland, Canada, Japan, China, and Australia.
- Developing countries negotiating with the European Union include Mexico, New Zealand, South Korea, Brunei, Papua New Guinea, Taiwan, Hong Kong, India, Saudi Arabia, Malaysia, Thailand, Indonesia, and the Philippines.

Standards Activities

As noted, many countries are becoming standards players. Some nations, like Argentina, are just starting to create a standards infrastructure, while others are actively negotiating mutual recognition agreements on both the standards and conformity assessment fronts. The following are some examples of ongoing standards activities worldwide. Special emphasis is given to countries where the United States has active involvement. Quality, especially ISO 9000 activities, will be outlined in the next section.

Former Soviet Union

The former Soviet Union has a fully developed standards and conformity assessment infrastructure. With a new emphasis on capitalism, Russian leaders are eager to move ahead with harmonization of Russian standards with those in the United States and elsewhere to facilitate trade. As noted in Chapter 3, U.S. government officials have been working with Russian counterparts since the early 1990s on these efforts. The following are some examples of ongoing standards and conformity assessment efforts taking place between Russia and the United States:

Russian Consumer Protection Law. The Russian Consumer Protection Law requires every commodity entering into the Russian marketplace to be certified for safety and health factors before the material or product can be sold. Almost every commodity, agricultural as well as nonagricultural, is covered.

The United States raised concerns about the impact of this law on exporters. Besides the expense of earning the certificate, there were the added costs of redundant testing and the need to provide proof of conformity assessment.

Product Standards and Conformity Assessment. On a larger scale, the United States and Russia have been cooperating in the areas of product standards and conformity assessment to avoid creation of nontariff trade barriers. Also involved is the intergovernmental Joint Business Development Committee that was established to resolve trade and investment issues.

• NIST and the Committee of the Russian Federation for Standardization, Metrology and Certification (GOSSTANDART of Russia) have established a memorandum of understanding on scientific and technical cooperation in the fields of standards and metrology.

• NIST signed similar agreements with the principal standards, metrology, and certification organizations in the Ukraine and the Czech Republic.

• GOSSTANDART agreed to directly accredit U.S. conformity assessment bodies to certify products. For example, the U.S. Conformity Assessment Company Testing of Hoboken received Russian accreditation. The Russian agency also entered into contractual relationships with Underwriters Laboratories and other conformity assessment companies.

• Many major U.S. conformity assessment bodies have been working with respective Russian standards and conformity assessment experts to conduct inspections, tests, and comparative analysis of U.S. and Russian standards. The aim was to gain confidence in each nation's standards and conformity assessment measures as a basis for future mutual acceptance. For example, in the area of pressure vessels, the American Society of Mechanical Engineers (ASME) set up contractual relationships for GOSSTANDART assessments under its de facto internationally recognized code for pressure vessels.

Laboratories and Testing. These agreements provide the basis for the cooperative efforts in laboratory accreditation that all governments continue to explore. GOSSTANDART and NIST have agreed to work toward the mutual acceptance of test data in the telecommunications and food industries.

Mutual confidences in legal metrology (measurements regulating mass, flow, and so on) also fall under national laboratory accreditation activities. Both the United States and Russia operate internationally recognized metrology programs under the auspices of the International Organization for Legal Metrology calibration programs.

Automobiles. The American Automobile Manufacturers Association (AAMA) and GOSSTANDART have agreed to accept "technical equivalents" of each other's motor vehicle requirements. The U.S. Department of Transportation (DOT) and the Environmental Protection Agency (EPA) assisted.

Drugs. The U.S. Food and Drug Administration (FDA) reached an agreement with Russia for the acceptance of FDA-approved drugs and other pharmaceuticals, eliminating the need for redundant or remote product testing of pharmaceuticals entering the Russian market.

Future Activities and Goals. Future goals include continued work toward further acceptance of U.S.-based conformity assessments measures, including product certification, testing, type approval, and quality assurance in the context of the ISO 9000 standards.

The Commerce Department is working to train their Russian counterparts in automotive, medical devices, telecommunications, and other U.S. standards areas. Training in U.S. conformity assessment measures and standards development was also offered through the auspices of ASME.

Latin America

In South America, countries like Brazil, Chile, and Argentina see international standards and conformity assessment practices as a means of improving international trade opportunities. Also, the Mercosur Agreement between Argentina, Brazil, Paraguay, and Uruguay includes standards-related issues. Other bilateral and multilateral agreements with standards-related provisions exist between and among Latin American countries.

Chile and Argentina are fast-developing South American countries. Both countries are working with U.S. and European officials to quickly develop standards infrastructures that will allow them to be players on the product standards, conformity assessment, and quality assurance fronts. Both countries are active participants within ISO and have adopted the ISO 9000 Standards Series. Companies within each country are currently pursuing ISO 9000 certification, and both countries are in the process of creating resident quality assessment certification bodies. Both countries are receiving help from European Union nations, particularly the United Kingdom, France, and Germany, in efforts to upgrade their industrial base.

As noted in Chapter 3, U.S. government officials are increasingly concerned that United States influence in this region lags behind that of the

European Union, Germany, and Japan, which are providing direct financial and technical support to Mercosur countries for standardization-related activities.

Example

U.S. standards documents are not available in the libraries of principal government or private-sector standards institutions in Argentina or Brazil. Germany and Japan, on the other hand, have standards experts on location in these countries to ensure adoption of their technologies as reflected in standards and conformity assessment activities important to trade.

Argentina. In Argentina, where an open economy is fairly recent, research and development, conformity assessment, and other underpinnings of standards activity are in the formative stages. The government plays a strong role in standards development. For example, quality assurance and conformity assessment measures take place under government mandate. The public and private sectors are establishing a joint quality infrastructure to address mutual concerns.

As of August 1994, the National Institute for Industrial Technology (INTI) is charged with creating a framework for conducting standards development and conformity assessment work in Argentina. Besides directing research grants, the INTI operates several basic research laboratories.

At this writing, Argentina's standards structure includes a charter council with both public- and private-sector representatives. Modeled after Britain's standards system, the council governs both standards development and conformity assessment activities, including laboratory accreditation, quality assurance, and product certification, as well as certifying auditors. The British are offering technical support in this endeavor, and the EU has provided the equivalent of $3 million in financial support.

INTI staff are also participating in various technical committees under Mercosur, working to harmonize standards and conformity assessment practices within the four member nations. A U.S.-Argentina Business Development Committee has been formed to establish working groups to address specific trade-related issues such as standardization. A main concern of this new committee is reducing standards-related trade barriers. Argentina is exploring becoming more involved with international standards institutions at the suggestion of NIST advisers. There is also talk of electronically linking Argentine standards bodies with ANSI.

Brazil. A tremendous amount of standards and conformity assessment and harmonization is taking place between NIST, ANSI, and the chief Brazilian standards organization, ABNT. Of particular concern to all parties is harmonization of electrical, petroleum, food, pharmaceutical, and metrological standards.

Example

The U.S. Food and Drug Administration (FDA) has concerns with contamination of Brazilian black pepper, cocoa beans, and coffee that are entering the United States. During a recent meeting, government officials from both countries agreed to examine testing practices governing these food categories on the Brazilian side. The Brazilians also registered complaints about American foodstuffs containing fruit flies after being imported into Brazil.

Example

U.S. and Brazilian officials agreed to work with each nation's health authorities on the development of standards, regulations, and conformity assessment practices governing pharmaceuticals. These standards would relate to both prescription and over-the-counter products.

Example

For testing and certification, Brazil and the United States have agreed to develop a list of products that each country wishes to trade or export. The next step is exchange of product-specific regulatory and market requirements for products that either Brazil or the United States wishes to trade or export, including related information on standards and conformity assessment activities or programs.

Chile. Chile is actively moving from a government-dominated economy that catered to multinationals to a system that promotes private-sector growth. The Chilean government is introducing advanced technologies in various industrialized sectors, efforts that eventually lead to standards and conformity assessment.

The country's entire science and technology infrastructure is undergoing massive change, with institutions now seeking half of their support from industry. Science and technology activities are being redirected to commercial use, rather than being strictly academic.

One of the most prominent technological institutions charged with technology transfer is Fundacion Chile, a private entity that works under the direction of the National Institute for Standards (INN). The main Chilean standards body, INN is part of the Ministry of Economy and Industries and accredits organizations to carry on testing and certification. Established in 1976, Fundacion Chile's work ranges from providing technical expertise and marketing guidance to companies to conducting management studies and training, certification, and test programs for acceptance of products in the national and international markets. Fundacion Chile is particularly active in the agribusiness and marine resources. When it comes to certification, Fundacion Chile serves both the private and public sectors. Most of its outside work is in product certification, including certification of food products and pharmaceuticals.

A number of private testing laboratories operate in Chile, including multinationals like SGS Laboratories of Geneva.

Mexico. Mexico is also creating an infrastructure for measurements, standardization, and conformity assessment under the 1992 Federal Law on Metrology and Standardization. In the spring of 1994, the Mexican Bureau of Standards published conformity assessment procedures for product certification to satisfy official Mexican standards.

In a spring of 1995 trilateral committee meeting, Mexico reported accrediting eight private-sector certification bodies, including the National Association for Standards and Certification for the Electrical Sector (ANCE). ANCE is accredited for the certification of household appliances and is also responsible for developing voluntary electrotechnical standards.

Despite being a primary signatory of the North American Free Trade Agreement (NAFTA), Mexico is not moving toward mutual recognition of outside conformity assessment schemes. Since becoming effective in 1994, NAFTA has been a problem for American exporters who complain that it ties them to Mexican importers. When they change customers, they have to repeat a product certification process. Redundant certification requirements mean increased costs and a possible barrier to trade.

Free Trade Area of the Americas. Work is underway to create a Free Trade Area of the Americas (FTM). Thirty-four countries have now agreed to support the concept. An action plan was being developed in the spring of 1995. The United States has proposed that standards and conformity assessment appear for immediate action on an FTM agenda.

For ongoing efforts, the United States is recommending that FTM countries implement the principles of the Agreement on Technical Barriers to Trade (TBT) that are part of the Uruguay Round to the General Agreement on Tariffs and Trade, now under the auspices of the World Trade Organization. The TBT is designed to eliminate the use of standards-related measures as barriers to trade and encourage the transparent development of international standards and conformity assessment systems without compromising national, safety, health, or security measures.

Interamerican Metrology System. The Organization for American States (OAS) in the beginning of 1995 agreed to create the Interamerican Metrology System (SIM). At present, twenty-seven of the thirty-four signatories to the FTM are participating in this ongoing effort to unify measurements throughout this hemisphere. Of special concern are those measurements that are known as legal metrology, "weights and measures," and govern commercial transactions.

Pacific Rim

As one of the fastest-growing export markets in the world, the Pacific Rim region holds particular interest for the United States. The U.S. Trade Representative's office has also identified this region as problematic in terms of the proliferation of trade barriers, in which standards and conformity assessment play a large role. U.S. trade retaliation has forced the removal of some of these barriers, but the U.S. government (as noted in Chapter 3) has been working hard on mutual recognition of testing and certification practices with other members of the Asia Pacific Economic Cooperation Forum (APEC) since 1994.

APEC members include most of the principal nations bordering the Pacific Ocean: the United States, Canada, Japan, South Korea, Taiwan, Hong Kong, Singapore, China, Australia, New Zealand, and the members of the Association of Southeast Asian Nations (Malaysia, Indonesia, the Philippines, Thailand, Brunei, and Singapore). Chile joined APEC in 1994.

Meeting in Jakarta, Indonesia, in November 1994, APEC leaders endorsed the broad concept of mutual recognition agreements (MRAs) and proposed to work for regionwide open trade by the year 2020. Among the elements cited for development were the following:

- Clearly defining the scope of testing and certification procedures mutually accepted by the parties to the MRA
- Creating criteria for identifying competent, acceptable laboratories and certifiers in each country
- Establishing provisions for information exchange, joint monitoring, and dispute resolution
- Getting commitments from government authorities in each country to oversee the performance of conformity assessment organizations and, if necessary, terminate their accreditation if they fail to maintain technical competence

Because of economic and other disparities, APEC leaders do not envision achieving complete harmonization of standards and conformity assessment practices for quite some time. Some have recommended an incremental approach to build confidence in testing laboratory practices throughout the region as a means of building eventual confidence in product certification—very much the approach the United States and the European Union are adopting.

Example: Indonesia

Indonesia is a rapidly growing export market that highlights the importance of harmonizing standards and conformity assessment practices as a means of improving foreign trade. Since 1985, rapid economic growth in Indonesia has led to a series of domestic and foreign policy reforms, including liberalization of Indonesia's foreign trade policies. Domestic markets have been deregulated, and the Indonesian economy has been opened to foreign investment.

Industrial modernization has involved policy changes affecting standards and conformity assessment. Through the National Standardization Council of Indonesia (Dewan Standardisasi Nasional, or DSN), the government is creating a new framework for the development, adoption, and dissemination of product and other standards. Also being constructed are new procedures and institutions for product testing and certification, oversight rules for laboratory and certifier accreditation, and rules to accredit the competence of ISO 9000 quality system auditors in Indonesia.

Standards and conformity assessment systems are being revised to meet increasing demands for efficiency at home and because foreign customers are requiring higher quality levels. Outsiders are keenly watching Indonesia's evolving standards infrastructure for signs of future economic growth and for indications that Indonesia's private sector will continue to grow.

Of 3,550 Indonesia standards in use, only about 20 percent are based on international standards. As a GATT signatory, Indonesia will be required to consult the International Organization for Standardization (ISO) and International Electrotechnical Commission (IEC) before creating national standards. The government standards body is determined to increase the number of national standards based on international ones.

India

In 1991, the Indian government both liberalized the economy and launched a major movement to improve the country's competitiveness. Since the early 1990s, a national accreditation board has been established to test and calibrate national and state laboratories to ensure they follow international criteria. The government is also helping modernize and upgrade test houses and laboratories to bring them up to international standards so that India's test certificates will be accepted internationally.

Common Standards and Conformity Assessment Issues Companies Can Expect to Face Worldwide

U.S. government officials are not addressing standards and conformity assessment issues in a vacuum. If talks are taking place worldwide to harmonize standards and conformity assessment practices it is at the request of U.S. companies trying to improve trade in those regions. Following are some of the standards-related problems companies can expect to face around the world until harmonization and mutual recognition agreements are in place:

• *Russia, Ukraine, and Newly Independent States.* National conformity assessment requirements have not been abolished and differ from country to country and even state to state. Foreigners are required to have testing done either on site or in specially designated labs. For example, manufacturers of portable telephones face quite a few redundant testing requirements in this region.

• *European Union.* Meeting CE Marking requirements is a major issue for U.S. companies. There is also continued fear that U.S. interests will not be represented in the development of European standards and conformity assessment practices.

• *China.* National standards are not harmonized to international standards, and other national or regional standards are not accepted. Also, U.S. government officials are candid about the Chinese "cheating" when it comes to intellectual property and other aspects of standards. For example, Chinese manufacturers have been known to forge Underwriters Laboratories stickers.

• *Pacific Rim.* Countries like Malaysia and the Philippines are willing to accept and adopt U.S. standards. There are few issues.

• *Latin America.* In countries like Argentina, Brazil, and Chile it is important to be aware of their national standards and be prepared to adopt them. For example, Brazil maintains its own electrical codes. However, Brazil has been most involved in adopting U.S. standards, especially auto industry standards, because of ongoing sourcing work for the Big Three automakers.

Advice to Companies

U.S. standards officials warn companies not to depend on local government officials or standards bodies when attempting to apply foreign standards or conformity assessment practices. These are areas where local consultants can make a major difference because of their knowledge of the cultures, for their contacts, and because of language barriers.

NIST has foreign desk officers based in the United States (see Chapter 2) and resident foreign commercial services to help American companies seek out qualified consultants abroad. Commerce Department officials will provide lists, but no recommendations. Once consultant names are provided, insist on references and make sure there is follow-up.

ISO 9000 Worldwide Efforts

ISO 9000 is by far the most widely accepted international standards series. Although the bulk of ISO 9000 certificate holders are Europeans, there are thirty-two national accreditation bodies worldwide accrediting registrars to issue ISO 9000 certificates.

Seventy-six countries have accepted ISO 9000 standards as a national standard and thirty-two nation members have accreditation boards. There are about 70 certification bodies (registrars) operating internationally.

Although ISO publishes and sells standards through national accreditation bodies, it does not maintain a country-by-country breakdown of standards sales. To determine how many ISO 9000 certificates have been issued worldwide means culling information from each of these accreditation bodies.

As ISO 9000 continues to grow in acceptance internationally, private entities are tracking its development. For instance, Ernst and Young's Australian office recently surveyed more than one thousand manufacturers in ten countries to determine ISO 9000's global impact. Countries selected were Australia, Brazil, Canada, France, Germany, Japan, Korea, Sweden, the Netherlands, and the United Kingdom.

As part of this survey, respondents were asked (1) why they pursued ISO 9000 certification, (2) the benefits of ISO 9000, and (3) whether they would encourage their suppliers to become certified.

More than 60 percent of manufacturers from the ten countries surveyed had either earned ISO 9000 certification or were in the process of doing so. Few respondents reported having no intention of pursuing ISO 9000 certification.

As is the case with many American companies, the most common reasons foreign companies reported for pursuing ISO 9000 were to gain a competitive edge and to achieve continuous improvement. Many companies also considered ISO 9000 certification an integral part of TQM (Total Quality Management) and other continuous improvement processes.

Here are some additional findings:

- More than 70 percent of respondents reported gains in productivity, customer satisfaction, and staff morale as a result of pursuing ISO 9000 certification.
- Seventy-nine percent of companies surveyed reported that they actively encourage their suppliers to achieve certification.

As noted, ISO 9000 has been gaining worldwide acceptance with rapid growth taking place in Latin America and the Pacific nations. Following are some examples of ISO 9000 developments in various nations worldwide:

- *Australia.* In Australia, the government actively encourages quality certification and has played a key role in raising ISO 9000 awareness. In certain Australian states, Queensland, for example, ISO 9000 certificate holders get higher consideration for government contracts. At this writing, 3 percent of Australian companies have achieved quality standard certification. That percentage is expected to rise to at least 50 percent of all companies over the next five years.

- *Argentina, Chile, and Brazil.* ISO 9000 has taken hold in Argentina, Chile, and Brazil, countries that are actively pushing foreign trade. All have many companies pursuing ISO 9000. None have a mechanism in place for accrediting certifiers, but all three nations are developing plans for such entities. At present, twenty-three Argentinian companies are ISO 9000 certified. Brazil leads the way on ISO 9000 in South America; more than 450 Brazilian companies have earned certification. Chilean standards officials have been promoting ISO 9000. Registrars were being sought from other countries, and about five companies have earned certification.

- *Indonesia.* The government plays a major role in standards and conformity assessment in Indonesia, where most of the large testing laboratories are government owned and operated.

Indonesia is building a new standards infrastructure to promote and support quality systems management, especially ISO 9000. The country adopted the ISO 9000 series as national standards in 1992. In 1994, a national accreditation body was created and that same year one quality systems registration body earned official accreditation. More applications for accreditation were pending.

As of August 1994, twenty-five manufacturing firms and one service-sector company had earned ISO 9000 certification.

- *India.* The Indian quality movement escalated in 1991 with the liberalization of the Indian economy and simultaneous government initiatives to encourage implementation of ISO 9000 in both the industrial and service sectors. The Bureau of Indian Standards (BIS) is the agency responsible for these efforts, as well as for setting up a Quality System Certification

Scheme in 1991 to accredit ISO 9000 registrars. At least ten Indian registrars were offering ISO 9000 services at this writing and more than eighty companies had earned ISO 9000 certification, with many others in the process of pursuing certification. Among those that had earned certification were testing laboratories, financial institutions, and companies from the engineering, chemical, textile, and food industries.

The Indian government offers financial assistance to small companies pursuing ISO 9000 certification in the form of reimbursements of registration, consultation, and training fees. Individual state governments have been following suit, though support differs from state to state.

• *Portugal.* Until Portugal entered the European Union, most quality efforts were product oriented. Entrance into the European Union brought more government and private-sector awareness of quality assurance and the need to promote quality as a competitive tool for entering world markets. The government and private sector began to actively promote quality efforts.

In 1993, a National Quality Management System was created (later renamed the Portuguese Quality System). The system operates under the auspices of the Portuguese Institute for Standardization, which handles all standardization, accreditation, certification, and metrology-related activities in Portugal. The Excellence Prize (PEX), which requires applicants to earn ISO 9000 certification, was created in 1994.

Foreign ISO 9000 registrars operate in Portugal along with IPQ, the country's one home-based ISO 9000 registrar. IPQ participates in the EQNet (European Network for Quality System Assessment and Certification), which guarantees mutual recognition of ISO 9000 certificates among registrars in member countries.

The first Portuguese company earned ISO 9000 certification in 1989. By the end of 1994, 220 companies had their ISO 9000 certificates, with many more in the ISO 9000 pipeline. Electrical and electronics industries represent about 40 percent of ISO 9000 certificate holders, followed by textiles, cork, and wood, which are Portugal's traditional industries. The Portuguese service sector is showing increased interest in ISO 9000.

Summary of Worldwide Standards Issues

Harmonized standards and conformity assessment practices are a means of uniting the industrial world, opening the doors to vastly increased international trade. By the same token, quality assurance standards like ISO 9000 are expected to provide an assurance of quality that will level world markets.

There is a direct correlation between countries that are known international traders and countries that are players on the standards scene. International trade experts would not be surprised to learn that Malaysia, India, Chile, and Brazil are actively developing standards infrastructures to match, and compete with, the bigger players'. These are countries that in recent years have become major U.S. export markets.

That many countries are entering the standards arena in force has tremendous advantages to world trade as long as the purpose is harmonization, not trade retaliation. As recent disputes between Japan and the United States on automobiles, software, and other industries indicate, the "new world order" is not necessarily going to be peaceable. Countries and regional blocs still must defend their markets and their products. Standards and conformity assessment practices can easily turn into barriers to trade.

Chapter 12 addresses trade barriers and how recent treaties aim to defuse this issue. Future trends in standards and conformity assessment are presented, along with advice to companies on how to cope in this new global trade environment.

Resources

International Organization for Standardization, "ISO 9000 News," April 1995.
Standards, Conformity Assessment and Trade.
Warshaw, Stanley, ITA press releases.

Appendix

Countries Investigating Mutual Recognition Agreements With the European Union

<u>AUSTRIA</u>

OVQ	Austrian Association for Quality (Osterreichische Vereinigung fur Qualitatssterung)

<u>BELGIUM</u>

AWQ	Association Wallone pour la gestion de la Qualite (Walloon Quality Association)
BCK-CBQ	Belgisch Centrum voor Kwaliteitszorg—Centre Belgique pour la gestion de la Quality (Belgium Centre for Quality)
BENOR	Belgian conformance mark
BIN-IBN	Belgisch Institut voor Normalisatie–Institute Belge de Normalisation—Belgian Standards Institute
BQS	Belgian Committee for Quality Systems
CEBEC	Belgian Electrotechnics Organisation
CKZ	Centrum voor Kwaliteitszorg—Flemish Quality Centre
CQ	Centre pour le Gestion de la Qualit—Walloon Quality Centre
NACQS	National Accreditation Council for Quality Systems in Belgium
NBN	Belgisch Norm Belge—Belgian Standard
RAPS	Regulatory Affairs Professionals Society (Belgium)

VCK	Vlaams Centrum voor Kwaliteitszorg—Flemish Centre for Quality (Belgium)

<u>BRITAIN</u>

ABCB	Association of British Certification Bodies
ACB	Association of Certification Bodies (UK)
AQMC	Association of Quality Management Consultants (UK)
BABT	British Approvals Board for Telecommunications
BEAMA	Federation of British Electrotechnical and Allied Manufacturers Associations
BFPSA	British Fire Protection Systems Association
BMIF	British Marine Industries Federation
BNFMF	British Non-Ferrous Metals Federation
BPE	British Plastics Federation
BSI	British Standards Institute
BS	British Standards
AMA	British Value & Actuator Manufacturers Association
BQA	British Quality Association (UK)
CITAC	Cooperation in International Traceability in Analytical Chemistry
	CITAC Secretariat LGC-B006, Queens Road, Teddington, Middx. TW11 OLY United Kingdom. Fax 44 81 943 2767
CPDA	Clay Pipe Development Association (UK)
CUI	Committee of User Inspectives (UK)
EARA	Environmental Auditor's Registration Association (UK)
EECS	Electrical Equipment Certification Service (UK)
FIRA	Furniture Industry Research Association (UK)
IQA	Institute of Quality Assurance (UK)
PC	Loss Prevention Council (UK)
LPGITA	Liquefied Petroleum Gas Industries Technology Association (UK)
METCOM	Mechanical & Metal Traders Confederation (UK)
NACCB	National Accreditation Council for Certification Bodies (UK)
NAMAS	National Measurement & Accreditation Service (UK)
NWML	National Weights & Measures Laboratory (UK)
US	Quasi autonomous non-governmental organisations (UK)

RBA	Registration Board for Assessors (UK/IQA)
QSRMC	Quality Scheme for Ready Mixed Concrete (UK Certification Body)
STL	Short-Circuit Testing Liaison (UK)

DENMARK

DS	Dansk Standardiseringsrad—Danish Standards Association

FRANCE

AFAQ	Association Francaise de Assurance de Quality
AFNOR	Association Francaise de Normalisation
AG	Agreement Group
IFAE	Institute Francais des Auditeurs de l'Environement
LNE	Laboratoire National d'Essais (France)
UPIP	Union Francais des Industries Petrolieres (France)
UIC	Union des Industries Chemiques (France)

GERMANY

AUS	Arbeitskreis Uberwachungsbedurftige Anlagen (Germany)
BAM	Bundesanstalt fur Materialforschung und prufung (Federal Institute for Materials Research & Testing)
DGQ	Deutsche Gesellschaft fur Qualitat e. V (German Society for Quality)
DIN	Deutsches Institut fur Normung (German Standards Authority)
DVGW	German Gas and Water Certification Authority

GREECE

ELOT	Hellenic Organisation for Standardization

ITALY

CEI	Comitato Eletrotecnico Italiano—Italian Standards Institute
CSITO	Centro Servizi Informazione Tecnologica Organizzata (Italy)
SCI	Sistema de Calibracion Industrial—System of Industrial Calibration
SINAL	Sistema Nazionale per l'Accreditamento di Laboraton—National Systems for the Accreditation of Laboratories

SINCERT	Sistema Italiano di l'Accreditamento degli Organismi de Certificazione—National System for the Accreditation of Certification Organisations
SIT	Sistema Italiano di Taratura—Italian Testing Service
LTM	Ente Nationale Italiano di Unificazione—Italian Standards Institute

PORTUGAL

APQ	Associacao Portuguesa para a Qualidade—Portuguese Quality Association
IPQ	Instituto Portugues da Qualidade—Portuguese Institute for Quality
NP	Normas Portuguesas—Portuguese Standards

SCANDINAVIA

| NORDTEST | Nordic Cooperation Body for Technical Testing |

SPAIN

ADLNB	Association of Designated Laboratories and Notified Bodies
AENOR	Asociacion Espanola de Normalizacion y Certification—Spanish Association for Standardization and Certification
AECC	Asociacion Espanola para la Calidad—Spanish Association for Quality
REDLE	Red Espanola de Laboratorios de Ensavo—Spanish Network of Test Laboratories
UNE	Una Norma Espanola—Spanish Standards

SWEDEN

| SWEDAC | Swedish Board for Technical Accreditation |

SWITZERLAND

| SAS | Swiss Accreditation Service |

THE NETHERLANDS

KDI	Stichting Kwaliteitsdienst—Quality Foundation
NVK	Netherlandse Vereniging voor Kwaliteit—Dutch Association for Quality Management
NNI	Netherlands Normaalistic Institut—Netherlands Standards Institute
RvC	Stichting Raad voor Certificatiee—Dutch Council for Certification

| STERLAB | Netherlandse Stichtung voor de Erkenning van Laboratoria—Institute for the Recognition of Laboratories |
| WEID | Werkgroep Eigen Inspectia Diensten (Holland) |

EASTERN EUROPE

| COOMET | Metrology Cooperation of Central & Eastern European States |

AMERICA

AALA	American Association of Laboratory Accreditation
ANSI	American National Standards Institute
AOTC	Associated Offices Technical Committee
ASME	American Society of Mechanical Engineers
ASQC	American Society for Quality Control
ASTA	ASTA Certification Services
ASTM	American Society for Testing and Materials
AWS	American Welding Society
ACS	Association of Consulting Scientists
CIA	Chemical Industry Association
CPSC	Consumer Product Safety Commission (USA)
FDA	Federal Drug Administration (USA)
IAAR	Independent Association of Accredited Registrars (US)
ICSP	Interagency Committee on Standards Policy (USA)
ITES	International Test & Evaluation Association (USA)
NADCAP	National Aerospace & Defense Contractors Accreditation Program (USA)
NBBPVI	National Board of Boiler & Pressure Vessel Inspectors (USA)
NIST	National Institute of Standards and Technology
NVLAP	National Voluntary Laboratory Accreditation Program (NIST/US)
OSHA	Occupational Safety and Health Administration (USA)
OSHA/NRTL	OSHA Nationally Recognised Testing Laboratory Program
RAB-ANSI	Registrar Accreditation Board jointly operated (US)
USNC	United States National Committee

US TAG   United States Technical Advisory Group

<u>CANADA</u>

CIGOS   Canadian Interest Group On Open Systems
SCC   Standards Council of Canada

<u>NORTH AMERICA</u>

NADBANK   North American Development Banks
NAFTA   North American Free Trade Association
NAOSTC   North American Open Systems Testing &
     Certification Policy Council
NAPCTC   North American Policy Council for OIS Testing
     and Certification

<u>CARIBBEAN</u>

ACS   Association of Caribbean States

<u>AFRICA</u>

SADC   South African Development Community
     [11 Member States]

<u>ASIA</u>

APEC   Asia-Pacific Economic Cooperation. 18 coun-
     tries. ASEAN members plus U.S., Japan, Aus-
     tralia, New Zealand, Canada, South Korea,
     Mexico, Papua New Guinea, and the three
     Chinas [China, Taiwan, and Hong Kong]
ARF   Asia Regional (Security) Forum
ASEAN   Association of Southeast Asian Nations
     (Malaysia, Thailand, Singapore, Brunei, In-
     donesia, and the Philippines)

<u>MALAYSIA</u>

SIRIM   Standards & Industrial Research of Malaysia
SMM   Laboratory Accreditation Scheme of Malaysia
     (Skim Accreditasi Makmal Malaysia)

<u>JAPAN</u>

INTAP   Interoperability Technology Association for In-
     formation Processing (Japan)
JSA   Japan Standards Association
MITI   Ministry of International Trade and Industry
     (Japan)
MPT   Ministry of Posts and Telecommunications
     (Japan)

PACIFIC RIM
PASC   Pacific Area Standards Congress

AUSTRALIA
NATA   National Association of Testing Authorities
                                (Australia)

NEW ZEALAND
TELARC   New Zealand Accreditation Authority for Qual-
                                ity Assurance Laboratory Testing and Indus-
                                trial Design

INDIA
BIS   Bureau of Indian Standards

SAUDI ARABIA
SASO   Saudi Arabian Standards Organisation

12

Standards in the New Order, the Impact of Treaties, International Trends, and How to Plan for Their Effects in Your Global Strategy

Questions the Reader Will Find Addressed in This Chapter

1. What are the costs of trade barriers?
2. What are existing standards and conformity assessment barriers to trade?
3. What is the impact of major treaties on standards and conformity asessment practices? GATT? NAFTA?
4. What work is the World Trade Organization performing related to standards and reducing trade barriers?
5. How can your company manage in an era of ongoing standards developments?
6. What are developments the ISO is pushing that your company should consider?
7. What are ongoing international standards developments your company should address?
8. What are recommendations for the U.S. standards system for your company to consider?
9. What are recommendations for U.S. involvement in global standards activities your company should consider?

10. How can your company plan strategically in this new global environment?
11. What is Strategic Standardization Management?

Introduction

Companies today cannot afford to overlook international standards and conformity assessment practices. This chapter provides specific information on the current and future threats companies face in this arena and the methods businesses can use to control their destiny in this changing world market.

The advent of a global economy does not yet signify a united world. Competition in this transitional world order is fierce. Korea, for example, is fast surpassing Japan in the semiconductor market. The United States automobile industry is just inching back into dominance after several decades of European and Japanese competitive battering. With traditional protectionist trade tactics on the ostensible decline—duties, tariffs, quotas, and so forth—standards and conformity assessment practices are fast joining the world economic arsenal.

This is the atmosphere in which harmonization of standards and conformity assessment practices are taking place. In the best of all worlds countries and economic blocs would universally applaud harmonization of standards and conformity assessment practices. After all, international harmonization of standards provide many advantages, including:

- Enabling manufacturers to produce more efficiently for a larger, combined market
- Conveying information to customers about products and services in a technically precise, consistent manner
- Promoting global communications
- Supporting international health, safety, and environmental goals
- Increasing global trade opportunities

The Cost of Trade Barriers

In this less than ideal world the issue of standards and conformity assessment practices as trade barriers is very real. Countries and regional economic blocs still want to defend their markets. Many use standards and conformity assessment practices as protectionist weapons.

When standards and conformity assessment practices vary, manufacturers invariably pay higher costs in redundant testing and certification activities. Lack of harmonization means potential time delays when entering foreign markets. Delays can produce a number of effects, mostly negative, from added costs to having a product shut out altogether as a foreign product gains market control.

Also, when different countries or regions have different technical standards for essentially the same product, manufacturers selling into multiple markets are forced to produce multiple versions of the same product.

Examples

- Producing automobiles for the United Kingdom and continental Europe means switching between right-hand- and left-hand-drive cars.
- Differing electric standards between the United States and Europe means producing appliances that are adaptable to both markets.

When conformity assessment practices vary, that can also mean added costs. For example,

- U.S. exporters are forced to ship products abroad for costly, wasteful retesting.
- Exporters may have to support the costs associated with bringing foreign inspectors to visit and inspect U.S. manufacturing facilities.
- Costs of goods imported to the United States may rise if this country imposes unreasonable conformity assessment demands on foreign competition.

Foreign trade experts recognize that nontariff trade barriers negatively affect production costs in manners similar to more obvious forms of market protectionism, such as tariffs. Nontariff barriers

- Increase the price of imported materials and components.
- Reduce a manufacturer's ability to profit from economies of scale.
- Block more competitive and efficient producers from selling superior products in export markets.

Standards, Conformity Assessment, and Barriers to Trade

The U.S. Trade Representative (USTR) annually produces the National Trade Estimate (NTE) Report on Foreign Trade Barriers, which outlines foreign use of discriminatory standards, testing, and certification requirements as barriers to U.S. exports. Because other countries want to slow the on-slaught of foreign goods into their market, trade barriers more often exist between countries or trading blocs where one or even several countries/blocs enjoy substantial competitive market advantage.

Example

U.S. industry faces more possible trade barriers in high tech, transportation equipment, electrical machinery, biotechnology, and pharmaceuticals because U.S. industry is preeminent in these markets. These are just some of the areas the USTR has identified as trouble zones.

Attempts to estimate the impact of standards and conformity assessment barriers on U.S. trade are fairly recent. The Commerce Department is tracking nontariff trade barriers, but has only collected preliminary data at this writing. In the United States there have been no comprehensive analyses of standards and conformity assessment systems as nontariff barriers to trade. However, authors of a major National Research Council study conclude that many barriers to trade are embedded in existing standards.

These conclusions are based, in part, on the following observations about world standards practices:

- Countries employ standards that differ from international norms to protect domestic products.
- Standards are often written to match the design features of domestic products, rather than designed to improve performance.
- In many nations, foreign exporters have unequal access to the testing and certification systems of the market they are entering.
- Test results and certifications performed by competent foreign organizations are often refused in many markets.

Note: Government studies indicate that foreign conformity assessment schemes can create more problems for U.S. exporters than standards. This is because products such as food additives and medical devices require complicated testing and certification before release in any market. As noted, redundant testing and certification means additional work and expenditures.

The USTR has culled examples of trade barriers to U.S. exports. These are outlined in Figure 12-1.

As discussed in Chapter 9, EU officials have been concerned with lowering barriers to trade among all member states. As early as 1983, the then EU adopted information procedures for standards and technical regulations on industrial, agriculture, pharmaceutical, cosmetic, and food products for the purpose of harmonizing standards in these sectors. Under the standards information procedures, each national standards body must in-form the European Commission and all other member state standardization bodies of its proposed draft standards or amendments to existing ones.

Note: U.S. industry leaders are keeping tabs on Great Britain, whose standards bodies are actively creating conformity assessment schemes. Sometimes, as in the case of ISO 14000, there is a push for compliance even before the standard is set.

Treaties and Their Impact on Standards and Conformity Assessment

With one foot still in the protectionist mode and another moving toward creating a truly functioning global economy, governments and regional economic blocs are making strides to harmonize standards and conformity assessment practices. The next sections of this chapter will examine how treaties are working to accomplish harmonization, and how major standards bodies such as ISO are joining forces to create a more unified world economy.

GATT: General Agreement on Tariffs and Trade

Since 1979 there have been two major rounds of talks under the auspices of the General Agreement on Tariffs and Trade (GATT). The Tokyo Round of GATT trade negotiations, which ended in 1979, reduced tariffs between the United States, Japan, and Europe to about 3.8 percent.

In 1994, the Uruguay Round of negotiations cut tariffs in major industrial markets to zero in many sectors. These include construction, agricultural and medical equipment, pharmaceuticals, paper, toys, and furniture, among others. In semiconductors and computer components, tariff cuts ranged from 50 to 100 percent, and many developing countries committed to cutting tariffs in these industrial sectors.

GATT negotiators in 1994 recognized that nontariff trade barriers were not only increasing in response to drops in direct protectionist activities, but that these sorts of barriers can be tremendously costly. For this reason, standards and conformity assessment issues featured prominently in the Uruguay Round of GATT. Significant progress was made in reducing barriers related to discriminatory standards and national product testing and certification systems.

In short, GATT accomplished the following in areas related to standards:

- Established new World Trade Organization (WTO) Codes on Technical Barriers to Trade (the Standards Code) and on Trade and the Environment

Figure 12-1. An overview of trade barriers by country to U.S. exports.

Country/Region	Trade Barriers
European Union (EU)	In 1989, the EU banned meat and meat products produced from livestock treated with natural or artificial (biotechnology-derived) growth hormones. The EU has stated its recognition that there is no scientific evidence to support the ban; however, it remains in effect. Damage to U.S. exporters is measured at $97 million per year. *STATUS:* Unresolved; U.S. retaliation under Section 301 remains in effect.
	The EU's "Global Approach to Testing and Certification," instituted in 1990, mandates that certification of regulated products be performed by European testing laboratories and certifiers. This system imposes unbalanced costs on non-European manufacturers for obtaining product approvals. (U.S. government accreditation, by contrast, does not discriminate between U.S. and foreign laboratories.) In some sectors, testing can be performed by a U.S. laboratory under subcontract to a European laboratory. Success in U.S.-EU mutual recognition agreement (MRA) negotiations, which began in 1994, would remove or reduce this barrier. *STATUS:* MRA negotiations ongoing.
Japan	Prescriptive design standards under the High Pressure Gas Law favor Japanese producers. Affected sectors include air conditioners, refrigeration equipment, supercomputers, and aircraft support equipment. Performance standards would be less trade restrictive and more flexible in accommodating technological innovations. *STATUS:* Ongoing.
	Barriers to imported wood producers were estimated, in 1989, to restrict U.S. exports between $500 million and $2 billion annually. Key among the barriers were restrictive fire and building codes and refusal to accept foreign testing procedures. The National Forest Products Association petitioned the USTR to initiate a Super 301 case against Japan. *STATUS:* Case was resolved in April 1990. Japan agreed to increase reliance on

	performance-based standards and to accept foreign test data. International technical committees monitor implementation, which has been largely successful.
China	China does not accept U.S. certifications of quality. Procedures for obtaining a required "quality license" are costly and discriminatory, often imposing higher standards for imports than domestic goods. Many regulatory requirements are unknown or unavailable to non-Chinese firms. *STATUS:* In 1991, USTR self-initiated a Section 301 investigation of these and other Chinese trade practices. China agreed to publish notice of regulations and to discuss other issues. Implementation remains unclear.
Indonesia	Acceptance of new pharmaceutical imports can take more than a year. Copied products are often available on the local market before the original is accepted. *STATUS:* Ongoing.
Mexico	Beginning in July 1994, Mexico mandated that testing and certification for regulated products be through laboratories accredited by the Mexican Director General for Standards (DGN) or by DGN itself. In practice, DGN has accredited no non-Mexican laboratories and very few Mexican ones. Under the North American Free Trade Agreement (NAFTA), it is not obligated to accredit or recognize foreign organizations until 1998.
Republic of Korea	Many regulatory standards, such as shelf-life standards for processed foods, differ substantially from international practices without scientific basis. Public notice of rule making is often inadequate. Some standards are applied unequally to imported and domestic products. Medical equipment and processed agricultural products are among imports facing nontransparent or unclear standards. *STATUS:* Ongoing.
Taiwan	Agricultural imports are routinely tested, unlike domestic products. Complex registration procedures exist for approval of imported pharmaceuticals, medical devices, and cosmetics. *STATUS:* Ongoing.

- Provided new enforcement mechanisms through the WTO's Technical Barriers to Trade (TBT) Committee to prevent standards and conformity assessment-related barriers to trade
- Expanded the number of countries bound by standards regulations under the Tokyo Round

Figure 12-2 shows the countries where the two rounds of GATT talks resulted in changes to trade and thus standards issues.

Note: The TBT agreement does not provide for an automatic right to gain recognition under another country's laboratory accreditation, inspection, or quality system registration scheme. It does encourage signatories to negotiate mutual recognition agreements in the area of conformity assessment and quality assurance registration.

NAFTA: North American Free Trade Agreement

U.S. government officials recognize that standards are the building blocks of hemispheric, as well as international economic integration. NAFTA, which involves the United States, Canada, and Mexico, supports the elimination of technical barriers to trade, or nontariff barriers.

Through creation of a trilateral governmental committee on Standards-Related Matters (SRM), NAFTA places tremendous emphasis on standards and even exceeds GATT stipulations against creation of standards-related barriers. Specific product sectors are identified under NAFTA for standards harmonization efforts. These include land transportation, telecommunications, textile and apparel goods, and automotive products.

NAFTA Harmonization Efforts. NAFTA signatories are moving ahead on harmonization of electrotechnical standards under the auspices of the Council for Harmonization of Electrotechnical Standards (CANENA). Representatives from all three NAFTA member states serve on CANENA, which may soon enter the standards development arena.

Other groups and organizations working to harmonize standards in NAFTA countries include:

- North American Trilateral Standards Forum
- International Accreditation Forum
- American National Standards Institute (ANSI)
- Pan American Standards Commission (COPANT), to which ANSI serves as the U.S. member
- SRM intergovernmental committee
- Commerce Department's National Voluntary Conformity Assessment Systems Evaluation (NVCASE) Program

Figure 12-2. GATT members subject to standards provisions.

Tokyo Round: Standards Code Signatories
(as of November 1993)

Argentina	France	Luxembourg	Singapore
Australia	Germany	Malaysia	Slovak Republic
Austria	Greece	Mexico	Spain
Belgium	Hong Kong	Morocco	Sweden
Brazil	Hungary	Netherlands	Switzerland
Canada	India	New Zealand	Thailand
Chile	Indonesia	Norway	Tunisia
Czech Republic	Ireland	Pakistan	United Kingdom
Denmark	Israel	Philippines	United States
Egypt	Italy	Portugal	Yugoslavia
European Union	Japan	Romania	
Finland	Korea, Republic of	Rwanda	

Uruguay Round Signatories
(as of April 1994)

All of the above,* plus the following:

Angola	Costa Rica	Liechtenstein	Qatar
Algeria	Cote d'Ivoire	Macau	Saint Lucia
Antigua and Barbuda	Cuba	Madagascar	Senegal
Bahrain	Cyprus	Malawi	South Africa
Bangladesh	Dominican Rep.	Mali	Sri Lanka
Barbados	El Salvador	Malta	Suriname
Belize	Fiji	Mauritania	Tanzania
Benin	Gabon	Mauritius	Trinidad and
Bolivia	Ghana	Mozambique	Tobago
Botswana	Guatemala	Myanmar	Turkey
Brunei Darussalam	Guinea-Bissau	Namibia	Uganda
Burundi	Guyana	Nicaragua	United Arab
Cameroon	Honduras	Niger	Emirates
Central African Republic	Iceland	Nigeria	Uruguay
China	Jamaica	Paraguay	Venezuela
Colombia	Kenya	Peru	Zaire
Congo	Kuwait	Poland	Zambia

---

*Except Rwanda and Yugoslavia

ISO and International Standards Trends
for Companies to Consider

Although the International Organization for Standardization (ISO) does not represent all international standards activities, it is a definite standards trend setter. What ISO is planning today may very well have a major impact on companies throughout this decade and the millennium to come. For this reason, companies must pay attention to ongoing ISO standards development.

ISO officials have identified five areas for strategic action from 1996 to 1998. These five major action areas are:

1. *Enhance Market Relevance.* Increase ISO's market relevance through improvements in program management, priority setting, secretariat resource commitments, individual project management, and leadership training.

2. *Speed Up Time to Market.* Decrease total system costs and time to market (standards publication) through improved cost management, elimination of administrative system inefficiencies, better use of human resources, process reengineering, and better utilization of computerization throughout the system.

3. *Improve Promotional Efforts.* Effectively promote the ISO system and its standards through introduction of an expanded industrial outreach program highlighting the benefits of consensus standardization.

4. *Create New Self-Sustaining Program Elements.* This would include expansion and promotion of ISO mechanisms for adopting standards, encouraging new work in services to service industry sectors, building special technical support relationships with the World Trade Organization (WTO), facilitating conversion of governmental procurement specifications to ISO standards, and meeting global expectations for conformity assessment recognition.

5. *Upgrade National Standards Infrastructures in Developing Countries.* This would involve offering ISO help in building threshold-level standardization infrastructures in partnership with other ISO members and donor agencies.

Global Outreach

Besides these major action points, ISO officials have plans for increased global outreach and increased involvement in efforts to halt use of international standards—especially ISO standards—as nontariff trade barriers. Some of the areas outlined for future attention and consideration are:

1. *Cooperation with WTO.* ISO officials propose establishing a collaborative mechanism with the WTO, also based in Geneva, to administer the standards code of the Technical Barriers to Trade provision of the 1994 GATT negotiations (Uruguay Round).

ISO recognizes the WTO policy of encouraging and adopting international standards whenever possible. It intends to continue its role as the international leader in standards information services and standards development, and conformity assessment programming, while providing a special technical support role to the WTO in relation to its standards activities.

2. *International partnerships.* ISO will continue to improve its working relationships with the International Electrotechnical Commission and other international standardizing bodies. The aim is to further develop a coherent and effective "International Standardization System."

3. *Consumer organizations.* ISO will strive to strengthen its cooperation with consumer organizations that support ISO's objectives. The aim is twofold: to build consumer awareness of and confidence in international standardization and to gain consumer input for national delegations to ISO technical committees.

4. *Promoting ISO standards for services.* There is increased emphasis on free and open international trade within the service sector, including services such as insurance, finance, tourism, education, and so forth. Requests are increasing from this sector for international standards to benefit consumers operating internationally. ISO is exploring means of providing standards relevant to this sector.

5. *Advancing global conformity assessment recognition.* ISO standards are increasingly the basis for conformity assessment certification services. ISO recognizes the need to ensure that requirements for conformity assessment build worldwide customer confidence and do not become trade barriers. Models for addressing this issue are still evolving.

6. *Moving government procurement standards to the private sector.* There is a general trend worldwide to privatize standards development. As is the case with the U.S. military, this means altering government procurement practices that rely on standards. ISO and IEC are considering a role to play in these privatization efforts.

7. *Upgrading national standards infrastructures in developing countries.* Helping developing countries establish "threshold-level" standardization infrastructures in areas like metrology, calibration, standards information, testing, and certification is a main concern of ISO. Officials envision the ISO working alongside international aid agencies and others in an educational capacity.

8. *Regional support.* Many of the ISO's members are also members of

regional organizations that focus on standardization and standards-related fields. At present, such relationships exist with regional standardization bodies including AIDMO (Arabic region), ACCSQ (Southeast Asia region), ARSO (African region), CEN (European region), COPANT (Latin American region), and PASC (Pacific Rim countries).

Ongoing International Standards Issues for Companies to Address

The concern that standards and conformity assessment practices could be manipulated as nontariff trade barriers is a subtext running through this guide. Trade barriers are serious matters, but they are hardly the only concern that standards developers are encountering as they face a new millennium.

As new economic blocs form to meet the demands of globalization—as well as protect hemispheric interests—other questions arise that companies should be addressing through their trade associations and even legislators:

- Who will run this new world order?
- Who will be in charge of a truly integrated international standards system?
- How will this system operate?

Standards developers worldwide, from U.S. government officials, to industry and ISO officials, already recognize the need to tackle these questions. There is concern that the current consensus system that ISO and IEC employs, while ideal in the long run, is not designed for speedy resolution of crises. The following are some of the issues these experts have defined and are tackling:

- Safeguards must be built into an international standards system to avoid creation of nontariff barriers.
- Checks and balances have to be constructed so no one party dominates the standards-setting process, and standards participants must be better defined as the field grows.
- A fair and open standards system has to be defined to encompass different cultures and different attitudes.
- The role of governments in standards development should be unified worldwide, with governments and industry together defining an international norm.
- A system must be designed so that standards development and im-

plementation can take place at a pace that matches technological change.

- Small and midsize companies need better representation in the standards-setting process.

Recommendations for the U.S. Standards System for Companies to Consider

U.S. government officials are keenly aware of the role that standards and conformity assessment are playing in binding the New World Order. They are equally keen to ensure that this country has a substantial role in defining that order through, among other things, a coherent standards policy that will protect American businesses and American markets.

The recent decision to grant the American National Standards Institute (ANSI) a memorandum of understanding is a major step toward presenting a stronger, more unified presence to the international standards arena. However, there are many other changes these officials must make to ensure that the United States is positioned to protect its market interests abroad on the standards and conformity assessment fronts.

The following are some recommendations for implementation at this writing. Companies should bring these issues before relevant lobbying bodies, whether trade associations, industry forums, or legislators, to ensure their interests are being protected:

- Policy makers cite an "urgent need" for increased federal data gathering and analysis on standards and conformity assessment.
- An ongoing capacity to analyze the economic effects of developments in domestic and international standards and conformity assessment systems is required.
- The United States must be able to monitor and anticipate international developments in key emerging areas such as environmental management.
- There is a need for improved and greater dissemination of information to U.S. companies about standards and certification requirements in global markets. This is especially important for small and midsize companies.
- The National Institute of Standards and Technology (NIST) should increase educational and information dissemination resources for the benefit of U.S. industry.
- NIST should develop programs focusing on product acceptance in domestic and foreign markets. These efforts should include both

print and electronic information dissemination, as well as seminars, workshops, and other outreach efforts.

- NIST should establish a permanent analytical office with economics expertise to analyze emerging U.S. and international conformity assessment issues.
- All federal regulatory and procurement agencies should become dues-paying members of ANSI. Dues will support the government's fair share of ANSI's administrative expenses.

Recommendations for U.S. Involvement in Global Standards Activities

The following are a series of government expert recommendations regarding the U.S. government's involvement in global standards activities. Once again, business tax dollars go into supporting government outreach efforts so it behooves companies to study these concerns and address them in business forums (see Chapter 3 for additional recommendations).

1. The Office of the U.S. Trade Representative (USTR) should continue ongoing mutual recognition agreement negotiations with the European Union. If talks break down with the European Union it is recommended that the U.S. take unilateral action to remove trade barriers to European markets based on standards or conformity assessment practice.

2. The USTR should also expand efforts to negotiate mutual recognition agreements (MRAs) with other U.S. trading partners in markets and product sectors that represent significant U.S. export opportunities. Priority should be given to conclusion of MRAs on conformity assessment through the Asia Pacific Economic Cooperation forum.

3. The USTR should use its authority under Section 301 of the Trade Act of 1974 to self-initiate retaliatory actions against foreign trade practices involving discriminatory or unreasonable standards and conformity assessment criteria.

4. U.S. government agencies should, whenever possible, provide technical assistance to developing countries to help them construct standards and conformity assessment infrastructures that match the U.S. model.

5. The United States must take an active role in ensuring follow-through on GATT provisions regarding standards and conformity assessment.

6. Creation of a network of global mutual recognition agreements is the ultimate goal for facilitating international trade.

How Companies Can Plan Strategically in This New Global Environment

For too long American industry has taken an isolationist posture. In the last decade, a shrinking U.S. market has forced many companies into foreign markets for the first time. Importing and exporting may be lucrative, but it is also a tricky business that requires constant monitoring of foreign markets, their regulatory climate, and standards and conformity assessment practices.

Reading this guide should be the basis of an ongoing effort. Any American company venturing overseas must keep a vigilant eye on the sorts of changes just outlined, with foreign standards and conformity assessment trends topping the list.

In Europe, for example, companies must be certified for product performance (CE Mark) to enter the EU while still meeting a variety of rules and regulations. Some industries must also meet ISO 9000 requirements.

Five suggestions follow for coping with this new order:

1. Companies should become directly involved in the standards development and conformity assessment process. If possible, someone in-house should be appointed to:

- Continuously monitor regional and international standards practices in affected markets
- Create in-house mechanisms to allow for quick design and other changes to meet foreign demands
- Represent company interests in industry, regional, national, and international standards bodies

2. Through industry trade associations or other groups, companies should band together and ensure their interests are represented in the international standards and conformity assessment arena. For example, the electronics industry worldwide is successfully altering how ISO 9000 and other registration schemes are implemented.

3. Recognize that most standards and conformity assessment practices have intrinsic value. Those companies that jump ahead of the pack and pursue new standards programs may themselves be standards setters.

4. View government as a potentially positive force in the international standards and conformity assessment arena rather than a threat. In some cases, only the U.S. government or its agencies can offer the clout needed when negotiating MRAs or other agreements.

5. Practice what the American National Standards Institute calls Strategic Standardization Management (SSM).

Strategic Standardization Management

Strategic Standardization Management is a management discipline and methodology that investigates all aspects of standardization across a business and/or industry, then defines, recommends, and implements appropriate strategies and policies to leverage standardization in a way by which a company can gain competitive advantage or avoid competitive disadvantage.

There is no one way for a company to practice SSM. That will depend on its personal corporate agenda and overseas market strategies. However, Diego Betancourt, manager of Polaroid's Office of Strategic Standardization Management, and Robert Walsh of ANSI have teamed up to provide tools for companies that want to better track standards developments worldwide that will affect their businesses.

In working with a number of companies, these experts find that many businesses need a practical methodology and strategy for assessing and managing the broad spectrum of critical global standardization issues. For example, when critical standardization issues like ISO 9000 and ISO 14000 are grouped together with an organization's quality initiative and analyzed with a strategic unified corporate approach, they yield a very different decision impact value from the traditional "engineering standards" thinking. These issues also require a different discipline and infrastructure for appropriate evaluation and consequent action processes.

Here are some questions Betancourt and Walsh have designed that companies can apply to get an in-house SSM program up and running. Does your company:

- Know what the critical standardization business issues are?
- Know who is in charge of coordinating activities on which issue?
- Know the potential impact to the business?
- Have a strategy and plan for participating in standardization activities? Is it part of the corporate strategy? Part of the business plan?
- Know which standardization meetings are attended by which employees?
- Know that the persons attending these meetings represent a corporate position?
- Have a process for tracking and budgeting standardization activities?
- Know how much it spends on standardization activities?
- Know how many people participate across the entire organization?
- Know who the people are?
- Know what activities these people are involved in?
- Know what happened at those meetings?

Figure 12-3. Strategic standardization management infrastructure model.

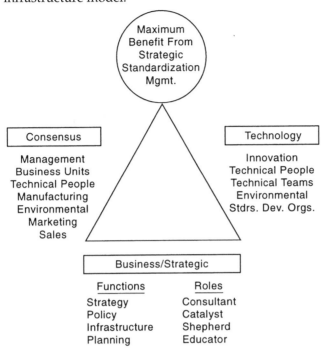

In general, it is recommended that companies form a centralized Office of SSM or an SSM Council that gathers input from all the organizations, then recommends a cohesive strategy for corporate approval. A centralized organization can be more responsive, accountable, and provide more timely action than a decentralized operation.

Within a company, Figure 12-3 shows an infrastructure that is balanced from the business and strategic foundation upward and results in a concerted group effort toward SSM objectives.

ANSI's Center for Strategic Standardization Management

In March of 1995 ANSI opened its Center for Strategic Standardization Management (CSSM) to offer customized assistance to companies seeking strategies for best tracking standards trends. The aim is to enable U.S. corporations to determine the best way to leverage their resources on the standards front and maximize their competitive position in existing and emerging markets.

Note: Companies can learn more about help ANSI offers in forming a Strategic Standardization Management effort by calling 212-642-4915.

Resources

Betancourt, Diego, *Strategic Standardization Management: A Strategic Macroprocess Approach to the New Paradigm in the Competitive Business Use of Standardization.*

International Organization for Standardization, "ISO's Long-Range Strategies 1996–1998, Agenda Item 6.1 Endorsement of Strategic Actions for 1996–1998," Executive Summary.

Warshaw, Stanley, ITA release, Nov. 18, 1994.

Index